12/15/15



To Jenn!

261/1000

# *Greed and Evil*

*

**Robert Platshorn**

Editing, additional content by Mercy Pilkington
Cover design and art by Ashley McCullum Swanson
Cover photo by Liam Crotty



ISBN: 978-0-990-9001-1-5

CONTENTS

# Introduction

By Neill Franklin, Executive Director, LEAP

Failed drug management policy and disastrous laws are obviously problematic in and of themselves, but when such laws are enacted on a foundation of profiteering and corruption, that's an entirely different scenario. *Greed and Evil* exposes the sinister schemes, people and corporations behind decades of marijuana prohibition laws responsible for the arrest and imprisonment of millions of otherwise law-abiding citizens. As a retired Maryland state trooper who has made countless marijuana possession arrests while working undercover, reading this book makes me feel somewhat dirty, knowing that I unwittingly contributed to such a diabolical plan.

I believe that if citizens knew the historical truth behind our marijuana prohibition laws, they would call for their immediate repeal. "Greed and Evil" is one of the best history lessons you will ever receive on marijuana policy, but you must read it to learn the truth. I highly recommend this book for everyone, mainly our elected officials, those possessing the power to end the reefer madness.

# Foreword

Every 37 seconds, someone is arrested for a marijuana related offense. The federal government has for decades been focusing their attention and your tax dollars on cracking down on all levels of marijuana offenses. They've created a system in which federal agencies, state agencies, police forces, and police officers are rewarded financially for high numbers of arrests. Instead of using our tax dollars as they should be used—to keep communities thriving—they're wasted on putting citizens in jail for non-violent offenses involving a plant less harmful than alcohol and which has, for over three thousand years, been used worldwide as a safe and effective medicine.

How this disastrous war on a plant came about and why it still exists is the subject of this book.

My biggest problem in putting pen to paper, or fingers to the keys, was determining who I was writing for. My motive for writing *Greed and Evil* is to expose the greed, corruption and self-serving motives of today's anti-cannabis movement. Most activists are well acquainted with the history of marijuana prohibition. But the majority of mainstream Americans, especially our law makers, do not have a clue. So, although that was not my plan, I have to start from the beginning. No one has ever told that story with the passion for truth of the late great Jack Herer. His book, *The Emperor Wears No Clothes*, has captivated and inspired people all over the world to demand that governments restore access to this important plant. So with the kind permission of Jack's family, I will quote liberally from a book I hope everyone will read in its entirety.

Being a pragmatist, I want to be able to say that this work will make a significant difference in the fight to end cannabis prohibition. That means that I must write this book for politicians, law enforcement and mainstream voters. First and foremost, the book must be readable and entertaining. By necessity, it will be filled with facts, figures and charts virtually all of which was collected by reporters and researchers. I have never believed in rewriting or taking credit for other people's work. As a result a great deal of this book is cut and paste excerpts. So I will attempt to provide original content with stories and personal experiences gathered from my thirty years in federal prisons and prison factories, as well as five years traveling America as an activist for legalization while promoting my first book, *Black Tuna Diaries*, and doing PR for the movie *Square Grouper* that tells the story of my years as a marijuana smuggler.

# Chapter 1: History

Most activists are familiar with this history and can skip to the next chapter. For those who aren't already aware of the ramifications and the reasons why marijuana access was revoked from the public, this chapter will highlight the truth about marijuana's status as an illegal drug.

Interestingly, the torrid history of marijuana's criminalization had nothing to do with drug use by the American public or a concern for the public welfare, and everything to do with economic politics. Citizens have been charged with criminal possession and imprisoned, and unwell people have been denied access to a potentially life-saving and natural health aide, all so those who have an interest in keeping hemp from gaining ground as an industry can make a buck.

## Why You Can No Longer Buy Marijuana at Your Corner Drug Store

The truth is, it was never about marijuana. The major motive for criminalizing marijuana was to eliminate the growing hemp industry before it could take hold and undermine other industries like cotton and wood. The other driving force was blatant racism.

## History According to Jack Herer

In 1619, America's first marijuana law was enacted at Jamestown Colony, Virginia, "ordering" all farmers to "make tryal of" (grow) Indian hempseed. More mandatory (must-grow) hemp cultivation laws were enacted in Massachusetts in 1631, in Connecticut in 1632, and in the Chesapeake Colonies into the mid-1700s. Cannabis hemp was legal tender (money) in most of the Americas from 1631 until the early 1800s. Why? To encourage American farmers to grow more. You could actually pay your taxes with cannabis hemp throughout America for over 200 years.

The founding fathers were intent on developing a thriving economy in the New World and saw the potential for this cash crop, not for its illicit properties but for its ability to contribute to industry and economy as a renewable resource. This is why both George Washington and Thomas Jefferson grew cannabis on their plantations. Jefferson, while envoy to France, went to great expense and even considerable risk to himself and his secret agents, to procure particularly good hemp seeds smuggled illegally into Turkey from China. The Chinese Mandarins (political rulers) so valued their hemp seed that they made its exportation a capital offense.

Benjamin Franklin started one of America's first paper mills with cannabis. This allowed America to have a free colonial press without having to beg or justify the need for paper and books from England.

1. *Diaries of George Washington; Writings of George Washington, Letter* ***to Dr. James Anderson, May 26, 1794, vol. 33, p. 433, (U.S. govt. pub., 1931); Letters to his caretaker, William Pearce, 1795 & 1796; Thomas Jefferson, Jefferson's Farm Books; Abel, Ernest, Marijuana: The First 12,000 Years, Plenum Press, NY, 1980; Dr. Michael Aldrich***

When these original growers built the industry in the newly formed country, hemp was needed for its characteristics as the strongest, most-durable, longest-lasting natural soft-fiber on the planet. Its leaves and flower tops (marijuana) were, depending on the culture, one of the most important and most widely-used medicines for two-thirds of the world's people for at least 3,000 years. That all changed at the turn of the 20th century.

## A Brief Summary of the Uses of Hemp

Radical scientists have called for a ban on all fossil fuels and their derivatives, along with trees harvested for paper and construction, in order to save the planet, reverse the Greenhouse Effect, and stop deforestation. While that day may be a long way off, if it did come to pass then there is only one known annually renewable natural resource that is capable of replacing those resources. It can provide the overall majority of the world's paper and textiles, and meeting all of the world's transportation, industrial, and home energy needs while simultaneously reducing pollution, rebuilding the soil, and cleaning the atmosphere, all at the same time. Interestingly, that substance is the same one that did it all before, that met the public's textile, building, and fiber needs, cannabis hemp.

Cannabis extract medicines were produced by Eli Lilly, Parke-Davis, Tildens, Brothers Smith (Smith

Brothers), Squibb, and many other American and European companies and apothecaries. During this time there was not one reported death from cannabis extract medicines, and virtually no abuse or mental disorders reported, except for first-time or novice-users occasionally becoming disoriented or overly introverted.

"The earliest known woven fabric was apparently of hemp, which began to be worked in the eighth millennium (8,000-7,000 B.C.)." (*The Columbia History of the World, 1981, page 54.)*

The body of literature (i.e., archaeology, anthropology, philology, economy, history) pertaining to hemp is in general agreement that, at the very least from more than 1,000 years before the time of Christ until 1883 A.D., cannabis hemp, indeed marijuana, was our planet's largest agricultural crop and most important industry, involving thousands of products and enterprises. It produced the overall majority of Earth's fiber, fabric, lighting oil, paper, incense, and medicines. In addition, it was a primary source of essential food oil and protein for humans and animals.

## Great Wars Were Fought to Ensure the Availability of Hemp

The primary reason for the War of 1812 (fought by America against Great Britain) was over access to Russian cannabis hemp. Russian hemp was also the principal reason that Napoleon (our 1812 ally) and his "Continental Systems" allies invaded Russia in 1812.

In 1942, after the Japanese invasion of the Philippines cut off the supply of Manila (Abaca) hemp, the U.S. government distributed 400,000 pounds of cannabis seeds to American farmers from Wisconsin to Kentucky, who produced 42,000 tons of hemp fiber annually until 1946 when the war ended.

## Why Has Cannabis Hemp Been So Important in History?

Cannabis hemp is one of the strongest, most-durable, longest-lasting natural soft-fibers on the planet. Botanically, hemp is a member of the most advanced plant family on Earth. It is a dioecious (having male features, female features, and sometimes hermaphroditic, or male and female on same plant), woody, herbaceous annual that uses the sun more efficiently than virtually any other plant on the planet, reaching a robust 12 to 20 feet or more in one short growing season. It can be grown in virtually any climate or soil condition on Earth, even marginal ones that don't lend themselves well to vegetation and agriculture.

Hempseed can be pressed for its highly nutritious vegetable oil, which contains the highest amount of essential fatty acids in the plant kingdom. These essential oils have been shown to be responsible for our immune responses and clear the arteries of cholesterol and plaque.

Because one acre of hemp produces as much cellulose fiber pulp as 4.1 acres of trees,* hemp is the perfect material to replace trees for pressed board, particle board and for concrete construction molds.

*Dewey & Merrill, Bulletin #404, United States Dept. of Agricultural., 1916.

**Footnotes:** 1. Clark, V.S., History of Manufacture in the United States, McGraw Hill, NY 1929, Pg. 34.

2. Ibid.

3. Diaries of George Washington; Writings of George Washington, Letter to Dr. James Anderson, May 26, 1794, vol. 33, p. 433, (U.S. govt. pub., 1931); Letters to his caretaker, William Pearce, 1795 & 1796; Thomas Jefferson, Jefferson's Farm Books; Abel, Ernest, Marijuana: The First 12,000 Years, Plenum Press, NY, 1980; Dr. Michael Aldrich, et al.

## Hemp Was Doomed by a New Machine that Would Slash Costs

**February 1938 – *Mechanical Engineering* Magazine:**

## "THE MOST PROFITABLE & DESIRABLE CROP THAT CAN BE GROWN"

Jack Herer

"The Most Profitable and Desirable Crop that Can be Grown" *Mechanical Engineering*, February 26, 1937

"Flax and Hemp: From the Seed to the Loom" was published in the February 1938 issue of Mechanical Engineering magazine.

It was originally presented at the Agricultural Processing Meeting of the American Society of Mechanical Engineers in New Brunswick, NY of February 26, 1937 by the Process Industries Division.

*Flax and Hemp: From the Seed to the Loom*

*By George A. Lower*

*This country imports practically all of its fibers except cotton. The Whitney gin, combined with improved spinning methods, enabled this country to produce cotton goods so far below the cost of linen that linen manufacture practically ceased in the United States. We cannot produce our fibers at less cost than can other farmers of the world. Aside from the higher cost of labor, we do not get as large production. For instance, Yugoslavia, which has the greatest fiber production per are in Europe, recently had a yield of 883 lbs.*

*Comparable figures for other countries are Argentina, 749 lbs.; Egypt 616 lbs.; and India, 393 lbs.; while the average yield in this country is 383 lbs.*

*To meet world competition profitably, we must improve our methods all the way from the field to the loom.*

*Flax is still pulled up by the roots, retted in a pond, dried in the sun, broken until the fibers separate from the wood, then spun, and finally bleached with lye from wood ashes, potash from burned seaweed, or lime. Improvements in tilling, planting, and harvesting mechanisms have materially helped the large farmers and, to a certain degree, the smaller ones, but the processes from the crop to the yarn are crude, wasteful and land injurious. Hemp, the strongest of the vegetable fibers, gives the greatest production per acre and requires the least attention. It not only requires no weeding, but also kills off all the weeds and leaves the soil in splendid condition for the following crop. This, irrespective of its own monetary value, makes it a desirable crop to grow.*

*In climate and cultivation, its requisites are similar to flax and like flax, should be harvested before it is too ripe. The best time is when the lower leaves on the stalk wither and the flowers shed their pollen.*

*Like flax, the fibers run out where leaf stems are on the stalks and are made up of laminated fibers that are held together by pectose gums. When chemically treated like flax, hemp yields a beautiful fiber so closely resembling flax that a high-power microscope is needed to tell the difference - and only then because in hemp, some of the ends are split. Wetting a few strands of fiber and holding them suspended will definitely identify the two because, upon drying, flax will be found to turn to the right or clockwise, and hemp to the left or counterclockwise.*

*Before [World War I], Russia produced 400,000 tons of hemp, all of which is still hand-broken and hand-scutched. They now produce half that quantity and use most of it themselves, as also does Italy from whom we had large importations.*

*In this country, hemp, when planted one bu. Per acre, yields about three tons of dry straw per acre. From 15 to 20 percent of this is fiber, and 80 to 85 percent is woody material. The rapidly growing market for cellulose and wood flower for plastics gives good reason to believe that this hitherto wasted material may prove sufficiently profitable to pay for the crop, leaving the cost of the fiber sufficiently low to compete with 500,000 tons of hard fiber now imported annually.*

*Hemp being from two to three times as strong as any of the hard fibers, much less weight is required to give the same yardage. For instance, sisal binder twine of 40- lb. Tensile strength runs 450 ft. To the lb. A better twine made of hemp would run 1280 ft. To the lb. Hemp is not subject to as many kinds of deterioration as are the tropical fibers, and none of them lasts as long in either fresh or salt water.*

*While the theory in the past has been that straw should be cut when the pollen starts to fly, some of the best fiber handled by Minnesota hemp people was heavy with seed. This point should be proved as soon as possible by planting a few acres and then harvesting the first quarter when the pollen is flying, the second and third a week or 10 days apart, and the last when the seed is fully matured. These four lots should be kept separate and scutched and processed separately to detect any difference in the quality and quantity of the fiber and seed.*

*Several types of machines are available in this country for harvesting hemp. One of these was brought out several years ago by the International Harvester Company. Recently, growers of hemp in the Middle West have rebuilt regular grain binders for this work. This rebuilding is not particularly expensive and the machines are reported to give satisfactory service.*

*Degumming of hemp is analogous to the treatment given flax. The shards probably offer slightly more resistance to digestion. On the other hand, they break down readily upon completion of the digestion process. And excellent fiber can, therefore, be obtained from hemp also. Hemp, when treated by a known chemical process, can be spun on cotton, wool, and worsted machinery, and has as much absorbency and wearing quality as linen.*

*Several types of machines for scutching the hemp stalks are also on the market. Scutch mills formerly operating in Illinois and Wisconsin used the system that consisted of a set of eight pairs of fluted rollers, through which the dried straw was passed to break up the woody portion. From there, the fiber with adhering shards - or hurds, as they are called - was transferred by an operator to an endless chain conveyer. This carries the fiber past two revolving single drums in tandem, all having beating blades on their periphery, which beat off most of the hurds as well as the fibers that do not run the full length of the stalks. The proportion of line fiber to tow is 50% each. Tow or short tangled fibers then go to a vibrating cleaner that shakes out some of the hurds. In Minnesota and Illinois, another type has been tried out. This machine consists of a feeding table upon which the stalks are placed horizontally. Conveyor chains carry the stalks along until they are grasped by a clamping chain that grips them and carries them through half of the machine.*

*A pair of intermeshing lawnmower-type beaters are placed at a 45-degree angle to the feeding chain and break the hemp stalks over the sharp edge of a steel plate, the object being to break the woody portion of the straw and whip the hurds from the fiber. On the other side and slightly beyond the first set of lawnmower beaters is another set, which is placed 90-degrees from the first pair and whips out the hurds.*

*The first clamping chain transfers the stalks to another to scutch the fiber that was under the clamp at the beginning.*

*Unfortunately, this type of scutcher makes even more tow than the so-called Wisconsin type. This tow is difficult to re-clean because the hurds are broken into long slivers that tenaciously adhere to the fiber.*

*Another type passes the stalks through a series of graduated fluted rollers. This breaks up the woody portion into hurds about 3/4 inch long, and the fiber then passes on through a series of reciprocating slotted plates working between stationary slotted plates.*

*Adhering hurds are removed from the fiber which continues on a conveyer to the baling press. Because no beating of the fiber against the grain occurs, this type of scutcher make only line fiber. This is then processed by the same methods as those for flax.*

*Paint and lacquer manufacturers are interested in hempseed oil which is a good drying agent. When markets have been developed for the products now being wasted, seed and hurds, hemp will prove, both for the farmer and the public, the most profitable and desirable crop that can be grown, and one that can make American mills independent of importations.*

*Recent floods and dust storms have given warnings against the destruction of timber. Possibly, the hitherto waste products of flax and hemp may yet meet a good part of that need, especially in the plastic field which is growing by leaps and bounds.*

**February 1938 – *Popular Mechanics* Magazine:**
***"NEW BILLION-DOLLAR CROP"***

*"AMERICAN farmers are promised a new cash crop with an annual value of several hundred million dollars, all because a machine has been invented which solves a problem more than 6,000 years old. It is hemp, a crop that will not compete with other American products. Instead, it will displace imports of raw material and manufactured products produced by underpaid coolie and peasant labor and it will provide thousands of jobs for American workers throughout the land.*

*The machine which makes this possible is designed for removing the fiber-bearing cortex from the rest of the stalk, making hemp fiber available for use without a prohibitive amount of human labor.*

*Hemp is the standard fiber of the world. It has great tensile strength and durability. It is used to produce more than 5,000 textile products, ranging from rope to fine laces, and the woody "hurds" remaining after the fiber has been removed contain more than seventy-seven percent cellulose, and can be used to produce more than 25,000 products, ranging from dynamite to Cellophane.*

*Under old methods, hemp was cut and allowed to lie in the fields for weeks until it "retted" enough so the fibers could be pulled off by hand. Retting is simply rotting as a result of dew, rain and bacterial action. Machines were developed to separate the fibers mechanically after retting was complete, but the cost was high, the loss of fiber great, and the quality of fiber comparatively low. With the new machine, known as a decorticator, hemp is cut with a slightly modified grain binder. It is delivered to the machine where an automatic chain conveyor feeds it to the breaking arms at the rate of two or three tons per hour. The hurds are broken into fine pieces which drop into the hopper, from where they are delivered by blower to a baler or to truck or freight car for loose shipment. The fiber comes from the other end of the machine, ready for baling.*

*From this point on almost anything can happen. The raw fiber can be used to produce strong twine or rope, woven into burlap, used for carpet warp or linoleum backing or it may be bleached and refined, with resinous by-products of high commercial value. It can, in fact, be used to replace the foreign fibers which now flood our markets."*

*Until the invention of the new harvester, called a decorticator, hemp was too labor intensive to threaten established manufacturing. But in an instant, the cost of producing hemp and hemp products was cut by 50-75%. High quality paper could now be produced for half the price and without harvesting a single tree. One acre of hemp produced more paper than four acres of trees. Superior cloth, oils for paint and varnish, building materials, and fuels could all be made at substantial savings.*

Modern technology was about to be applied to hemp production, making it the number-one agricultural resource in America. Two of the most respected and influential journals in the nation, popular mechanics and mechanical engineering, forecast a bright future for American hemp. Thousands of new products creating millions of new jobs would herald the end of the great depression. Instead hemp was persecuted, outlawed, and forgotten at the bidding of W. R. Hearst, who branded hemp the "Mexican killer weed, marihuana."

# Chapter 2:

# A Conspiracy to Wipe Out the Natural Competition

Until the invention of the new harvester, called a decorticator, hemp was too labor intensive to threaten established manufacturing. But in an instant, the cost of producing hemp and hemp products was cut by 50 to 75 percent. High quality paper could now be produced for half the price and without harvesting a single tree. One acre of hemp produced more paper than four acres of trees. Superior cloth, oils for paint and varnish, plastics, building materials, and fuels could all be made at substantial a savings.

**More from Jack Herer**

> In the mid-1930s, when the new mechanical hemp fiber stripping machines and machines to conserve hemp's high-cellulose pulp finally became state-of-the art, available, and affordable, the enormous timber acreage and businesses of the Hearst Paper Manufacturing Division, Kimberly Clark (USA), St. Regis, and virtually all other timber, paper, and large newspaper holding companies stood to lose billions of dollars and perhaps go bankrupt.
>
> Coincidentally, in 1937, DuPont had just patented processes for making plastics from oil and coal, as well as a new sulfate/sulfite process for making paper from wood pulp. According to DuPont's own corporate records and historians,* these processes accounted for

over 80 percent of all the company's railroad car loadings over the next 60 years, into the 1990s.

*Author's research and communications with DuPont, 1985-1996.

If hemp had not been made illegal, 80% of DuPont's business would never have materialized and the great majority of the pollution which has poisoned our Northwestern and Southeastern rivers would not have occurred.

In an open marketplace, hemp would have saved the majority of America's vital family farms and would probably have boosted their numbers, despite the Great Depression of the 1930s.

But competing against environmentally-sane hemp paper and natural plastic technology would have jeopardized the lucrative financial schemes of Hearst, DuPont, and DuPont's chief financial backer, Andrew Mellon of the Mellon Bank of Pittsburgh.

## "Social Reorganization"

A series of secret meetings were held. In 1931, Mellon, in his role as Hoover's Secretary of the Treasury, appointed his future nephew-in-law, Harry J. Anslinger, to be head of the newly reorganized Federal Bureau of Narcotics and Dangerous Drugs (FBNDD), a post he held for the next 31 years.

These industrial barons and financiers knew that machinery to cut, bale, decorticate (separate the fiber from the high-cellulose hurd), and process hemp into paper or plastics was becoming available in the mid-1930s. Cannabis hemp would have to go.

In DuPont's 1937 Annual Report to its stockholders, the company strongly urged continued investment in its new, but not readily accepted, petrochemical synthetic products. DuPont was anticipating "radical changes" from "the revenue raising power of government ... converted into an instrument for forcing acceptance of sudden new ideas of industrial and social reorganization." *

*(DuPont Company, annual report, 1937, our emphasis added.)

In *The Marijuana Conviction* (University of Virginia Press, 1974), Richard Bonnie and Charles Whitebread II detailed this process:

"By the fall of 1936, Herman Oliphant (general counsel to the Treasury Department) had decided to employ the taxing power [of the federal government], but in a statute modeled after the National Firearms Act and wholly unrelated to the 1914 Harrison [narcotics] Act. Oliphant himself was in charge of preparing the bill. Anslinger directed his army to turn its campaign toward Washington.

"The key departure of the marijuana tax scheme from that of the Harrison Act is the notion of the prohibitive tax. Under the Harrison Act, a non-medical user could not legitimately buy or possess narcotics. To the dissenters in the Supreme Court decisions upholding the act, this clearly demonstrated that Congress' motive was to prohibit conduct rather than raise revenue. So in the National Firearms Act, designed to prohibit traffic in machine guns, Congress 'permitted' anyone to buy a machine gun, but required him to pay a $200 transfer tax* and carry out the purchase on an order form.

"The Firearms Act, passed in June 1934, was the first act to hide Congress' motives behind a prohibitive tax. The Supreme Court unanimously upheld the anti-machine gun law on March 29, 1937. Oliphant had undoubtedly been awaiting the Court's decision, and the

Treasury Department introduced its marihuana tax bill two weeks later, April 14, 1937."

Thus, DuPont's** decision to invest in new technologies based on "forcing acceptance of sudden new ideas of industrial and social reorganization" makes sense.

*About $5,000 in 1998 dollars.

** It's interesting to note that on April 29, 1937, two weeks after the Marihuana Tax Act was introduced, DuPont's foremost scientist, Wallace Hume Carothers, the inventor of Nylon for DuPont, the world's number-one organic chemist, committed suicide by drinking cyanide. Carothers was dead at age 41.

### Hearst, His Hatred, and Hysterical Lies

Concern about the effects of hemp smoke had already led to two major governmental studies. The British governor of India released the Report of the Indian Hemp Drugs Commission 1893-1894 on heavy bhang smokers in the subcontinent. And in 1930, the U.S. government sponsored the Siler Commission study on the effects of off-duty smoking of marijuana by American servicemen in Panama. Both reports concluded that marijuana was not a problem and recommended that no criminal penalties apply to its use.

In early 1937, Assistant U.S. Surgeon General Walter Treadway told the Cannabis Advisory Subcommittee of the League of Nations that, "It may be taken for a relatively long time without social or emotional breakdown. Marihuana is habit-forming...in the same sense as ... sugar or coffee."

But other forces were at work. The war fury that led to the Spanish American War in 1898 was ignited by William Randolph Hearst through his nationwide chain of newspapers, and marked the beginning of "yellow journalism"* as a force in American politics.

*Webster's Dictionary defines "yellow journalism" as the use of cheaply sensational or unscrupulous methods in newspapers and other media to attract or influence the readers.

In the 1920s and '30s, Hearst's newspapers deliberately manufactured a new threat to America and a new yellow journalism campaign to have hemp outlawed.

For example, a story of a car accident in which a "marijuana cigarette" was found would dominate the headlines for weeks, while alcohol-related car accidents (which outnumbered marijuana-connected accidents by more than 10,000 to 1) made only the back pages.

This same theme of marijuana leading to car accidents was burned into the minds of Americans over and over again in the late 1930s by showing marijuana-related car accident headlines in movies such as "Reefer Madness" and "Marijuana – Assassin of Youth."

## Blatant Bigotry

Starting with the 1898 Spanish American War, the Hearst newspaper had denounced Spaniards, Mexican-Americans, and Latinos. After the seizure of 800,000 acres of Hearst's prime Mexican timberland by the "marihuana" smoking army of Poncho Villa,* these slurs intensified.

*The song "La Cucaracha" tells the story of one of Villa's men looking for his stash of "marijuana por fumar!" (to smoke!)

Non-stop for the next three decades, Hearst painted a picture of the lazy, pot-smoking Mexican, still one of our most insidious prejudices. Simultaneously, he waged a similar racist smear campaign against the Chinese, referring to them as the "Yellow Peril."

From 1910 to 1920, Hearst's newspapers would claim that the majority of incidents in which blacks were said to have raped white women could be traced directly to cocaine. This continued for ten years until Hearst decided it was not "cocaine-crazed negroes" raping white women – it was now "marijuana-crazed negroes" raping white women.

Hearst's and other sensationalistic tabloids ran hysterical headlines atop stories portraying "negroes" and Mexicans as frenzied beasts who, under the influence of marijuana, would play anti-white "voodoo-satanic" music (jazz) and heap disrespect and "viciousness" upon the predominantly white readership. Other such offenses resulting from this drug-induced "crime wave" included stepping on white men's shadows, looking white people directly in the eye for three seconds or more, looking at a white woman twice, laughing at a white person, etc. For such "crimes," hundreds of thousands of Mexicans and blacks spent, in aggregate, millions of years in jails, in prisons, and on chain gangs under brutal segregation laws that remained in effect throughout the U.S. until the 1950s and '60s. Hearst, through persuasive and repetitive use, pounded the obscure Mexican slang word "marijuana" into the English-speaking American consciousness. Meanwhile, the word "hemp" was discarded and "cannabis," the scientific term, was ignored and buried.

The actual Spanish word for hemp is "cáñamo." But using a Mexican "Sonoran" colloquialism–marihuana, often Americanized as marijuana–guaranteed that few would realize that the proper terms for one of the chief natural medicines (cannabis), and for the premiere industrial resource (hemp), had been pushed out of the language.

## The Prohibitive Marijuana Tax

In the secret Treasury Department meetings conducted between 1935 and 1937, prohibitive tax laws were drafted and strategies plotted. Marijuana was not banned outright; the law called for an "occupational excise tax upon dealers, and a transfer tax upon dealings in marijuana."

Importers, manufacturers, sellers, and distributors were required to register with the Secretary of the Treasury and pay the occupational tax. Transfers were taxed at $1 an ounce; $100 an ounce if the dealer was unregistered. The new tax doubled the price of the legal "raw drug" cannabis which at the time sold for one dollar an ounce.2

The year was 1937. The state of New York had exactly one narcotics officer.*

*New York currently has a network of thousands of narcotics officers, agents, spies, and paid informants – and 20 times the penal capacity it had in 1937, although the state's population has only doubled since then.

After the Supreme Court decision of March 29, 1937, upholding the prohibition of machine guns through taxation, Herman Oliphant made his move. On April 14, 1937, he introduced the bill directly to the House Ways and Means Committee instead of to other appropriate committees such as food and drug, agriculture, textiles, commerce, etc.

His reason may have been that Ways and Means is the only committee that can send its bills directly to the House floor without being subject to debate by other committees. Ways and Means Chairman Robert L. Doughton,* a key DuPont ally, quickly rubber-stamped the secret Treasury bill and sent it sailing through Congress to the President.

*Colby, Jerry, The DuPont Dynasties, Lyle Stewart, 1984.

## "Did Anyone Consult the AMA?"

However, even within his controlled Committee hearings, many expert witnesses spoke out against the passage of these unusual tax laws. Dr. William C. Woodward, for instance, who was both a physician and an attorney for the American Medical Association, testified on behalf of the AMA.

He said, in effect, the entire fabric of federal testimony was tabloid sensationalism and that no real testimony had been heard. This law, passed in ignorance, could possibly deny the world a potential medicine, especially now that the medical world was just beginning to find which ingredients in cannabis were active.

Woodward told the committee that the only reason the AMA hadn't come out against the marijuana tax law sooner was that marijuana had been described in the press for twenty years as "killer weed from Mexico."

The AMA's doctors had just realized "two days before" these spring 1937 hearings that the plant Congress intended to outlaw was known medically as cannabis, the benign substance used in America with perfect safety to treat scores of cases of illness for over one hundred years.

"We cannot understand yet, Mr. Chairman," Woodward protested, "why this bill should have been prepared in secret for two years without any intimation, even to the profession, that it was being prepared." He and the AMA* were quickly denounced by Anslinger and the entire Congressional committee, and curtly excused.3

* The AMA and the Roosevelt Administration were strong antagonists in 1937.

When the Marijuana Tax Act bill came up for oral report, discussion, and vote on the floor of Congress, only one pertinent question was asked from the floor: "Did anyone consult with the AMA and get their opinion?" Representative Vinson, answering for the Ways and Means Committee replied, "Yes, we have. A Dr. Wharton [mistaken pronunciation of Woodward?] and [the AMA] are in complete agreement."

With this memorable lie, the bill passed, and became law in December 1937. Federal and state police forces were then created, which have incarcerated hundreds of thousands of Americans, adding up to more than 16 million wasted years in jails and prisons–even contributing to the deaths of inmates–all for the sake of poisonous, polluting industries, prison guards unions, and to reinforce some white politicians' policies of racial hatred.

(Mikuriya, Tod, M.D., Marijuana Medical Papers, 1972; Sloman, Larry, Reefer Madness, Grove Press, 1979; Lindesmith, Alfred, The Addict and the Law, Indiana U. Press; Bonnie & Whitebread; The Marijuana Conviction, U. of VA Press; U.S. Cong. Records; et al.)

## Protecting Special Interests

As the AMA's Dr. Woodward had asserted, the government's testimony before Congress in 1937 had, in fact, consisted almost entirely of Hearst's and other sensational and racist newspaper articles read aloud by Harry J. Anslinger,* director of the Federal Bureau of Narcotics (FBN). (This agency has since evolved into the Drug Enforcement Administration [DEA]).

*Harry J. Anslinger was director of the new Federal Bureau of Narcotics from its inception in 1931 for the next 31 years, and was only forced into retirement in 1962 by President John F. Kennedy after Anslinger tried to censor the publications and publishers of Professor Alfred Lindesmith ("The Addict and the Law", Washington Post, 1961) and to blackmail and harass Lindesmith's employer, Indiana University. Anslinger had come under attack for racist remarks as early as 1934 by a U.S. Senator from Pennsylvania, Joseph Guffey, for such things as referring to "ginger-colored niggers" in letters circulated to his department heads on FBN stationery.

Prior to 1931, Anslinger was Assistant U.S. Commissioner for Prohibition. Anslinger, remember, was hand-picked to head the new Federal Bureau of Narcotics by his uncle-in-law, Andrew Mellon, Secretary of the Treasury under President Herbert Hoover. The same Andrew Mellon was also the owner and largest stockholder of the sixth largest bank (in 1937) in the United States, the Mellon Bank in Pittsburgh, one of only two bankers for DuPont* from 1928 to the present.

*DuPont has borrowed money from banks only twice in its entire 190-year history, once to buy control of General Motors in the 1920s. Its banking business is the prestigious plum of the financial world.

In 1937, Anslinger testified before Congress saying, "Marijuana is the most violence-causing drug in the history of mankind." This, along with Anslinger's outrageous racist statements and beliefs, was made to the Southern-dominated Congressional committee and is now an embarrassment to read in its entirety.

For instance, Anslinger kept a "Gore File," culled almost entirely from Hearst and other sensational tabloids, which contained stories of axe murders where one of the participants reportedly smoked a joint four days before committing the crime.

Anslinger pushed on Congress as a factual statement that about 50% of all violent crimes committed in the U.S. were committed by Spaniards, Mexican-Americans, Latin Americans, Filipinos, African-Americans, and Greeks, and these crimes could be traced directly to marijuana.

(From Anslinger's own records given to Pennsylvania State University, ref.: Li Cata Murders, etc.)

Not one of Anslinger's marijuana "Gore Files" of the 1930s is believed to be true by scholars who have painstakingly checked the facts.4

## Self-Perpetuating Lies

In fact, FBI statistics, had Anslinger bothered to check, showed at least 65-75% of all murders in the U.S. were then – and still are – alcohol related. As an example of his racist statements, Anslinger read into U.S. Congressional testimony (without objection) stories about "coloreds" with big lips luring white women with jazz music and marijuana. He read an account of two black students at the University of Minnesota doing this to a white coed "with the result of pregnancy." The Congressmen of 1937 gasped at this and at the fact that this drug seemingly caused white women to touch or even look at a "negro."

Virtually no one in America other than a handful of rich industrialists and their hired cops knew that their chief potential competitor–hemp–was being outlawed under the name "marijuana."

That's right. Marijuana's reputation, created intentionally through fear-mongering, was just a pretext for hemp prohibition and economic suppression.

The water was further muddied by the confusion of marijuana with "loco weed" (Jimson Weed). The situation was not clarified by the press, which continued to print the misinformation into the 1960s.

At the dawn of the 1990s, some of the most extravagant and ridiculous attacks on the hemp plant drew national media attention, such as a study widely reported by health journals* in 1989 that claimed marijuana smokers put on about a half a pound of weight per day. Now in 2007, they just want to duck the issue.

Meanwhile, serious discussions of the health, civil liberties, and economic aspects of the hemp issue are frequently dismissed as being nothing but an "excuse so that people can smoke pot" – as if people need an excuse to state the facts about any matter. One must concede that, as a tactic, lying to the public about the beneficial nature of hemp and confusing them as to its relationship with "marijuana" has been very successful.

**Footnotes:**

*1. Dewey & Merrill, Bulletin 404, US Department of Agriculture 1916; "Billion-Dollar Crop", Popular Mechanics, 1938; U.S. Agricultural Indexes, 1916 thru 1982; New Scientist, November 13, 1980 .2. Uelmen & Haddox, Drug Abuse and the Law, 1974. 3. Bonnie, Richard & Whitebread, Charles, The Marijuana Conviction, Univ. of Virginia Press, 1974; Congressional testimony, 1937 (See full testimony in Appendix); et al. 4. Sloman, Larry; Reefer Madness, 1979; Bonnie and Whitebread, The Marijuana Conviction, Univ. of Virginia Press, 1974.*

## Man-Made Fiber, the Toxic Alternative to Natural Fibers

The late 1920s and 1930s saw continuing consolidation of power into the hands of a few large steel, oil, and chemical (munitions) companies. The U.S. federal government placed much of the textile production for the domestic economy in the hands of its chief munitions maker, DuPont.

The processing of nitrating cellulose into explosives is very similar to the process for nitrating cellulose into synthetic fibers and plastics. Rayon, the first synthetic fiber, is simply stabilized guncotton, or nitrated cloth, the basic explosive of the 19th century.

"Synthetic plastics find application in fabricating a wide variety of articles, many of which in the past were made from natural products," beamed Lammot DuPont (*Popular Mechanics*, June 1939).

"Consider our natural resources," the president of DuPont continued, "The chemist has aided in conserving natural resources by developing synthetic products to supplement or wholly replace natural products."

DuPont's scientists were the world's leading researchers into the processes of nitrating cellulose and were in fact the largest processor of cellulose in the nation in this era.

The February 1938 *Popular Mechanics* article stated, "Thousands of tons of hemp hurds are used every year by one large powder company for the manufacture of dynamite and TNT." History shows that DuPont had largely cornered the market in explosives by buying up and consolidating the smaller blasting companies in the late 1800s. By 1902, it controlled about two-thirds of industry output.

They were the largest powder company, supplying 40% of the munitions for the allies in WWI. As cellulose and fiber researchers, DuPont's chemists knew hemp's true value better than anyone else. The value of hemp goes far beyond line fibers; although recognized for linen, canvas, netting, and cordage, these long fibers are only 20% of the hemp stalk's weight. Eighty percent of the hemp is in the 77% cellulose hurd, and this was the most abundant, cleanest resource of cellulose (fiber) for paper, plastics, and even rayon.

The empirical evidence in this book shows that the federal government – through the 1937 Marijuana Tax Act – allowed this munitions maker to supply synthetic fibers for the domestic economy without competition. The proof of a successful conspiracy among these corporate and governing interests is simply this: in 1997, DuPont was still the largest producer of man-made fibers, while no American citizen has legally harvested a single acre of textile grade hemp in over sixty years (except during the period of WWII).

An almost unlimited tonnage of natural fiber and cellulose would have become available to the American farmer in 1937, the year DuPont patented Nylon and the polluting wood-pulp paper sulfide process. All of hemp's potential value was lost.

Simple plastics of the early 1900s were made of nitrated cellulose, directly related to DuPont's munitions-making process. Celluloid, acetate, and rayon were the simple plastics of that era, and hemp was well known to cellulose researchers as the premier resource for this new industry to use. Worldwide, the raw material of simple plastics, rayon, and paper could be best supplied by hemp hurds.

Nylon fibers were developed between 1926 and 1937 by the noted Harvard chemist Wallace Carothers, working from German patents. These polyamides are long fibers based on observed natural products. Carothers, supplied with an open-ended research grant from DuPont, made a comprehensive study of natural cellulose fibers. He duplicated natural fibers in his labs and polyamides–long fibers of a specific chemical process–were developed. (Curiously, Wallace Carothers committed suicide in April of 1937, one week after the House Ways and Means Committee had the hearings on cannabis and created the bill that would eventually outlaw hemp.)

Coal tar and petroleum-based chemicals were employed, and different devices, spinnerets, and processes were patented. This new type of textile, Nylon, was to be controlled from the raw material stage, as coal, to the completed product: a patented chemical product. The chemical company centralized the production and profits of the new "miracle" fiber. The introduction of Nylon, the introduction of high-volume machinery to separate hemp's long fiber from the cellulose hurd, and the outlawing of hemp as "marijuana" all occurred simultaneously.

The new man-made fibers (MMFs) can best be described as war material. The fiber-making process has become one based on big factories, smokestacks, coolants, and hazardous chemicals, rather than one of stripping out the abundant, naturally available fibers.

Coming from a history of making explosives and munitions, the old "chemical dye plants" now produce hosiery, mock linens, mock canvas, latex paint, and synthetic carpets. Their polluting factories make imitation leather, upholstery, and wood surfaces, while an important part of the natural cycle stands outlawed.

The standard fiber of world history, America's traditional crop, hemp, could provide our textiles and paper and be the premier source for cellulose. The war industries–DuPont, Allied Chemical, Monsanto, and others–are protected from competition by the marijuana laws. They waged war on both the natural cycle and the common farmer.

**Sources:** Encyclopedia of Textiles, 3rd Edition by the editors of American Fabrics and Fashions Magazine, William C. Legal, Publisher Prentice-Hall, Inc., Englewood Cliffs, NJ, 1980; The Emergence of Industrial America Strategic Factors in American Economic Growth Since 1870, Peter George State University, NY; DuPont (a corporate autobiography published periodically by E.I. DuPont De Nemours and Co., Inc., Wilmington, DE.; The Blasting Handbook, E.I. DuPont De Nemours & Co., Inc., Wilmington, DE; Mechanical Engineering Magazine, Feb. 1938; Popular Mechanics, Feb 1938; Journal of Applied Polymer Science, Vol. 47, 1984; Polyamides, the Chemistry of Long Molecules (author unknown); U.S. Patent #2,071,250 (Feb. 16, 1937), W.H. Carothers; DuPont Dynasties, Jerry Colby; The American Peoples Encyclopedia, the

## Moving to Crush Dissent

After the 1938-1944 New York City "LaGuardia Marijuana Report" refuted his argument by reporting that marijuana caused no violence at all and citing other positive results, Harry J. Anslinger, in public tirade after tirade, denounced Mayor Fiorello LaGuardia, the New York Academy of Medicine, and the doctors who researched the report.

Anslinger proclaimed that these doctors would never again do marijuana experiments or research without his personal permission, or risk being sent to jail.

He then used the full power of the United States government, illegally, to halt virtually all research into marijuana while he blackmailed the American Medical Association (AMA)* into denouncing the New York

Academy of Medicine and its doctors for the research they had done.

Why, you ask, was the AMA now on Anslinger's side in 1944-45, after being against the Marijuana Tax Act in 1937? Answer: Since Anslinger's FBN was responsible for prosecuting doctors who prescribed narcotic drugs for what he, Anslinger, deemed illegal purposes, they (the FBN) had prosecuted more than 3,000 AMA doctors for illegal prescriptions through 1939. In 1939, the AMA made specific peace with Anslinger on marijuana. The result: only three doctors were prosecuted for illegal drugs of any sort from 1939 to 1949.

To refute the LaGuardia report, the AMA, at Anslinger's personal request, conducted a 1944-45 study; "of the experimental group, 34 were negroes and one was white" (for statistical control) who smoked marijuana, became disrespectful of white soldiers and officers in the segregated military. (See Appendix, "Army Study of Marijuana," Newsweek, Jan. 15, 1945.)

This technique of biasing the outcome of a study is known among researchers as "gutter science."

## Pot and the Threat of Peace

However, from 1948 to 1950, Anslinger stopped feeding the press the story that marijuana was violence-causing and began "red baiting," typical of the McCarthy era.

Now the frightened American public was told that this was a much more dangerous drug than he originally thought. Testifying before a strongly anti-Communist Congress in 1948 and thereafter continually to the press–Anslinger proclaimed that marijuana rendered its users not violent at all, but so peaceful–and pacifistic!–

that the Communists could and would use marijuana to weaken our American fighting men's will to fight.

This was a 180-degree turn-around of the original pretext on which "violence-causing" cannabis was outlawed in 1937. Undaunted, however, Congress now voted to continue the marijuana law based on the exact opposite reasoning they had used to outlaw cannabis in the first place.

It is interesting and even absurd to note that Anslinger and his biggest supporters–Southern Congressmen and his best senatorial friend, Senator Joseph McCarthy* of Wisconsin–from 1948 on constantly received press coverage on the scare.

*According to Anslinger's autobiographical book, *The Murderers*, and confirmed by former FBN agents, *Anslinger had been supplying morphine illegally to U.S. Senator Joseph McCarthy for years.*

The reason given by Anslinger in his book? So the Communists would not be able to blackmail this great American Senator for his drug-dependency weakness. (Dean Latimer, *Flowers In The Blood*; Harry Anslinger, *The Murderers*.)

Anslinger told Congress the Communists would sell marijuana to America's boys to sap their will to fight, to make us a nation of zombie pacifists. Of course, the Communists of Russia and China ridiculed this US marijuana paranoia every chance they got, both in the press and at the United Nations.

Unfortunately, the idea of pot and pacifism got so much sensational world press for the next twenty years that eventually Russia, China, and the Eastern Bloc Communist countries (who grew large amounts of cannabis) outlawed marijuana for fear that America would sell it or use it to make the Communist soldiers docile and pacifistic.

This was strange because Russia, Eastern Europe, and China had been growing and ingesting cannabis as a medical drug, relaxant, and work tonic for hundreds and even thousands of years, with no thought of marijuana laws.

(The J.V. Dialogue Soviet Press Digest, Oct., 1990, reported a flourishing illegal hemp business, despite the frantic efforts by Soviet law enforcement agencies to stamp it out. "In Kirghizia alone, hemp plantations occupy some 3,000 hectares." In another area, Russians were traveling three days into "one of the more sinister places in the Moiyn-Kumy desert," to harvest a special high-grade, drought resistant variety of hemp known locally as anasha.)

## A Secret Program to Control Minds & Choices

Through a report released in 1983 under the Freedom of Information Act, it was discovered (after forty years of secrecy) that Anslinger was appointed in 1942 to a top-secret committee to create a "truth serum" for the Office of Strategic Service (OSS), which evolved into the Central Intelligence Agency (CIA). (*Rolling Stone*, August 1983.)

Anslinger and his spy group picked, as America's first truth serum, "honey oil," a much purer, almost tasteless form of hash oil, to be administered in food to spies, saboteurs, military prisoners, and the like, to make them unwittingly "spill the truth."

Fifteen months later, in 1943, marijuana extracts were discontinued by Anslinger's group as America's first truth serum because it was noted that they didn't work all the time. The people being interrogated would often giggle or laugh hysterically at their captors, get paranoid, or have insatiable desires for food (the munchies?). Also, the report noted that American OSS agents and other interrogation groups started using the honey oil illegally themselves and would not give it to the spies. In Anslinger's OSS group's final report on marijuana as a truth serum, there was no mention of violence caused by the drug. In fact, the opposite was indicated. The OSS and later the CIA continued the search and tried other drugs as truth serum, psilocybin or amanita muscaria mushrooms and LSD, to name a few. For twenty years, the CIA secretly tested these concoctions on American agents. Unsuspecting subjects jumped from buildings, or thought they'd gone insane.

Our government finally admitted doing all this to its own people in the 1970s, after 25 years of denials; drugging innocent, non-consenting, unaware citizens, soldiers, and government agents was all in the name of national security, of course. However, these American "security" agencies constantly threatened and even occasionally imprisoned individuals, families, and organizations that suggested the druggings had ever occurred.

It was three decades before the Freedom of Information Act forced the CIA to admit its lies through exposure on TV by CBS's *60 Minutes* and others. However, on April 16, 1985, the U.S. Supreme Court ruled that the CIA did not have to reveal the identities of either the individuals or institutions involved in this travesty.

The court said, in effect, that the CIA could decide what was or was not to be released under the Freedom of Information Act, and that the courts could not overrule the agency's decision.

As an aside, repealing this Freedom of Information Act was one of the prime goals of the Reagan/Bush/Quayle Administration.

(L.A. Times, The Oregonian, etc. editorials 1984; The Oregonian, January 21, 1985; Lee, Martin & Shlain, Bruce, Acid Dreams, Grove Press, NY, 1985.)

**Criminal Misconduct**

Before Anslinger started the pacifist zombie-marijuana scare in 1948, he publicly used jazz music, violence, and the "Gore Files" for five to seven more years (1943-50) in the press, at conventions, at lectures, and in Congressional hearings. We now know that on the subject of hemp, disguised as marijuana, Anslinger was a bureaucratic police liar.

For more than seventy years now, Americans have been growing up with and accepting Anslinger's statements on the herb, believing in everything from its power to incite violence and evil pacifism, and finally in the corrupting influence of music.

Whether this was economically or racially inspired, or even because of up-beat music or some kind of synergistic (combined) hysteria, is impossible to know for sure. But we do know that for the US government, specifically the DEA, information disseminated on cannabis was then, and continues to be, a deliberate deception.

As you will see in the following chapters, the weight of empirical fact and large amounts of corroborating evidence indicate that the former Reagan/Bush/Quayle administrations, along with their unique pharmaceutical connections, have conspired at the highest levels to withhold information and to disinform the public, resulting in the avoidable and needless deaths of tens of thousands of Americans, not to mention the legal and criminal ramifications of marijuana's status.

And they did it, it seems, with the intention of saving their own investments and those of their friends in the pharmaceutical, energy, and paper industries; and to give these poisonous, synthetic industries an insane advantage over natural hemp and protect the billions of dollars in annual profits that they stood to lose if the hemp plant and marijuana were not prohibited.

As a result, millions of Americans have wasted millions of years in jail time, and millions of lives have been and continue to be ruined by what started out as Hearst's, Anslinger's, and DuPont's shameful economic lies, vicious racial libels, and bigoted musical taste.

# Chapter 3: The New Enemies

Starting in the mid-1960s and continuing in the 70s, the American public began to learn that the government's decades-long propaganda condemning marijuana was pure fiction or to be more precise, deliberate lies. The use of cannabis, which had been for the most part limited to musicians and ethnic minorities, now became the symbol of rebellion for American youth. I was born on November 22, 1942, and so got to spend my teens bridging the two most important movements that rebelled against a long list of government deceptions and persecutions: the Beatniks and the Hippies. We knew marijuana would not lead down the path of destruction. It became the common denominator of a generation of people who would think for themselves and question the status quo.

We can date the beginning of the new lies and new liars with the presidency of Richard M. Nixon. Two things took place that changed everything. Nixon commissioned an in-depth study of all aspects of marijuana, and appointed former Pennsylvania Governor Raymond Shafer to chair the effort. My generation had great hope that the truth would finally emerge. It did, and we were not disappointed by the commission's report. Here are the most relevant parts.

**National Commission on Marihuana and Drug Abuse**

March 22, 1972

To The President and Congress of the United States:

As Chairman of the National Commission on Marihuana and Drug Abuse, I am pleased to submit to you our first year Report in conformance with the mandate contained in Section 601 of Public Law 91-513, The Comprehensive Drug Abuse Prevention and Control Act of 1970.

This Report "Marihuana, A Signal of Misunderstanding" is an all-inclusive effort to present the facts as they are known today, to demythologize the controversy surrounding marihuana, and to place in proper perspective one of the most emotional and explosive issues of our time. We on the Commission sincerely hope it will play a significant role in bringing uniformity and rationality to our marihuana laws, both Federal and State, and that it will create a healthy climate for further discussion, for further research and for a continuing advance in the development of a public social policy beneficial to all our citizens.

Whatever the facts are we have reported them. Wherever the facts have logically led us, we have followed and used them in reaching our recommendations. We hope this Report will be a foundation upon which credibility in this area can be restored and upon which a rational policy can be predicated.

By Direction of the Commission
Raymond P. Shafer
COMMISSION MEMBERS
The Honorable Raymond Philip Shafer, Chairman
Dana L. Farnsworth , M.D., Vice Chairman
Henry Brill, M.D.

The Honorable Tim Lee Carter, U.S. Representative, Kentucky

Mrs. Joan Ganz Cooney

Charles o. Galvin, S.J.D.

John A. Howard , Ph. D.

The Honorable Harold E. Hughes, U.S. Senator, Iowa

The Honorable Jacob K. Javits, U.S. Senator, New York

The Honorable Paul G. Rogers, U.S. Representative, Florida

Maurice H. Seevers, M.D., Ph. D.

J. Thomas Ungerleider, M.D.

Mitchell Ware, J.D.

Here are excerpts of what was discovered by President Nixon's Commission. Some emphases are those of the author.

The Report of the National Commission on Marihuana and Drug Abuse

Marihuana: A Signal of Misunderstanding

Commissioned by President Richard M. Nixon, March, 1972

No objective evidence of specific pathology of brain tissue has been documented. This fact contrasts sharply with the well-established brain damage of chronic alcoholism.

There is no systematic empirical evidence, at least that drawn from the American experience, to support the thesis that the use of marihuana either inevitably or generally causes, leads to or precipitates criminal, violent, aggressive or delinquent behavior of a sexual or nonsexual nature.

Scientific evidence has clearly demonstrated that marihuana is not a narcotic drug, and the law should properly reflect this fact.

*We recommend that cannabis be removed from the existing single convention and consideration be given to listing it in the psychotropic convention among drugs which have similar effects.*

IV. Therapeutic Uses

*Recommendation: increased support of studies which evaluate the efficacy of marihiuana in the treatment of physical impairments and disease is recommended.*

Historical references have been noted throughout the literature referring to the use of cannabis products as therapeutically useful agents. Of particular significance for current research with controlled quality, quantity and therapeutic settings would be investigations into the treatment of glaucoma, migraine, alcoholism and terminal cancer. The NIMII-FDA Psychotomimetic Advisory Committee's authorization of studies designed to explore the therapeutic uses of marihuana is commended.

The Commission recommends only the following changes in federal law:

- *possession of marihuana for personal use would no longer be an offense, but marihuana possessed in public would remain contraband subject to summary seizure and forfeiture.*
- *casual distribution of small amounts of marihuana for no remuneration, or insignificant remuneration not involving profit would no longer be an offense.*

All the component parts of the recommended policy of the Commission should be consistent with its objective of non-interference with casual transfers and possession and use which is essentially and fundamentally private and personal.

The contraband device, the not-for-profit sale, and public possession of some reasonable amount which should be presumed to be necessarily incident to private use should all be removed from the ambit of legal sanction. To do so would be to strike down "symbols" of a public policy which had never been adequately justified in the first instance. Such steps would in no way jeopardize the firm determination of the Commission that the use of marihuana ought to be discouraged.

*"That some of these original fears were unfounded and that others were exaggerated has been clear for many years. Yet, many of these early beliefs continue to affect contemporary public attitudes and concerns."*

National Commission on Marihuana and Drug Abuse

March 22, 1972

Talk about happy hippies, we were ecstatic. Surely the Shafer report would free the weed.

Not so fast. The President of The United States had his own agenda. True to his name, Tricky Dick tossed the report in the garbage and declared a new War on Drugs, mainly a war on marijuana. I doubt his reason was greed or even the normal political corruption engendered by the need for big campaign contributions. It was pure evil. Richard M. Nixon, President of the United States, was a bigot, a drunk, a homophobe, a racist, an anti-Semite, and a tool of the mob. He was a paranoid who feared and hated people under thirty and members of the press who dared to criticize his actions. He believed that all those who demonstrated against his policies were crazed stoners and even worse, Jewish physiatrists.

In 2002, thirty years after the Shafer Commission released its report, the government declassified Oval Office tapes from 1971-1972 demonstrating that the foundation of marijuana criminalization is misinformation, culture war, and prejudice.

## White House Conversations Reveal Truth behind Nixon's Drug War

"We need, and I use the word 'all-out war,' on all fronts..."

The year after Nixon's "all-out war," marijuana arrests jumped by over 100,000 people.

(Download a PDF copy of the text transcripts of portions of Nixon White House taped conversations, including the portions excerpted here. Review the Shafer Commission's report, “Marihuana, A Signal of Misunderstanding.”)

Nixon blamed the calls for marijuana legalization on Jews; Nixon blamed the decline and fall of ancient

Rome, and of the Catholic Church, on homosexuality; and Nixon criticizing the CBS sitcom *All in the Family* as a show which promoted homosexuality. (Check out some of these transcripts.)

Nixon made clear several times that he wanted a report which supported his views and 'tough on crime' policies, no matter what the facts might be. To his credit, Governor Shafer delivered instead an honest report, with conclusions based on all the evidence, even though at the time he was being considered for a federal judgeship (needless to say, he didn't get it). Ever since the Commission issued its recommendation that marijuana offenses not be a crime, millions of Americans have been arrested on marijuana charges. Today, there is a marijuana arrest every thirty-seven seconds.

President Nixon, speaking with Bob Haldeman in the Oval Office one month after he had been told his national commission would urge marijuana decriminalization, had a different agenda: "I want a goddamn strong statement about marijuana. Can I get that out of this sonofabitching, uh, Domestic Council? ...I mean one on marijuana that just tears the ass out of them."

Highlights of Nixon comments on marijuana:

Nixon: "I see another thing in the news summary this morning about it. That's a funny thing, every one of the bastards that are out for legalizing marijuana is Jewish. What the Christ is the matter with the Jews, Bob, what is the matter with them? I suppose it's because most of them are psychiatrists."

Nixon: "You see, homosexuality, dope, immorality in general. These are the enemies of strong societies. That's why the Communists and the left-wingers are pushing the stuff, they're trying to destroy us."

Nixon compared marijuana to alcohol: marijuana consumers smoke "to get high" while "a person drinks to have fun." Nixon also saw marijuana leading to loss of motivation and discipline but claimed: "At least with liquor I don't lose motivation."

Nixon: “The [unintelligible] to these, uh, these, uh, more radical demonstrators that were here the last, oh, two weeks ago. [unintelligible] They’re all on drugs. Oh yeah, horrible, it’s just a -- when I say all, virtually all. Enforce the law, you’ve got to scare them."

Nixon: “Do you know what happened to the Romes, Romans? The last six Roman emperors were fags. The last six. Nero had a public wedding to a boy. Yeah. And they’d [unintelligible]. You know that. You know what happened to the Popes? It’s all right that, po-po-Popes were laying the nuns, that’s been going on for years, centuries, but, when the popes, when the Catholic Church went to hell, in, I don’t know, three or four centuries ago, it was homosexual.”

You might think from the above that Nixon hated everyone. Not true! He loved being around gangsters and organized crime figures. I first learned about this while paying a social call on some customers and a well-known mafia fixer who owned a famous restaurant in Ft Lauderdale. It was late at night and the boys had been drinking hard. The conversation turned to politics. Never having heard anyone say a good word about Richard Nixon, I was shocked to hear my friends describe the Nixon era as “the good old days.”

We were at the bar, which was three deep in wise guys. Our host was telling my partner Robby that whenever Nixon was at his Key Biscayne home, he would visit his favorite mob eateries. The doors would be locked and the public excluded, wise guys only. The

President would get blind drunk while expressing love for his gangster pals, and then rail against his enemies, both real and imagined. I listened to similar stories from half a dozen men along the bar. Then our host summed it up with these words, "We owned Nixon, lock, stock and barrel, thanks to Rebozo (Bebe Rebozo). We had a cast iron jacket on the President of the United States." At first I took this with a grain of salt. But on reflection, it had a ring of credibility. Why not? For years J. Edgar Hoover denied the existence of the Mafia, because thanks to Roy Cohn, the mob had a "jacket" on Hoover filled with embarrassing photos confirming Hoover's alleged sexual preferences for men. Like Hoover, Nixon was a very vocal homophobe.

*President Nixon with Bebe Rebozo (left) and J. Edgar Hoover (center) at the "Florida White House." Credit: National Archives.*

Nixon and Rebozo were likely to have been lovers. It wasn't until recently that these allegations began appearing in the press. When Nixon became President, Rebozo got his own office and bedroom at the White House, and a security clearance that allowed him to go in and out without being logged by the secret service.

Using a false name, Rebozo even got into Nixon's hotel suite during a trip to Europe.

Rebozo was not a high-ranking government employee who deserved or required such free space or services. In fact, the only government entity that knew much about Bebe was the FBI, which said he was cozy with Mafia biggies—especially Tampa Godfather Santos Trafficante and Alfred ("Big Al") Polizzi of Cleveland. Big Al was a drug trafficker associated with the syndicate's financial genius, Meyer Lansky. In 1964, the Bureau of Narcotics branded Polizzi "one of the most influential members of the underworld in the United States."

A new biography by Don Fulsom, a veteran Washington reporter who covered the Nixon years, suggests the 37th U.S. President had a serious drinking problem, beat his wife, and by the time he was inaugurated in 1969 had links going back two decades to the Mafia, including with New Orleans godfather Carlos Marcello.

Nixon was well aware that his Mafia pals were deep into the dope business, yet he publicly mimicked their traditional lies about being opposed to selling drugs. Was he protecting their illegal enterprises in return for the huge illegal campaign contributions held in Bebe's personal safe deposit box in Rebozo's own bank? Or was he protecting what had become the mob's biggest cash cow in return for keeping his homosexuality a secret and continuing his love affair with mafia bagman/banker Bebe Rebozo? A friendship that endured 44 years and ended at Nixon's side by his deathbed?

Last word on Tricky Dick: Despite the fact that Nixon left office in 1974, his mob partners still controlled the entire Nixon/Rebozo compound on Key

Biscayne Island in 1977. One day, Robby and I were escorted to the compound and offered the entire property as a landing place for thirty thousand pounds of Santa Marta's finest weed. It was an exciting prospect. But on sober reflection it was just too scary, even for the Black Tuna Gang.

Two years later while we were under indictment for pot smuggling as the leaders of the Black Tuna Gang, Robby and I were approached by a Nixon associate of a very different type. Frank Sturgis, Watergate burglar, CIA operative, and alleged Grassy Knoll shooter, offered to use his government connections to help us with our "problems." Frank and I spent a lot of time together; some of it is chronicled in my memoir, *Black Tuna Diaries*.

## The Unholy Triangle

GOP Mogul Behind Drug Rehab 'Torture' Centers Is Bankrolling Opposition to Pot Legalization in Colorado
Drug war profiteers attempt to stop marijuana legalization in Washington and Colorado

Mel and Betty Sembler were the vanguard of the modern anti-cannabis movement. They have advanced their personal wealth and political power by running drug abuse treatment centers that kidnapped, tortured, and brainwashed young children. Today they distribute misleading anti-drug propaganda and finance campaigns to block cannabis reform. The Semblers' organizations receive government grants to run federally-funded programs to help businesses test for drug use. If anybody has a vested interest in maintaining the status quo, it is the Semblers. As marijuana use becomes legal and socially acceptable, they stand to lose a lot. Not just money. Their anti-marijuana organizations are a source of personal political power.

## Straight, Inc.

Barely two years into Nixon's Drug War, wealthy political wannabe be couple Mel and Betty Sembler, having failed to further their fortunes and personal ambitions as Democrats, switched parties and reinvented themselves as the saviors of America's youth. They gave an entirely new meaning to the expression "bring them kicking and screaming" into sobriety.

Founded by Florida businessmen Mel Sembler and his wife Betty Schlesinger Sembler, along with Joseph Zappala, the program was praised by prominent figures such as President George H. W. Bush, former First Lady

Nancy Reagan, and Princess Diana, but was also subject to multiple accusations of abusive practices.

Straight has been the subject of numerous allegations of abuse. In every state that Straight had a facility, abuse was documented either by state investigators or was alleged in civil suits.

## Mel Sembler: The Teflon Ambassador, a Crack in Bush's Golden Egg?

by Wesley M. Fager

Oakton Institute for Cultic Studies, Oakton, Virginia

In 1974, the US Senate had conducted a study of Straight's predecessor program, The Seed, and had concluded that The Seed used methods similar to the "brainwashing" methods employed by North Koreans against American servicemen during the Korean War. And since The Seed was being funded by the National Institute on Drug Abuse, under NIH, which was then directed by Dr. Robert L. DuPont, Jr., the White House's second Drug Czar, Senator Sam Ervin, the chairman of the Senate investigating committee, directed Dr. DuPont and NIDA to require The Seed to issue NIDA human consent forms to Seed participants and to their parents acknowledging that they were participating in human experimentation as required by NIDA's own regulations. It was because of this stipulation, in large part, that Seed expansion programs like the one in Saint Petersburg shut down in the first place. Mel and Betty Sembler had a son in that Seed. When it closed, Mel, Betty, and some other Seed parents formed their own Seed, which they called Straight. A half dozen directors left the new Seed in the first 18 months, one of them publicly comparing Straight to The Seed, and inferring that Straight was worse than The Seed.

Straight was founded in 1976 in a donated warehouse with 25 plastic chairs, $100,000 in federal grants, and a case of Vaseline. For the next 17 years, Straight operated the world's biggest chain of juvenile rehabilitation programs, with centers in major metropolitan areas all over America. Straight made nearly $100 million as a charity, but there is a dark side to Straight. Straight is one of the most destructive drug rehabilitation programs the world has ever known. It relied on traditional Chinese thought reform technologies to strip a child of his self-esteem before trying to build him up again in the Straight image. Food and sleep deprivation, making kids sit in their own feces, urine, and vomit, spitting in kids' faces and not allowing them to wipe the spit off, forced or cajoled sexual confessions open for common discussion, painful restraints—these are all trademarks of Straight treatment. Many former students have committed suicide subsequent to their confinement at Straight. As many as 50,000 kids may have been held captive at Straight. These are the charges that ISAC wants the UN to look into.

SOURCE: "Suicide or Murder? The destruction of young egos" by Wesley M. Fager (c) 2000

## DECLARATION OF MARCY SIZEMORE

I, Marcy Sizemore hereby state as follows:

1. I am a 17 year old resident of the State of Virginia, residing in Chantilly, Virginia. I presently attend Fairfax Baptist Temple Academy.

2. From December 27, 1980 until March 1982, I was enrolled in the Straight Inc. drug rehabilitation program in St. Petersburg, Florida.

3. I traveled to St. Petersburg, Florida, with my mother to enroll in the program. When I arrived at the Straight, Inc. headquarters in St. Petersburg, I was taken into a room by two other teenagers for intake. I was kept in the room for approximately five hours, and couldn't eat or use the bathroom during those five hours. Two girls sat in front of the exit door to the room. I couldn't leave, and I was told that if I didn't enroll in the program that they would put me in a mental institution. They also told me that if I didn't sign myself into the program that I would be put into the program by court order for a period of two years. I eventually signed myself into the program, was strip searched, and then entered into the Straight program.

4. During my 14 months in the program, I witnessed the types of abuses as set forth in the complaint in Collins v. Straight, Inc. Enrollees on first phase were not allowed to make any movement or to even use the bathroom without someone holding onto them, and they were kept under guard 24 hours a day. Individuals who did not cooperate were placed on prolonged diets of peanut butter sandwiches and water "choker sandwiches" and were placed in punitive isolation for weeks and months at a time. This was known as the time out room. The treatment consisted of 12 hours a day of sitting in straight back chairs, and participating in rap sessions which amounted basically to being confronted by other teenagers concerning drug and alcohol use. When I was in the program, the only exercise we got was once a week, which consisted of forced exercises, usually consisting of 100 pushups and other strenuous exercises.

5. The standard practice of Straight, Inc. is to prevent any individual who misbehaves in any way from progressing in the program. During my 14 months in the

program, I was put back to the beginning of the program at least four times. Each time I was put back to the beginning of the program I was put on "first phase, newcomer status" which meant that I was under guard 24 hours a day, and was in physical contact at all times with another enrollee.

6. Another standard practice of Straight, Inc. to punish those participants who "misbehave" was to subject the enrollee to a "marathon." In December of 1981, I had been placed on "no phase," which was meant I was frozen in the program and could not make any progress. I was accused of "misbehaving" because I simply sat in the rap session and did not participate. As punishment for this nonparticipation, I was taken into a bathroom by six or seven other girls, and I was kept in the bathroom from 12 noon until 9:30 that night. In the bathroom, the girls beat me, punched me, placed their fingers under my collar bone and twisted the bone, and verbally abused me for 9 1/2 hours. The girls would hold my arms out at the sides, while another girl would run across the room and ram her head into my stomach, and this was done continuously. I was thrown up against the wall, pushed back and forth, and was made to stand on my feet the entire 9 1/2 hours. I was told that I was crazy, that I would be put into a mental institution, and that if I did not participate I would be taken to a program where lesbians would get me and I would have to work in the fields.

7. During this marathon, I was so physically exhausted that I passed out twice. Whenever I passed out, the girls kicked me, pulled at me, and made me get to my feet and again continued to subject me to the beating. When I asked for water, I was told I could have water, and then they poured it on my head. The girls worked in shifts, and always kept at least six to eight

girls in the room with me at all times. After 9 1/2 hours, the marathon stopped, and I was taken to my "foster home." At that point, my entire body was covered with bruises.

8. This type of marathon is done regularly on the Straight, Inc. enrollees if they "misbehave." The other teenagers who carry out the punishment are "staff" or "trainees," who are former participants in the program.

9. Another type of punishment imposed on Straight, Inc. enrollees if they "misbehave" or do not do what they are told is to sleep-deprive the enrollees. We would be made to stay up until 3 a.m. on Friday night, participating in open session, stay awake all day Saturday, all day Saturday night, and all of Sunday night. I once observed one enrollee who was subjected to this type of sleep deprivation, and on Sunday night she fell on the floor and went into convulsions. Other enrollees were used to curse us and prod us to keep us awake so that we were unable to sleep during periods of 48 hours or more.

10. During my 14 months in Straight, I also suffered from specific medical problems. At that time I suffered from allergies and I needed shots every two weeks in order to treat the allergies. The Straight, Inc. people denied me access to these shots, and I received them only occasionally while I was in the program. In fact, I only saw a doctor once in the entire 14 months I was in the program.

11. While in the program, I also had a serious fungus problem with my feet. The fungus was so bad that my feet were swollen to the point where I couldn't walk and they also smelled very bad. I told my "foster mother" that I needed medical attention, but I received none. I was unable to wear my shoes, and I received no medical care until my mother took me to a doctor.

12. By the time I got out of the program in March of 1982, my physical condition had completely deteriorated. I had developed open sores all over my back and arms, and I was informed by my pediatrician that this condition is caused by the mental and physical debilitation I suffered while in the Straight, Inc. program.

I hereby affirm under penalty of perjury that the above statement is true and accurate.

Date: 12/5/82

### The Bad Memories Will Never End for Samantha Monroe

It was 1980. Monroe, 13, was a bright girl from a troubled home that had been visited by state child-welfare officers. She was in sixth grade. She never did drugs, she says. There had never been evidence of drug use. Nevertheless, she was forced into Straight. After two daring escapes from the program, she was "recaptured."

At Straight, she was taken directly to a windowless, bare closet called the "time-out room."

"I was in there for 14 days," Monroe says. "I had no shower, no trips to the bathroom. They brought me biscuits and water. Anybody who tried to touch me, I fought. I bit the inside of my mouth and would spit blood at them. I took off my shirt and used it as a weapon."

Periodically, other clients were sent into the time-out room to "motivate" Monroe: yell at her, tell her what a failure she was, how she had ruined her life.

Monroe had no choice but to soil her pants with urine, feces, and menstrual blood. She says Straight staffers called this punishment "humble pants." The room reeked, she recalls.

Finally one night, as parents and children held a meeting in the next room, Monroe heard her own mother pleading with her through a microphone to "be a good girl." She decided to cooperate.

Two parent volunteers gave her a bucket of water and a clean pair of underpants, then allowed her to go in another room to wash. She says they didn't seem shocked by her appearance.

"I had a busted lip and a black eye," she says. "The skin was peeling off my hands, I guess from malnutrition. My hair was falling out. I had bitten one finger each day, to mark the passage of time."

That night, a male Straight staffer came into her time-out room after the evening's program had ended and everyone had gone home. As she tells what happened next, Monroe's voice quivers.

"He said, 'I can make it easier on you if you do what I tell you to do.' Then he unzipped his pants. So I took my pants off, too."

That was Monroe's ticket out of the closet. But it started a whole new nightmare for her. She says the staffer continued to demand sexual acts several times a week, seeking her out usually in the kitchen, where she had earned the privilege of working.

"He'd walk in and say, 'Where's my pretty little girl?' I thought I had to do it. I thought everybody who had privileges was doing it."

A month shy of her 15th birthday, Monroe discovered she was pregnant. And that, finally, got her out of Straight.

"They brought me to the girls' rap room and they said, 'You're free to go.' "

Monroe had an abortion, paid for, she says, by the state. She claims she wasn't the only Straight client who was sexually abused.

"How did girls get herpes on their mouths? How did boys wind up with anal tears? There were yeast infections, urinary tract infections."

**What Professionals Say about the Straights**

*Straight is not a health care organization. It is a business posing as a health care organization and as a result hundreds of kids have been hurt. All of the business operations consist of fraud, double and triple billing of health insurance companies at the same time, and they bill government grants while telling parents they are not the recipients of any kinds of government money.*

Janet Kennedy, Ph.D. Pharmacy, MS, Hospital Administration, of Austin, Texas after a private, three-year investigation of Straight. [Channel 12, Eye on Tampa Bay Show, 1992]

*Straight officials have generously allowed me to witness some of their group sessions firsthand . . . I believe that Straight's treatment can be fairly compared with 'brainwashing' in prisoner-of-war camps as documented by Brown (1963, chap. 2)*. Thus, procedures that would be reprehensible in any context outside of a prisoner-of-war camp are considered acceptable 'treatment' in the case of drug addiction.*

Dr. Bruce K. Alexander of *Simon Fraser University* in *Peaceful Measures: Canada's Way Out of the 'War on Drugs'*, p. 75; [**Techniques of Persuasion:*

*From Propaganda to Brainwashing* by J. A. C. Brown

*Straight conducts a program that practices psychological coercion and physical assault against children under the guise of drug and alcohol treatment. I believe there is reason to fear for the physical and mental safety of any child sent to the program.*

Dr. Richard Ofshe, author and thought control specialist at the *University of California, Berkeley*

*Documentation on file indicates that there have been incidents where children have been subjected [to] unusual punishment, infliction of pain, humiliation, intimidation, ridicule, coercion, threat, mental abuse, or other actions of a punitive nature, including . . . interference with daily living functions such as eating, sleeping or toileting, or withholding of medication.*

Letter dated June 27, 1990 from Fred Dumont, Santa Ana, California District Manager for Dept. of Social Services to Straight National Headquarters, explaining why state authorities ordered the program closed.

*According to sworn testimony, Straight often left restrained group members sitting in their own urine, feces, or vomit until suitable concessions were extracted.*

From Treatment, Thought Reform, and the Road to Hell by Dr. Barry Beyerstein, a leading Canadian researcher on opiates and brain functioning who operates a laboratory at *Simon Fraser University* in British Columbia, Canada, first published in his report, in this report, *Strategies for Change, New Directions in Drug Policy (1992)*:

- Winter 1987 - Spring 1987 - Executive Staff, Springfield, VA
- Spring 1987 - Fall 1987 - Executive Staff, Cincinnati, OH
- Fall 1987 - Spring 1988 - Executive Staff, Springfield, VA
- Spring 1988 - Spring 1989 - Executive Staff, Atlanta, GA

There were brief periods between 1985 and 1989 that I was not employed by Straight, and I may have some of the months wrong above.

For 19 years, I gave very little thought to my actions as a staff member of Straight. Then, in the spring and summer of 2008, I began to interact with Straight survivors and listened to their experiences. As the weeks and months progressed, I became increasingly aware of the damage I caused to Straight survivors as a staff member. After much reflection on the events of the 1980s, I have become very much aware that many Straight survivors lost their integrity, innocence, sense of self-worth, youth, ability to trust others, family relationships, and more as a result of my actions as a staff member, and I deeply regret that I am responsible for this as a staff member.

I realize now that many survivors still suffer from diagnosed psychological disorders such as post-traumatic stress disorder, severe depression, social phobias, panic disorders, etc., caused by imprisonment in Straight, Inc, and that many survivors still endure vivid Straight, Inc. nightmares, can still hear the screams of children as they were abused, and cannot forget the abuse they personally endured or witnessed as vulnerable children. I am deeply ashamed of my role in this, including not putting a stop to it.

I am acknowledging to you that Straight, Inc. unjustly committed various crimes, abused children, and utilized extremely unethical practices against innocent young clients, which included, but were not limited to the following:

- Brainwashing (aka coercive thought reform)
- Physical abuse
- Usage of illegal and or unethical restraints - children routinely restrained children at the direction of staff for minor infractions (i.e. not motivating, not paying attention)
- Unethical forms of extreme humiliation, including but not limited to beltlooping, no privacy/watched while urinating, defecating, or bathing, motivating
- Food deprivation (ie. peanut butter diets, inadequate portions of food)
- Sleep deprivation caused by unwarranted, prolonged daily group hours (12), other time spent in the building (up to at least 3 additional pre and/or post group hours), lengthy commuting time, and in many cases, due to intentionally

withholding sleep as punishment for not "cooperating" to coerce compliance

- Verbal abuse - unduly harsh confrontational tactics that included swearing, screaming, yelling, spitting, belittling, humiliating, etc., a child in front of a large group of child clients
- Sexual abuse (while I was not aware of this while on staff, in recent months I have become aware, through the testimony of other Straight survivors, that this did happen)
- Psychological abuse
- Coerced confessions
- Unjustifiable and lengthy isolation in intake and/or time out rooms
- Denial of necessary medical care
- Kidnapping
- False imprisonment
- Accepting clients with little/no drug history (the so-called "dry druggie" theory); specifically, I was personally responsible for conducting client intakes that resulted in children with little history of drug or alcohol use
- Employing uneducated, unprofessional teenaged staff. Specifically, I allowed myself to be employed by Straight as a counselor, knowing full well that I had no outside training and no education.

Additionally, I apologize for allowing the abuse, unethical practices and crimes to continue for years, and lending my name to, sponsoring, recommending, and endorsing

Straight, Inc., and for admitting children, their siblings, and parents to Straight, Inc., and for failing to properly and adequately oversee and monitor Straight, Inc.

I regret my decision to go on staff and I regret my actions as a Straight staff member. I made the decision to go on staff and I made the decision to advance to Executive Staff. I am responsible for these actions and take full responsibility. As a former Straight client myself, I, of all people, should have known better.

I am aware of several former Straight clients who have taken their own lives as Steve did. Many of these people I knew personally, including Chris Weiss, Lisa D, Ira, Duane, and others. I can't begin to understand all of these deaths, but I damn sure know Straight is why Steve took his life. My heart aches for you and your mom. I wish I could bring him back.

I would like to turn the clock back to 1985 and make better decisions. However, I am unable to undo the damage I have caused. I am unable to make any financial restitution to former victims, as well. However, in recent months, thanks to you, I have had the honor and privilege of interacting with former Straight clients who were victims of my actions and the actions of other Straight staff.

It is my hope that these interactions have been a step toward healing the wounds that have remained for two decades.

Along those lines, there is something I can do; I can make myself available to you. If you or your mom or anyone else wants to talk or email with me about this, please do.

It is my hope that other Executive Staff and administrators will take this opportunity to acknowledge and apologize for their part in Straight, Inc. If you know of any former staff who would like to communicate with me privately for any reason, please pass my contact info on.

In closing, it is my sincere hope that survivors of Straight can find the healing and closure that they need and deserve. I look forward to being a part of that healing.

And thanks for making this possible.

Sincerely,
Richard Mullinax
Straight Inc. Staff1985 – 1989
richmullinax@gmail.com

**Straight Suicides**

This is a partial list of people who committed suicide while in Straight or after they got out. Many others tried to take their lives. I left last names out purposely for those who wish to maintain privacy. There are several others who have died reasons not disclosed. No doubt this list will continue to grow over time. These people did not die in vain and we are not going away until all these abusive facilities are shut down and the people responsible are held accountable *Denotes death but suicide unconfirmed.

**Springfield, VA Straight** Jon Guyton 1985, Greg Hughes 1985, Kristin Stottlemeyer 1986, Chris Weiss 1986, Chris Kelly 1987, Duane Rolfs 1987, Matthew

Hunter 1988, Charlie Griffith 1989/90, Greg T. 1989, Dan Brown late 80s, Ira Kauffman late 90s, Glen Steepleton 2000, Kevin Yriondo 2000, Kent H. 2009, Travis Stone, Paul Riffle, Terry L. Teddy B., Lisa D.

**Stoughton, MA Straight** Chris Ahlman 1988, Glenn Jenkins, Brandon E., Dale N.

**Atlanta, GA Straight** Brandon K.. Tara M.. Theresa S., Tracey G., Ron H., Michelle E., Ben L.

**Dallas, TX Straight** William F. 2001, Vance H. Shiela, C Michelle K.

**Cincinatti, OH Straight** Jeff Leugers 1990, Paul Price, Rob H., Dane W.

**St Pete, FL Straight** Jerry V., Geoffery R., Kent C.

**Sarasota, FL Straight** Reagan F.

**Orlando, FL Straight** Chris C., Aaron Rockey, Dave Gilman, James Mixon (died Oct 1989 -15 yrs old-possible suicide by cop), Matt Willingham, Chris Cybulski

## Some Civil Suits and Criminal Cases Against Straight, Inc. and Straight-descendent programs

(c) 5-27-2002 by Wesley M. Fager

Straight makes it a point to try to get from its young students their deepest, darkest secrets. If someone knew your deepest, darkest secret, would you sue him? In spite of the high-pressure coaxed confessions stated in one's own handwriting from MIs, COCs, and FOS lists; in spite of the fact that Straight has parents sign a fine print statement that they will not sue regardless what happens in Straight; in spite of the fact that Straight goes to great lengths to limit potential witnesses to the daily abuses; despite the fact that Straight makes oldcomers become part of the abuse in order to progress; in spite of the fact that Straight can call in former White House Drug Czar Robert DuPont time after time to testify on its behalf; despite the fact that many judges have made pro-Straight stances; in spite of all this, there have been many, many criminal charges and civil suits against Straight, just as Straight has successfully sued many parents for money owed who stopped payment after having learned of the abuse.

The first table in the Appendix includes a brief look at litigation involving Straight, Inc, including the nature of the allegations and the outcomes where available.

Also see: Mel Sembler (Straight's founder) and SLAPP suits against his detractors at: http://thestraights.net/articles/logansinjunction-encl4.htm.

The fact is there are so many suits involving the Straights that it is almost impossible to track them all.

Richard and Susan Ferris were among the 80 families sued by Straight - Saint Petersburg in one ten-month period. Straight sued them for $1,089. Mrs. Ferris says that her son had been seduced by his host mother so she refused to pay, but later settled with Straight anyway just to make them go away. Straight sued Patricia Neumann of Lake Alfred, but Mrs.

Neumann filed a court document stating that she had been coerced by Straight and that the coercion included being told her son would "die without Straight." Robert and Veronica McCallion of St. Petersburg wrote in a court document that Straight was "unprincipled" and "had no intention of living up to their promise of treatment and rehabilitation." Darlene Licate of Spring Hill said her daughter had been stripped-searched and verbally abused. "I don't pay for abuse," she said.

The following table is from the official web site from the Pinellas County Sixth Circuit Court. It shows lawsuits where Straight - St. Pete was the plaintiff. Did Straight have a bunch of bums for parents, or were they middle class white parents who like Darlene Licate say they won't pay for abuse?

(See Table 2 in Appendix.)

And there are many others. Interestingly, Fairfax Food Services & Caterers (In Step Corporation) was one that sued Straight. They were awarded $17,177.72 for food they had supplied plus interest, but Straight avoided collections until the judgment was eventually "discontinued and stricken" by the Fairfax County Courts.

Growing Together is a Sembler-based synanon in Lake Worth, Florida. Here are some Florida parents who have sued:

- Charles A. Parnell of Palm Beach Gardens
- Janet Knauss of West Palm Beach
- Ellie Madison of Fort Lauderdale
- Janice McIntyre of Singer Island
- Michael and Janice Peterson of Palm Beach Gardens
- Janette Thorin of Lake Worth

## Sembler's Companies, a Long History of Civil Suits

Straight was facing so many civil suits that it created a shell corporation to protect program assets and directors from civil judgments. The name was changed to Straight Foundation, Inc., and the mission changed to one of educating the public on the dangers of teenage drug use. Straight Foundation kept all the money so far collected from revenues and donations, plus it kept all the property. A new entity was then created called Straight, Inc., which was to provide substance abuse treatment to addicted kids. But the new Straight, Inc. had no property in which to treat clients and no money to pay staff salaries. So the shell corporation leased the property back to Straight, Inc. and gave it grants to meet payroll until it once again started paying for itself. The by-laws for the shell corporation were modified to allow foundation money to be used to defend foundation officers and directors should they be sued, and also to allow for the spending of foundation money to pay legal judgments in case any court judgments were made against foundation officers and directors.

Amazingly, Jeb Bush, the President's brother and governor of Florida, along with his wife Columba, his lieutenant governor Toni Jennings, his drug czar, James R. McDonough, and James T. "Tim" Moore, Commissioner of the Florida Department of Law Enforcement, are all on Straight's advisory board under its new name Drug Free America Foundation (DFAF), along with former drug czar Robert L. DuPont, Jr. who is in partnership with the former head of the DEA Peter Bensinger, Thomas Constantine, another former head of the DEA, and Richard M. Baker, mayor of Saint Petersburg.

DFAF no longer treats kids. Instead it is federally funded to give assistance to businesses to setup a Drug Free Workplace Environment. And DFAF also serves as a think tank for national and international drug policy where it continues to make a significant impact. For example, last spring the US Supreme Court decided to allow for suspicionless drug testing of kids who are involved in any school activity, including honor societies, in violation of their Fourth Amendment right protecting them against unreasonable searches and seizures. The court's decision was no doubt influenced by an Amicus Curie Brief signed by scores of national and international figures who urged the court to take the action it subsequently did. Philadelphia attorney David Evans of the Legal Foundation Against Illicit Drugs is the author of that brief. The Oakton Institute has learned that LFAID was co-founded by Calvina Fay, executive director of DFAF. What's more, Mr. Evans is a member of the Institute on Global Drug Policy—a DFAF front group.

**About DFAF, Inc.**

Drug Free America Foundation, Inc. is a drug prevention and policy organization committed to developing, promoting and sustaining national and international policies and laws that will reduce illegal drug use and drug addiction. It's a Non-Governmental Organization (NGO) in Special Consultative Status with the Economic and Social Council of the United Nations.

Front Divisions include:

The Institute on Global Drug Policy

The International Task Force on Strategic Drug Policy International Scientific and Medical Forum on Drug Abuse

The Drug Prevention Network of the Americas (DPNA)

Students Taking Action Not Drugs (STAND)

National Drug-Free Workplace Alliance (NDWA)

DFAF Annual Report 2013

Dear friend,

This past year has been bittersweet. Now, more than ever, we must remain steadfast in our commitment to educate key leaders about drug legislation, to reach students and our workforce and other community members with our prevention messages, and to assist families in finding help for their loved ones affected by drugs. Many of you may know that two states have legalized marijuana this year, against federal law and international drug treaties. Consequently, we must continue to push back against this trend and to educate the public on the harms of drug use and promote healthy alternatives. Every year more and more money is poured into the crusade to legalize drugs. Please take the time to read about our many successes detailed in this report. The generous support of friends like you allows Drug Free America Foundation to continue to help protect our loved ones from the devastation of drugs and alcohol. Thank you for helping us to make a difference.

Your support of our work at Drug Free America Foundation is very much appreciated!

Sincerely,

Betty S. SemblerCalvina Fay

Board Chair Executive Director

Founding Members:

Betty S. Sembler (proud to torture children)

Betty S. Sembler has dedicated the past three decades to fighting the war on drugs. In 1976, she was one of ten founding members of Straight, Inc., a nonprofit drug treatment program that successfully treated more than 12,000 young people with drug addiction in eight cities nationally from Dallas to Boston.

Mrs. Sembler is the founder and Board Chair of Save Our Society From Drugs (S.O.S.) and the Drug Free America Foundation, Inc. In 2009, she was inducted into the Florida Women's Hall of Fame by then Governor Charlie Crist.

The Honorable Mel Sembler (not too honorable)

Mel Sembler, Chairman of the Board of The Sembler Company, served as United States Ambassador to Italy from 2001 to 2005 and as Ambassador to Australia and Nauru from 1989 to 1993. In 1976, Sembler and his wife Betty co-founded STRAIGHT, an adolescent drug treatment program. During its 17 years of existence, STRAIGHT successfully graduated more than 12,000 young people nationwide from its remarkable program. He is nationally recognized as an activist in the anti-drug campaign and as a staunch, long-time supporter of the Republican Party and its candidates.

Calvina L. Fay

Executive Director (and queen of lies)

Calvina Fay is the Executive Director of Drug Free America Foundation and Save Our Society From Drugs (S.O.S.). Drug Free America Foundation provides education to the public about the dangers of drugs of abuse and efforts to legalize drugs. S.O.S. conducts political activities to combat drug legalization efforts. Professor Fay is also the Director of the International Scientific and Medical Forum on Drug Abuse, a brain-trust of the world's leading physicians and scientific scholars dedicated to advancing research on drug use and drug abuse. Professor Fay is the former Executive Director of the Drug Free Business Alliance (DBA), a Houston-based nonprofit coalition of member businesses involved in attacking the drug problem in the workplaces of the Texas Gulf Coast area. DBA has served as a model program for other U.S. cities and in several other countries. She falsely claims to be* a professor at the Argentina Universidad del Salvador.

- Citation provided further in the book.

Amy Ronshausen Manager of Congressional and Legislative Affairs

Karen Belanger Program Manager, National Drug-Free Workplace Alliance (NDWA)

Lana Beck Director of Communications

Sylvia Raymond Editor and Manager of Special Projects

## The Sembler's Remain Proud of Straight and Unrepentant for the Tortured Children

"In 1976 Betty and I helped found STRAIGHT, a non-profit, adolescent drug treatment and rehabilitation program with branches across the U.S., which successfully treated and graduated more than 12,000 young people nationwide. For 17 years, I served as chairman of the board of STRAIGHT. Other than our children, nothing was more rewarding than this effort. Betty and I initially agreed that if we helped one child it would be worth all the effort. With 12,000 successful graduates . . . It was a gratifying accomplishment."

--Calvina Fay

SOURCE: http://www.spoke.com/people/calvina-fay-3e1429c09e597c100885ce4c

**What She Tells the Public about Herself**

Director of the International Scientific and Medical Forum on Drug Abuse, a brain-trust of the world's leading physicians and scientific scholars dedicated to advancing research of drug use and drug abuse. Professor Fay is the former Executive Director of the Drug Free Business Alliance (DBA), a Houston-based nonprofit coalition of member businesses involved in attacking the drug problem in the workplaces of the Texas Gulf Coast area. DBA has served as a model program for other U.S. cities and in several other countries.

Professor Fay has been an outspoken advocate against the legalization of drugs for over 20 years. She was a founding board member of S.O.S. and she is the former president of Drug Watch International, a network engaged in combating the drug legalization movement globally. Professor Fay has served as an advisor to the White House Office of National Drug Control Policy as well as several political leaders, including President Bush, on drug policy issues.

Professor Fay has over 25 years of experience in the drug prevention field and is considered a pioneering expert on workplace drug abuse prevention programs. She has authored several books, including The Supervisor's Handbook For Preventing Drug Abuse in The Workplace and Starting a Drug Free Business Initiative, as well as numerous newsletters and publications in the field that have been published at regional and national levels. She was the managing editor and a co-author of A Report on Employer Attitudes and the Impact of Drug Control Strategies on Workplace Productivity. She also served as the managing editor of a monograph titled Drug Abuse in the Decade of the Brain.

Professor Fay holds a Master's degree in business administration, and she has founded, built, and sold two successful businesses. She is a professor at the Argentina Universidad del Salvador.

## The Truth about Calvina Fay

She always refers to herself in bios and PR blurbs, as Professor Calvina Fay, but after a dozen calls and emails to Argentina Universidad del Salvador where no one seemed to know her, I found several articles that claimed it was a donation to the university that bought her the honorary title of professor. It's only desperate ego driven con artists who call themselves professor, when in fact, they are not professors. One title Calvina did not have to buy is Honorary DEA Agent, awarded by the real DEA. She never uses this title in her misleading self-promotion because it might lead her gullible audiences to see that she is not quite the objective commentator she pretends to be.

Also very puzzling is the following that always appears in her bios: "She has founded, built, and sold two successful businesses." Not surprisingly, enquiries and web searches turn up no reference to her "successful businesses." Considering that The Queen of Lies blows her own trumpet louder than the late great Louis Armstrong, many details in her bio are suspiciously absent.

## The Queen of Lies and Her Cohorts the Semblers Continue to Promote a Litany of Lies

This information is reprinted from DFAF Website 2013, and outlines exactly what anti-marijuana advocates purport to be the truth about cannabis. In the interest of fairness, their position is outlined below; the section following the document includes the rebuttal and the cited sources that negate their myths.

From **"MARIJUANA: What Is The Truth?"**

Read what (their so-called) objective experts, scientific research, and well documented studies have discovered.*

*The preceding statement is not true.

*Truth: Increased Use*

- The number of teenage and adult users would increase if marijuana was legalized.1
- The number would probably at least double and most likely triple.
- There are 16.7 million regular marijuana users (6.7% of Americans 12 years old or older.)2
- The increase would mean an additional 17 to 34 million users in the United States.
- Colorado could have anywhere from 20% to 30% of its teenage population • regularly using marijuana.

Ask yourself: do you think increased marijuana use among teenagers and adults is good for the future of our country?

*Truth: Negative Impact on Youth*

- Signs that a youth may be using marijuana are apathy, disrespect, disinterest in activities, lower grades, frequent mood changes, depression, and isolation from the family.3
- Teens who use marijuana are more likely than non-users to engage in delinquent and dangerous behavior.4
- Those same teens experience increased risk of schizophrenia and greater levels of depression, including being three times more likely to have suicidal thoughts.5
- Marijuana-using teens are more likely to have multiple sexual partners and engage in unsafe sex.6
- Marijuana use has been shown to permanently impair brain development in youth.7 Learning skills such as problem solving, concentration, motivation, and memory are negatively affected.
- In 2007, 68% of youth in treatment nationally were there for marijuana use.8 In 2009, 830,000 youth displayed characteristics of marijuana addiction
- Colorado currently has the nation's third highest rate of marijuana use among youth ages 12 – 17.5.

Ask yourself: would you want your son or daughter to become involved in using marijuana?

*Truth: Impaired and Dangerous Driving*

- Stanford medical school research shows that tested pilots were still somewhat impaired on a simulator twenty-four hours after having smoked marijuana.9
- Marijuana use adversely affects concentration, coordination, and perception, all important skills to safe driving.10

- In 2009, 28% of all fatally-injured drivers tested positive for marijuana use.11
- In California, from 2005 to 2010, 1,240 persons were killed in traffic accidents where the driver had used marijuana.12
- Last year in Colorado, over fifty people were killed because of marijuana-impaired drivers.13
- More people driving on weekend nights were under the influence of marijuana (8.3%) than alcohol (2.2%).14
- A study of 182 truck accidents causing death found 12.8% of the drivers were under the influence of marijuana and 12.5% under the influence of alcohol.15
- A study revealed 28,000 high school seniors admitted to at least one accident after using marijuana.16

Ask yourself: do you want more impaired drivers on our interstates and roadways?

*Truth: Increased Risk for Employees*

- Safety, absenteeism, turnover rate, tardiness, productivity, work quality, and lawsuits are significant liabilities for employers with marijuana-using employees.
- Employees who tested positive for marijuana had 55% more industrial accidents and 85% more injuries compared to those that tested negative on a pre-employment exam.17
- Businesses with marijuana-impaired operators take a greater chance of causing injury to themselves, their shipments, and the traveling public. Accident records from one study showed that up to 12% of non-fatally injured drivers and up to 16% of fatally injured drivers had marijuana in their bloodstreams.18

• Drug using employees have 300% higher medical costs and benefits which increase insurance rates. Illicit drug users are 5 times more likely to file a claim under workers' compensation benefits.19

• Those testing positive for marijuana had absenteeism rates 75% higher than those that tested negative.20

Ask yourself: if you were an employer, would you want to hire an employee who uses marijuana? As an employee, do you want to work with drug users who put you at risk and run up healthcare costs?

*Truth: Skyrocketing Potency*

• In 2009, the average THC level was 10%, well over a 300% increase from the 70s when the THC potency was between 1.5-3%. 21 Marijuana samples tested from the University of Mississippi have levels exceeding 30%.22

• During the 70s, users would speak about being "stoned," "wasted," "out of it," or "spaced out," clearly indicating that even 3% potency causes intoxication.

• Increased potency is leading to higher admissions to emergency room visits and drug treatment programs. 20

Ask yourself: do you think this higher intoxicant level in marijuana is a positive factor for the health and safety of Americans?

*Truth: Additional Adverse Effects*

• Despite assertions to the contrary, marijuana is addictive. More than 4 million Americans are classified as meeting the criteria for marijuana addiction.23

- Of emergency room visits, 374,000 people were there because of a primary marijuana problem.24
- Marijuana smoke contains 50% to 70% more cancer-causing agents than smoked tobacco.25
- Only .7% of all state inmates are there for marijuana possession, with many pleading down from more serious crimes.26 In Colorado, possession of one ounce of marijuana, which produces between 30 – 60 marijuana cigarettes, although illegal, is only a citable offense with a $100 fine.
- Taxing marijuana to create revenue is "blind side" economics. Based on the experience with heavily taxed alcohol and cigarettes, revenue from marijuana would cover less than 15% of the cost associated with the adverse consequences of increased marijuana use.

Ask yourself: do you think legalizing marijuana would decrease its use?

If you answered "no" to any one of the above questions, then you should also say "no" to legalizing marijuana for recreational use."

*Adapted from: Healthy and Drug Free Colorado - Modified by: Drug Free America Foundation.

1 DEA, "Speaking Out Against Drug Legalization" 2010

2 SAMHSA, 2009 Annual Survey on Drug Use and Health, September 2010

3 ONDCP's National Youth Anti-Drug Media Campaign. Parents the Anti-Drug. Marijuana Facts

4 DEA, "DEA Position on Marijuana", July 2010

5 DEA, "DEA Position on Marijuana", July 2010

6 Bovassco, G., American Journal of Psychiatry, 2001

7 Dr. Christian Thurstone, M.D., Director, Denver Health – Substance Abuse, Treatment, Education and Prevention Program

8 SAMHSA, "Highlights for the 2007 Treatment Episode Data Set"

9 Government's Supplemental Sentencing Memorandum Re: Health Effects of Marijuana, U.S. v. Greyshock, United States District Court for the District of Hawaii, 1988.

10 Marijuana: Facts Parents Need to Know, Revised, NIDA, November 1998

11 Cesar Analysis of 2009 National Highway Transportation and Safety Administration FARS Data

12 Cramer and Associates, "Study Shows Passage of California Cannabis Initiative Will Increase Traffic Deaths"

13 "Drugged Driving Getting Worse in Colorado", 9News.com, 2011 February 17

14 National Highway Traffic Safety Administration Report, 2009

15 National Transportation Safety Board, (USA), (1990). Safety study: fatigue, alcohol, other drugs, and medical factors in fatal-to-the-driver heavy truck crashes (volume1) PBS()-917002NTSB/SS-90/91

16 O'Malley, Patrick and Johnston, Lloyd. "Unsafe Driving by High School Seniors: National Trends from 1976 to 2001 in Tickets and Accidents After Use of Alcohol, Marijuana and Other Illegal Drugs." Journal of Studies on Alcohol. May 2003

17 Zwerling and Associates. Journal of the American Medical Association. Vol. 264; pp. 2639-2643. 1990.

18 Mathias, R. "Marijuana Impairs Driving-Related Skills and Workplace Performance." NIDA Notes. Jan./Feb. 1996.

19 SmithKline Beecham Healthcare Services. "Substance Abuse in the Workplace II." Balanced Health Report. 12-96. Vol. 4., No. 3

20 U.S. Department of Health and Human Services, "Marijuana – April 26"

21 ONDCP, "New Report Finds Higher Levels of THC in U.S. Marijuana to Date", May 2009

22 CNN Health: Marijuana Potency Surpasses 10 Percent, US says by Jeanne Meserve and Mike M. Ahlers, May 14, 2009

23 National Institute of Drug Abuse, "Marijuana", 2010

24 ONDCP, Director Kerlikowske Speech, March 4, 2010

25 ONDCP, "Marijuana: Know the Facts", October 2010

26 Bureau of Justice Assistance Report, "Substance Abuse and Treatment, State and Federal Prisoners", January 1999

A glance at the sources of these statements clearly shows a poorly disguised attempt to present propaganda as fact. The two main sources of "research" cited in the footnotes are not research organizations. The DEA has, in order to retain funding, for years deliberately and knowingly lied about every facet of the marijuana debate. Early in the Carter administration, there were plans to defund and eliminate the DEA. It was clear even then that their phony "drug war" was a disaster whose only result was the ruin and incarceration of millions of American citizens.

The other authority most cited by the DFAF in their misleading propaganda is the ONDCP. The Office of National Drug Control Policy (ONDCP) was originally established by the National Narcotics Leadership Act of 1988, which mandated a national anti-drug propaganda campaign for youth. The Director of National Drug Control Policy, colloquially known as the Drug Czar, heads the office. "In addition to running the ONDCP, the director evaluates, coordinates, and oversees both the international and domestic anti-drug efforts of executive branch agencies and ensures that such efforts sustain and complement State and local anti-drug activities."

### Illegal Use of Video News Releases

In 2005, the Government Accountability Office found that the ONDCP had violated domestic propaganda and publicity prohibitions by preparing prepackaged news stories that did not disclose to television viewers that the government had produced them, and had illegally spent appropriations to develop, produce, and distribute the covert propaganda, but use of the term "drug czar" in the "video news releases" had not constituted unlawful self-aggrandizement. ONDCP supporters such as Representatives Tom Davis and Mark Edward Souder have dismissed such criticism on the grounds that the ONDCP is expressly authorized by law to conduct anti-drug media campaigns. According to Susan A. Poling, managing associate general counsel at the GAO, "What is objectionable about these is the fact the viewer has no idea their tax dollars are being used to write and produce this video segment."

In 2002, according to a multiyear study by the research firm hired by the office, teenagers exposed to federal anti-drug ads were no less likely to use drugs.

Some young girls said they were even more likely to give drugs a try. John P. Walters, ONDCP Director under George W. Bush, blamed poor ads that weren't resonating with teenagers. Walters promised in Senate testimony in 2002 that he would show results within a year or admit failure, and Congress agreed to extend the campaign through 2003 while cutting funding for the ads from $170 million in 2002 to $150 million in 2003. An entirely new advertising campaign was created.

In February 2005, a research company hired by the office and the National Institute on Drug Abuse reported that the government's ad campaign aimed at dissuading teens from using marijuana, a campaign that cost $1.4 billion between 1998 and 2006, did not work: "Greater exposure to the campaign was associated with weaker anti-drug norms and increases in the perceptions that others use marijuana." The research company was paid $42.7 million for the five-year study. After the February 2005 report was received, the office continued the ad campaign, spending $220 million on the anti-marijuana ads in fiscal years 2005 and 2006.

Let's breakdown the lies that are being told to concerned and undecided citizens:

LIE #1: DFAF CLAIMS OF INCREASED USE

"The number of teenage and adult users would increase if marijuana was legalized. The number would probably at least double and most likely triple."

THE REAL TRUTH - MARIJUANA USE BY YOUNG PEOPLE:

By Karen O'Keefe, Esq. Director of State Policies Marijuana Policy Project, and Mitch Earleywine, Ph.D.,

Professor of Psychology, University at Albany, State University of New York.

## The Impact of State Medical Marijuana Laws

All of the data in this report is from state and federal government surveys of drug use by young people. The most comprehensive nationally coordinated survey on teens' marijuana use on a state-by-state basis is the Youth Risk Behavior Surveillance System (YRBSS). The YRBSS is conducted by many (but not all) states in conjunction with the U.S. Centers for Disease Control and Prevention, and it includes data for all high schoolers, along with breakdowns of usage rates by grade level. The YRBSS has produced data for the majority of medical marijuana states with before-and-after data: Alaska, Hawaii, Maine, Michigan, Montana, New Mexico, Nevada, Rhode Island, and Vermont. It also produces national data.

In California—which has the longest-term, most detailed data available—data shows an overall decrease in teens' marijuana use. The number of seventh, ninth, and eleventh graders reporting marijuana use in the last six months and in their lifetimes all declined between 1996 (when the state's medical marijuana law passed) and 2008. An analysis commissioned by the California Department of Alcohol and Drug Programs found "no evidence supporting that the passage of Proposition 215 increased marijuana use during this period."

In Washington state (which passed its law in 1998), sixth and eighth graders' current and lifetime marijuana use has dropped significantly since the 1998 enactment of the state's medical marijuana law. The other surveyed grade levels have seen both lifetime and current marijuana use drop as well.

Data from Oregon (whose law passed in 1998) suggests modest declines in marijuana use among the two grades surveyed. Data from Alaska (which passed its law in 1998) show a moderate decrease in high schoolers' current marijuana use and a slight decrease in their lifetime use.

In Maine (which passed its law in 1999), available data on teen marijuana use suggests usage has decreased or stayed the same for every age group since Maine enacted its medical marijuana law. The Youth Risk Behavior Survey indicates a significant drop in both Maine high schoolers' current and lifetime marijuana use.

In Hawaii and Nevada (both passed laws in 2000), high schoolers' current and lifetime marijuana use has decreased since the enactment of the state laws. Colorado (which also passed its law in 2000) is the only state without an in-depth statewide survey; the limited data available suggests a modest decrease in Colorado teens' marijuana usage.

Data from Vermont (which passed its law in 2004) indicates a modest decline in teens' current marijuana use, as well as declines at all surveyed individual grade levels. Data from Montana suggest a small decline in high schoolers' lifetime marijuana use since the 2004 passage of the state's medical marijuana law and no change in their current marijuana use.

## Conclusions and Recommendations

45 Centers for Disease Control and Prevention, "2007 Michigan Youth Risk Behavior Surveillance System"; "2009 Michigan Youth Risk Behavior Surveillance System"; available at http://apps.nccd.cdc.gov/YouthOnline/App/Results.as

px?LID=MI. 46 Ammerman, Seth, M.D. "Medical Marijuana: Update for the Pediatrician," California Pediatrician, Vol. 27, No. 1 (Winter 2011): 11-13, available at: http://www.aap-ca.org/news/caPed/California%20Pediatrician%20-%20Winter%202011.pdf.

Since the mid-1990s, the U.S. has witnessed a well-publicized and sometimes emotional national debate over the medical use of marijuana. Contrary to the fears expressed by opponents of medical marijuana laws, there is no evidence that the enactment of medical marijuana laws in 16 (20 at the time of this writing) states and the District of Columbia have produced an increase in adolescent marijuana use in those states or nationwide. Instead, data from those states suggest a modest decline nationally and in medical marijuana states overall, with large declines in some age groups in some states. Only two of 13 states with operating medical marijuana programs have experienced an overall increase in youth marijuana use since passing a medical marijuana law, and both of those states have a modest amount of data since the programs are relatively new.

This data trend strongly suggests that the effect of state medical marijuana laws on teen marijuana use has been either neutral or positive. California researchers, who appear to be the only ones to specifically study the issue in the context of a survey of adolescent drug use, found no evidence of a "wrong message" effect. Legislators considering medical marijuana proposals should evaluate the bills on their own merits, without concern for unproven claims that such laws increase teen marijuana use.

## So What Is Really Going On?

First, what's behind this drop in reported marijuana use? After all, we not only have the "experts" issuing blanket, dire warnings that legalization even for medical reasons is going to kill our nation's youth. More importantly, there is some measure of logic—at least on the surface—that might lead people to believe in these claims. Wouldn't it be logical to assume that greater access to legal marijuana and the potential for even more citizens with access to it would translate into easier access to marijuana for teens and middle schoolers? Why are the numbers dropping if the access is increasing?

Let's take a look at the rest of the nation. According to an August 7, 2014, article (SOURCE: http://blogs.phoenixnewtimes.com/valleyfever/2014/08/marijuana_use_by_teens_down_in_colorado_health_department_focuses_on_risk_perception.php) in the *Phoenix New Times*, teens in Colorado are using less marijuana than before, but are also using less marijuana than their peers in states that have yet to legalize it medically.

You read that right. Teenagers in states that have not legalized medical marijuana report higher incidences of marijuana use than teens in Colorado.

So why then is the headline for the Colorado Department of Health 2013 Healthy Kids report, "New survey documents youth marijuana use, need for prevention," if marijuana use has actually decreased among young people in the state? Could it be that the officials in charge have an agenda?

Of course.

According to the department's report, "One in five Colorado high school students used marijuana in the past 30 days, and more than a third have used it at some point in their lives, the survey shows. Thirty-day marijuana use fell from 22 percent in 2011 to 20 percent in 2013, and lifetime use declined from 39 percent to 37 percent during the same two years. None of the declines shown in the preliminary data represent a statistically significant drop in rates."

So why choose to focus instead on the need for prevention? If the numbers are dropping, isn't that a sign that current efforts are sufficient?

Of course not.

If the current anti-marijuana groups were actually to acknowledge that teen use is in decline and that the state is actually faring better than most of the country in terms of teen marijuana use, they would stand to lose a lot of money on taxpayer-funded ad and awareness campaigns, a fact that Colorado's Department of Health and Environment spokesperson Mark Salley actually admitted when he spoke to the newspaper.

According to reporter Ray Stern, who spoke to Salley and wrote the resulting article, "Mark Salley, spokesman for the agency, tells Phoenix New Times that the department chose to go with the perception-of-risk angle, rather than the pot-use-is-falling angle, in order to tie the survey results to a youth marijuana-prevention campaign the agency intends to launch next month. He admits the disclaimer about how the declines aren't statistically significant applies equally to the stat about perception of risk."

What the report findings and the subsequent fear mongering are referring to is the decrease in the number of students—literally from 58% to 54%--who believe that marijuana use is risky. And why wouldn't that number decrease, when it's now being prescribed for a wide variety of medical uses? Should we expect teenagers to believe the state board-approved doctors in

Colorado are poisoning their patients? Or can we attribute the four percent drop to students widely recognizing that cannabis is now a prescribed medical treatment once again?

But even that understanding doesn't explain why fewer teens than in the past are using marijuana in states that have legalized it medically. What is causing teenagers to see marijuana as a "no big deal" drug, one that isn't worth bothering with?

One August 2014 article in the Washington Examiner may have summed it up nicely (SOURCE: http://washingtonexaminer.com/so-far-colorados-teens-are-actually-using-marijuana-less/article/2551843).

According to reporter Betsy Woodruff, "While these results might surprise some, they haven't really raised eyebrows in Colorado's cannabis business community. Kayvan Khalatbari, a businessman who co-founded the state's second-oldest marijuana dispensary, said people shouldn't have expected teen weed consumption to go up after legalization. 'Cannabis, now that it's legal, kind of is an old person's drug,' he said. 'It's something that kids are seeing adults use all over the place. It just doesn't seem as cool to kids anymore.'"

Are teenagers really shallow enough to turn away from a once-illicit drug for recreational purposes simply because their grandmothers now use it to treat their glaucoma? Why not? After all, look at the decline in Facebook use among teens and young people once their parents came along and took over. The social media site just became "uncool" once their mothers began using it to connect with their church groups and high school classmates.

While the report's findings might go deeper than simply rejecting marijuana because of its medical status, it may have become less of a peer pressure-related behavior. When the mystique and forbidden nature of it was lessened in the local culture, it became less of a draw. Added to that is the renewed understanding among younger citizens that cannabis is a medical drug with a long history of treatment applications, which changes the perception in students' minds that this isn't a party drug any more than something like penicillin is a party drug. There aren't a lot of ibuprofen-fueled raves going on in any neighborhoods, and that drug is legal for medical use, too. It's simply not just a recreational drug anymore in the eyes of consumers, regardless of their ages.

But given this information, which incidentally isn't new considering the 2012 report also showed a drop in marijuana use among teenagers (despite the CDPHE trying to simply gloss over that information by saying there was unusually high margin of error), why do officials continue to make outrageous claims that legalizing medical marijuana is going to cause an increase in the numbers of teenagers who use it? Quite frankly, because the war on drugs is very profitable for a lot of people, and employs millions of citizens in the fight. Researchers couldn't continue to conduct five-year studies for millions of dollars and ad campaign developers couldn't continue to charge the citizens of this country hundreds of millions of dollars to spread lies and half-truths to teenagers. Concentration camps like the one started by the founders of Straight, Inc. couldn't continue to take money from terrified parents if they couldn't convince those people that their children were one step from death's door if they so much as glanced at marijuana.

Even worse, entities like the state of Louisiana's for-profit privately contracted prison system couldn't continue to thrive, and their owners couldn't continue to line politicians pockets through lobbying and campaign contributions. If marijuana was decriminalized, a lot of wealthy and greedy business leaders and public figures would stand to lose, and they're not going to let that happen, even if it means cancer patients and AIDS patients needlessly die. There's too much money to be made off of fear for these officials to bother telling the truth.

Opponents of medical marijuana laws should cease making such unsubstantiated claims.

LIE #2: DFAF's CLAIM ABOUT IMPAIRED AND DANGEROUS DRIVING

• Stanford Medical School research shows that tested pilots were still somewhat impaired on a simulator twenty-four hours after having smoked marijuana.9

• Marijuana use adversely affects concentration, coordination, and perception, all important skills to safe driving.10

• In 2009, 28% of all fatally-injured drivers tested positive for marijuana use.11

• In California, from 2005 to 2010, 1,240 persons were killed in traffic accidents where the driver had used marijuana.12

• Last year in Colorado, over fifty people were killed because of marijuana impaired drivers.13

THE REAL TRUTH - DRIVING AND MARIJUANA

Investigators at Columbia University conducted a case-control study to assess the association between drug use and fatal crash risk. Of the substances identified by researchers, authors reported that depressants were most likely to be associated with crash risk (estimated odds ratio = 4:83). Estimated odds ratios for other specific drug categories were 3:57 for stimulants, 3:41 for polydrug use (excluding alcohol), and 3:03 for narcotics. Marijuana (1:83) possessed the lowest odds ratios of the substances identified.

The odds ratio for cannabis is similar to that reported in a 2012 meta-analysis of 66 separate studies which estimated that cannabis was associated with a nominally increased risk of accident (estimated odds ratio = 1:25). In that study, anti-histamines (1:12) and penicillin (1:12) were associated with comparable odds to cannabis. "Crash culpability studies have failed to demonstrate that drivers with cannabinoids in the blood are significantly more likely than drug-free drivers to be culpable in road crashes." [REFERENCE: G. Chesher and M. Longo. 2002. Cannabis and alcohol in motor vehicle accidents. In: F. Grotenhermen and E. Russo (Eds.) Cannabis and Cannabinoids: Pharmacology, Toxicology, and Therapeutic Potential. New York: Haworth Press. Pp. 313-323.]

Yes, automobile drivers who had used marijuana were only slightly more likely to have an accident while driving than someone taking over the counter allergy medicine in the same time frame, and someone taking prescription penicillin in comparable doses and in the same time frame.

In Colorado a new study by UC-Denver professor Daniel Rees and Montana State University professor D. Mark Anderson suggests stoned-driving limits don't impact traffic fatalities. Rees said he and Anderson looked at fatality data from 16 states that adopted marijuana-limit laws between 1990 and 2010 and found no statistically significant difference between states that did and didn't have such laws.

In fact, their findings have an even more shocking correlation:

"Our research suggests that the legalization of medical marijuana reduces traffic fatalities through reducing alcohol consumption by young adults," said Daniel Rees, professor of economics.

SOURCE:
http://www.ucdenver.edu/about/newsroom/newsreleases/Pages/Study-shows-medical-marijuana-laws-reduce-traffic-deaths.aspx

According to their research, Rees and Anderson have determined that greater access to marijuana has actually led to a decrease in alcohol-related automobile accidents.

Lie #3: DFAF's CLAIM ABOUT THE NEGATIVE IMPACT ON YOUTH

• Signs that a youth may be using marijuana are apathy, disrespect, disinterest in activities, lower grades, frequent mood changes, depression, and isolation from the family.3

• Teens who use marijuana are more likely than non-users to engage in delinquent and dangerous behavior.

THE REAL TRUTH - *California Marijuana Decriminalization Drops Youth Crime Rate to Record Low: Study*

(SOURCE:
http://www.huffingtonpost.com/2012/11/28/california-marijuana-decriminalization-_n_2205997.html)

By Aaron Sankin Posted: 11/29/2012 12:40 pm EST Updated: 12/01/2012 7:35 pm EST

Between 2010 and 2011, California experienced a drastic 20 percent decrease in juvenile crime—bringing the underage crime rate to the lowest level since the state started keeping records in 1954. According to a recently released study, much of that improvement can be credited to the decriminalization of marijuana.

The study, entitled "California Youth Crime Plunges to All-Time Low" and released by the San Francisco-based Center on Juvenile and Criminal Justice, looked at the number of people under the age of 18 who were arrested in the state over the past eight decades. The research not only found juvenile crime to be at its lowest level ever but, in the wake of then-Governor Arnold Schwarzenegger signing a bill reducing the punishment for possessing a small amount of marijuana from a misdemeanor to simply an infraction, the drop in rates was particularity significant.

In that one-year period, the number of arrests for violent crimes dropped by 16 percent, homicide went down by 26 percent, and drug arrests decreased by nearly 50 percent.

The category of drug arrests showed decreases in every type of crime; however, the vast majority of the drop resulted from far fewer arrests for marijuana possession. In 2010, marijuana possession accounted for 64 percent of all drug arrests, and in 2011, that number decreased to only 46 percent.

California's drop in serious youth crime has decreased faster than in the rest of the nation.

LIE #4: DFAF's CLAIM THAT MARIJUANA USE LEADS TO MENTAL ILLNESS

• Those same teens experience increased risk of schizophrenia and greater levels of depression including being three times more likely to have suicidal thoughts.

• Marijuana-using teens are more likely to have multiple sexual partners and engage in unsafe sex.

• Marijuana use has been shown to permanently impair brain development in youth. Learning skills such as problem solving, concentration, motivation and memory are negatively affected.

THE REAL TRUTH – NO BRAIN SIDE EFFECTS FOUND

"Teen Marijuana Use May Show No Effect On Brain Tissue, Unlike Alcohol, Study Finds"

Kathleen.Miles@huffingtonpost.com

huffingtonpost.com

Posted: 12/21/2012 3:18 am EST | Updated: 12/23/2012 2:04 pm EST

A teen who consumes alcohol is likely to have reduced brain tissue health, but a teen who uses marijuana is not, according to a new study.

Researchers scanned the brains of 92 adolescents, ages 16 to 20, before and after an 18-month period. During that year and a half, half of the teens -- who already had extensive alcohol and marijuana-use histories -- continued to use marijuana and alcohol in varying amounts. The other half abstained or kept consumption minimal, as they had throughout adolescence.

The before-and-after brain scans of the teens consuming typically five or more drinks at least twice a week showed reduced white matter brain tissue health, study co-author Susan Tapert, neuroscientist at University of California, San Diego, told HuffPost. This may mean declines in memory, attention, and decision-making into later adolescence and adulthood, she said.

However, the level of marijuana use -- up to nine times a week during the 18 months—was not linked to a change in brain tissue health.

Also controversial is whether chronic use of the drug causes brain damage. there are studies, like one from the Medicinal Cannabis Research Center, which found only minor differences from the control group, not only in regards to structure and metabolism but also with respect to intelligence testing, memory and concentration.

LIE #5: DFAF's CLAIM ABOUT THE PREVELANCE OF MARIJUANA USE

• Colorado currently has the nation's third highest rate of marijuana use among youth ages 12 – 17.5

THE REAL TRUTH – COLORADO TEENS USE LESS MARIJUANA THAN TEENS IN OTHER STATES

SOURCE:

http://www.huffingtonpost.com/2012/09/07/marijuana-usage-down-in-t_n_1865095.html

"Marijuana Usage Down Among Colorado Teens, Up Nationally: Study Shows"

Fortunately in Colorado, it appears that teen marijuana use is in decline while national use has gone up during the same period, according to data from the Youth Risk Behavior Surveillance System (YRBS) report compiled by the Center for Disease Control and Prevention. The drop in use by Colorado teens, a drop below the national average, coincides with the same period that the medical marijuana industry developed in the state, between 2009 and 2011.

"To put it simply, teen marijuana usage has been going down in Colorado since the passage of our comprehensive medical marijuana regulatory model," Mike Elliott, executive director of the Medical Marijuana Industry Group, told The Huffington Post. "This is exactly the opposite of what opponents of medical marijuana predicted. Colorado's teen marijuana usage rate is going down because this regulatory model has taken control away from the black market and given it back to our school districts, local and state governments, and the citizens of Colorado."

LIE #6: DFAF's CLAIM THAT MARIJUANA IS THE OVERWHELMING DRUG OF CHOICE FOR REHAB PATIENTS

- In 2007, 68% of youth in treatment nationally were there for marijuana use.8
- In 2009, 830,000 youth displayed characteristics of marijuana addiction.

THE REAL TRUTH – MARIJUANA IS NOT ADDICTIVE

Published in Psychology Today on May 5, 2012 by Dale Archer, M.D.

The vast majority of those who use marijuana do so occasionally and exhibit no addictive symptoms—no increased tolerance, no cravings, and no withdrawal. In other words, they can take it or leave it.

## Oreos: A Real Addiction

It should come as no surprise to anyone that Oreo cookies were found to be as addictive as cocaine in a recent study. "Our bodies are wired to like sugary, fatty foods. Our research supports the theory that high-fat/high-sugar foods stimulate the brain in the same way that drugs do," Schroeder told the Connecticut College News.

Why are so many youths in pot rehab?

Because the drug courts gave them the choice of rehab or prison. Rehab centers are a huge and lucrative business. The corporations that own rehabs spend millions to help elect judges who will fill their beds with marijuana offenders. These corporations, along with private prison companies, are among the largest contributors to organizations like DFAF and ALEC. Both organizations work to keep cannabis illegal and maintain draconian sentences that destroy thousands of American lives every year.

According to a federal study, the proportion of marijuana treatment admissions from all sources other than the criminal justice system—that is, the folks who weren't forced under threat of jail to attend—has been dropping since the 1990s.

According to the Substance Abuse Mental Health Services Administration (SAMHSA), more than a third of the 288,000 people entering "drug treatment for marijuana" hadn't even smoked any pot in the 30 days prior to the admission. Doesn't sound much like they were addicted, does it?

Another 16 percent admitted they'd only used marijuana three times or less in the month prior to their admission. That just doesn't sound much like the sort of out-of-control behavior we associate with drug addicts. Do these people meet the clinical standard of being in "the state of being psychologically and physiologically dependent on a drug"? Of course not.

## The Great Marijuana Rehab Scam: Feds Say You're Addicted to Pot, But They're Addicted To Cash

By Steve Elliott ~alapoet~ in Culture, News

"Any serious and impartial study of the adverse effects of marijuana use almost immediately runs into one striking and unavoidable fact: It's glaringly apparent that marijuana's potential negative effects are minor when compared to those of legal drugs such as opiates (physically habit-forming and capable of causing overdose deaths), alcohol (same on both counts) and tobacco.

A newly published clinical trial from the journal Drug and Alcohol Dependence raises serious doubts about the physical and psychological consequences of quitting pot.

So why does NIDA soberly claim that "therapeutic interventions" are necessary and important, "given the extent of use of cannabis in the general population"? (Adolescent pot use has actually been falling steadily since 1979.) Why is it so crucial to manufacture this bugaboo and to pretend it's scary?

Well, there are currently no accepted medications to aid in "quitting marijuana," and to help in combatting those fearsome CRDs (remember them?) And some companies (and, well, government officials) see a huge profit potential in fighting the marijuana monster.

On Nov. 3, Kentucky-based pharmaceutical corporation All Tranz Inc. announced it was the proud recipient of a $4 million NIDA grant to promote a "transdermal tetrahydrocannabinol (THC) patch" for the supposed "treatment of marijuana dependence and withdrawal."

THE BIGGEST LIE: DFAF's CLAIM ABOUT SKYROCKETING POTENCY

• In 2009, the average THC level was 10%, is well over a 300% increase from the 70s when the THC potency was between 1.5-3%.21 Marijuana samples tested from the University of Mississippi have levels exceeding 30%.22

• During the 70s users would speak about being "stoned," "wasted," "out of it," or "spaced out," clearly indicating that even 3% potency causes intoxication.

• Increased potency is leading to higher admissions to emergency room visits and drug.

THE REAL TRUTH

The statement that street marijuana used to be just 1.5-3% is ludicrous. That is barely above the THC level of legal hemp and is not likely to do much for anyone. On a personal level, the Santa Marta Gold that my Black Tuna's brought in from Colombia in the 1970s was every bit as potent as the better strains available today. In fact, it became the mother strain for many medical strains grown today. Of course, back then there was also Thai Stick, Maui, Kona Bud, Panama Red, Lamb's Breath from Jamaica, and several potent strains from the interior of Mexico. Most of those were 8-16% THC, about the same as the best varieties sold in dispensaries today.

Equally ridiculous, is Mohamed El Sohly's assertion to have seen cannabis with "well over 30% THC." The highest THC strains are grown mainly for the High Times Cannabis Cup competition. Growers spend years cultivating one or two high THC plants in order to win this prestigious contest. They do it strictly for bragging rights.

In a recent article by *High Times* Grow Editor and Cannabis Cup Judge Danny Danko:

"Last night on CNN's premiere of Dr. Sanjay Gupta's documentary *Weed*, it was reported that the University of Mississippi claims to have tested a strain of cannabis that clocked in at a whopping 37 percent THC.

"This is far higher than any pot we here at HIGH TIMES have encountered after ten North American Cannabis Cups in the last three years. Our lab testing, which includes multiple labs using gas and liquid chromatography, tops out at 25.49 percent THC for flowers (OG Ghost Train Haze, which was entered in the 2011 Denver Medical Cannabis Cup).

No strain we've had tested ever came close to 30 percent THC.

So, we'd like to challenge the University of Mississippi to reveal the method and results of their testing (or at least tell us the name of the strain with 37 percent THC so that we can, um... further study it).

We'll even offer the University of Mississippi a free entry in our upcoming Seattle Cannabis Cup (September 7-8) so they can compete with other high potency strains."

One man, Mahmoud El Sohly at the University of Mississippi, has the exclusive right to grow marijuana for all federally approved research and medical use. Since 1968 the United States has had a federally funded medical marijuana farm and production facility. The National Institute on Drug Abuse (NIDA) contracts with the university the production of the cannabis for the use in approved research studies. NIDA also manages the distribution of cannabis to the four surviving medical patients grandfathered into the Compassionate Investigational New Drug program (established in 1978 and canceled in 1991). The federal government, as it has ruthlessly at times gone after dispensaries that are legally operated under state law, has had, all of this time, millions and millions of dollars' worth of marijuana growing and stored at the University of Old Miss.

El Sohly is concerned about the unregulated market for marijuana. He said that without some type of regulation in place people are subjected to dangerously high levels of THC, the main psychoactive chemical in marijuana. He also admits that his real fear is the loss of his government protected exclusive license (and the millions of tax payer dollars that supports his personal fiefdom if the federal government ever allows upstarts like Harvard Medical School to grow their own marijuana for medical research).

**Irvin Rosenfeld, Federal Marijuana Patient and Author of My Medicine**

*"My own dealings with 'The Partnership For Drug Free America' and their leaders."*

*As the longest surviving of the final four Federal Medical Cannabis patients, I have been a thorn in their ass for decades. You can read in my book My Medicine about my experience in April of 1997 when I was allowed to attend their conference in Orlando that was teaching people about how to go against the growing approval of cannabis in states around the country. I was not welcomed with open arms. They let me in because of the media attention that I generated before the conference. But that was then, however history does repeat itself, especially those who twist the truth for their own well-being.*

*Now to the present. In May of 2013, I attended a community discussion put on by the Urban League of*

*Greater Miami and Concerned African Women where the subject was, "How will a medical marijuana law in Florida affect the children of Liberty City, both good and bad?" They invited six speakers made up of police officers, a judge, a drug rehab spokesperson, clergy, and a community leader. The special keynote speaker during lunch was Calvina Fay. I had asked to speak but was told the program was set. However I was told that everyone attending would get their three minutes to share their opinion.*

*Sure enough after each speaker, the audience of almost 200 got to say their peace both pro and con. I spoke and the crowd was very friendly to me once they heard that I had taken on the Federal government to gain access to my much needed medicine. This give and take continued until Calvina Fay spoke.*

*Her Power Point presentation was full of mistruths, so much so by the time she finished speaking there were maybe 75 people left. We all kept our mouths shut until she said that no one in the United States had a prescription for marijuana. I stood up and said, "Here is my Federal prescription (holding up my baggy of twelve joints) and you are as wrong about what you just said and all the other mistruths." She said she was right, that I did not have a prescription. I was then asked to sit down by the moderator as he smiled at me, letting me know that I would be allowed to ask her the first question after her presentation as was the procedure after each speaker.*

*Sure enough, I was allowed to ask her the first question, at which time she said she had to leave and would not answer any questions. Those people will never have a frank discussion with anyone who has any intelligence that can debate their position. As I said, history repeats itself when you use the same flawed rhetoric."*

Irv's book is available at www.mymedicinethebook.com.

**But What about the Children?!**

If you were fortunate enough to be a teenager in the 80s when Nancy Reagan decided to send young people out into the world armed with nothing more intellectually potent than "just say no," then you probably remember TV commercials with frying eggs and afro-tastic dads who demanded to know who taught their sons to smoke weed. "I learned it by watching you!" became a catchphrase for all that was wrong with adults with bad hair.

But what are we really supporting if we work to decriminalize marijuana? Are we leading children down a path of destruction by convincing them that the side effects of marijuana are trivial, that it is not a gateway drug, and that—much like the dad from the TV commercial—marijuana is a "do as I say, not as I do" habit?

Of course not. Because compared with the current status of marijuana in many teens' opinions and compared with the dangers of the illicit behaviors that teens currently face—such as underaged drinking, driving while impaired, tobacco, and the abundance of readily available prescription drugs to abuse—any potentially harmful effects from marijuana are low on the list of dangerous behaviors that teens could engage in.

Reports have already shown a decrease in the allure of marijuana for the teenaged demographic. Sociologists have begun to investigate whether this is because teens see it as an "old fogey" drug from their parents' and even grandparents' generation, or whether the growing legalization efforts for medical cannabis have helped shape marijuana into a medical treatment in young people's opinions. However teens view marijuana, one thing is certain: teen marijuana use is dropping around the country.

According to an article by Victoria Bekiempis for *Newsweek* (9/2/2014), we may have more to fear from other more widely available forms of recreational activity. As she states, "The researchers, from New York University's Center for Drug Use and HIV Research, analyzed data from 7,437 high school seniors who had responded to a national, annual behavioral questionnaire, called the 'Monitoring the Future' study. Two-thirds of the teens reported drinking alcohol and fifty percent said they smoked pot. The researchers found that both groups experienced adverse psychosocial impacts, but that the specific impacts differed depending on the drug. For example, with regard to relationships, marijuana tended to compromise teens' relationships with teachers and bosses more than alcohol, whereas alcohol typically compromised their relationships with friends and significant others. In this data set, marijuana was also more closely linked with lower school or job performance; alcohol, on the other hand, is more likely to lead to teens 'engaging in behaviors they regretted.'"

This study would indicate that teenagers who regularly use marijuana may have less respect for authority, but that when they turn to another widely available option, alcohol, they engage in behaviors that they later regret. Let's see, questioning authority and not holding teachers in high regard, versus having unprotected sex with strangers or driving a car while under the influence? Which one was supposed to be more harmful again?

The article continued with a further examination of the link between teen alcohol consumption and driving, compared to teen marijuana use and driving.

"Probably the most important finding, at least when it comes to overall public health, is the relationship between frequent imbibing and driving under the influence. 'The most alarming finding was that alcohol use was highly associated with unsafe driving, especially among frequent drinkers,' Joseph J. Palamar, PhD and lead study author, said in a statement about the research. 'Compared to non-drinkers, frequent drinkers were over 13 times more likely to report that their alcohol use has led to unsafe driving. Marijuana users, compared to non-users, were three times more likely to report unsafe driving as a direct result of use.'"

So what we can take away from this is that marijuana may have scientifically unproven long-term effects on developing adolescent brains, but that teens who drink alcohol are more likely to drive while under the influence and are capable of overdosing to the point of death. According to Teen Treatment Center, which proclaims itself to be one of the nation's "top" teen rehab centers—you know, those places that are reportedly saving America's youth—"alcohol is the most commonly abused substance among youth in the United States. It's one of the leading causes of abuse of other drugs, car crashes, unwanted or unplanned pregnancy, high-risk suicide and homicide."

There's a rampant belief being propagated that teenagers are trying marijuana for the first time at younger and younger ages. But according to another well-known treatment center, CRC Health Group,

"Youths aged 12 to17 have constituted about two-thirds of the new users of marijuana in recent years, with young adults aged 18 to 25 constituting most of the remaining third. Recent rates of new use among youth in 1996-1998 (averaging 86.4 initiates per 1000 potential new users) were higher than they have ever been. Rates of new use for both youth and young adults decreased between 1998 and 1999 (from 85.2 to 73.0, and from 44.1 to 31.7, respectively)."

The CRC Health Group goes on to say, "The average age of initiation of marijuana use in 1999 was 17.0 years. Since 1992, the average age has ranged from 16.5 to 17.4."

Well, which is it? Are more people smoking marijuana now, and are more teens trying it practically before they lose all their baby teeth? No. According to the very twisted wording from this inpatient treatment facility, less people are using marijuana and they're actually getting older before they try it for the first time. In 1992, the average age was between sixteen and seventeen; in 1999, it was seventeen.

## If Not Marijuana, Then What?

One other constant argument from the anti-marijuana-because-we're-pro-child crowd is the gateway drug aspect that they report to be indicative of marijuana use. Under this logic, teens who experiment with marijuana then move on to harder and harder drugs of abuse. One inpatient rehab facility, Promise Treatment Centers, had this to say:

"The Substance Abuse and Mental Health Services Administration (SAMHSA) released the findings from the latest fully analyzed version of the National Survey on Drug Use and Health in late 2013. These findings show that just under 3 million Americans age 12 or older took an improperly used or illegal drug in 2012 (SAMHSA does not include nicotine or alcohol use in this calculation). Split evenly over the year, this amounts to 7,900 individuals on any given day. Almost two-thirds (65.6 percent) of the reported new drug users took marijuana in one form or another; altogether, slightly less than 2.4 million people started using this drug.

"The next most popular targets for first-time drug use in 2012 were opioid painkillers; almost 1.9 million teenagers and adults started abusing these prescription medications. In descending order, the other substances most likely to function as first targets for drug use were prescription tranquilizers (over 1.4 million users), MDMA (869,000 users), stimulants other than cocaine (676,000 users), cocaine (639,000 users), inhalants (584,000 users), LSD (424,000 users), prescription sedative-hypnotics (166,000 users), heroin (156,000 users) and PCP (90,000 users)."

Again, let's look at the breakdown of what's being reported. Certainly, their data states that marijuana is at the top of the list for first-time drug use. Remember, these teens' initial experimentation into the world of "drugs of abuse" as categorized by SAMHSA is a plant that has been proven to be non-addictive, has been linked to only one auto accident in history, and is impossible to overdose on.

But for those teens who decided to skip the "gateway" baby step of marijuana, they headed straight to opioid painkillers, tranquilizers, cocaine, LSD, heroin, PCP, and other drugs.

Let's look at this logically from a parent's perspective, since these treatment centers are touting frightening statistics intended to lure parents into turning over their children and their checking accounts for "treatment."

If the police called and said, "We have your son in custody. He was picked up at a party and we've taken him to the hospital because there are drugs in his system," WHICH OF THOSE DRUGS WOULD YOU RATHER IT WAS? Right now, if you had to answer this question today, which of those drugs—marijuana, cocaine, heroin, PCP, LSD, or tranquilizers—would you rather your child had consumed? And yet, all of those are treated as equally serious when one of them has none of the addictive or potentially deadly consequences of the others.

The criminalization of marijuana is what lumps it together into those categories. Notice that M&Ms candies is nowhere on the list, despite the fact that the AMA reported years ago that marijuana is no more addictive than chocolate. Of course a parent receiving a phone call from the police would rather her child had been eating M&Ms than experimenting with drugs, but who made the official determination that marijuana was as harmful as heroin? Or as addictive as cocaine? Or as potentially deadly as PCP?

But of course, the purpose here is to understand more fully why cannabis has been banned for medical use, and why it's still so vilified in the eyes of the public thanks to lawmakers and lobbyists. When did marijuana stop being a viable prescription medication and start being the bad guy? The day corporate fat cats realized there was money to be made in scaring the population into turning their backs on it.

## Crime and Punishment of Children

Just as is illustrated elsewhere in this book, the for-profit prison system and the private rehab industry in the US don't extend only to adult offenders. Juvenile offenders are in just as much danger of being incarcerated against their will for minor infractions thanks to our "tough on drugs" policies in this country.

One case has recently shed light on just how deep the corruption goes. A Pennsylvania judge has finally been brought to justice after nearly a decade of selling children to the for-profit prison system.

You read that right. The judge was SELLING CHILDREN to private lock-up facilities who were willing to line his pockets, not in "campaign contributions" or donations to a cause, but in cold hard cash that went directly to the judge's personal account.

In exchange for millions of dollars in bribes over the course of the last ten years, Judge Mark Ciavarella Jr. sentenced children as young as ten years old to serve multi-year sentences in juvenile correctional and detention facilities, often for petty crimes. In one particular case, a ten-year-old was sentenced to two years in a facility for driving his mom's car, an infraction that elsewhere might have been seen as a case of poor supervision or "boys will be boys." A story that would be laughed about around the Thanksgiving dinner table twenty years later resulted in a child being locked up for two years alongside juveniles who've committed murder, all because Judge Ciavarella was paid by two separate for-profit prison corporations to make sure that they filled the bed spaces, which are paid for with tax dollars.

Over the course of Judge Ciavarella's "illustrious" and lucrative career, more than 5,000 teenagers—both male and female—were sentenced unjustly to lengthy jail time for minor infractions in exchange for money paid directly to the judge. The Pennsylvania Supreme Court has already overturned 4,000 of his convictions of children, but more remain in detention facilities and rehab centers while they wait for the wheels of justice to undo what has been done to them.

Again, it might be tempting for some voters to have little sympathy. After all, these children ended up in the judge's courtroom of their own doing, and it wasn't for selling Girl Scout cookies without a permit. But when a judge knows that the next twenty kids who appear in his courtroom are getting the maximum sentence he can impose because he's got to make a payment on his beach house, we have a legal system that is in shambles.

But how does any of this relate to marijuana decriminalization?

Even without child slave traders like Judge Ciavarella, our system is setup to teach children that they might as well go whole-hog when it comes to breaking the law because there will be no mercy or leniency, at least where drugs are concerned. The common street phrase "a little bit of weed" has no bearing in a courtroom—regardless of whether bribe money is changing hands—because of our lawmakers' efforts to throw the book at individuals who are caught possessing even small amounts of a drug that has been used medicinally by world cultures for thousands of years, a drug that has been proven non-addictive and non-tolerance building.

That's not to say that we should open the doors of the dispensaries and invite children to come in and sample the wares, but when we continue to treat marijuana as if it's the worst possible thing an individual can consume, we perpetuate a lie that leads to a criminal mindset. Young people being to think, "I'm already a lawbreaker...so what's a little more crime?"

## Who Is Paying DFAF to Send Americans to Prison for Pot?

DFAF 2012 Donors and Funders - A partial list of big funders

**$250,000+**

AbbVie - *makers of Vicodin, Vicoprofen, Marinol, Dronabinol*

Cardinal Health Foundation

Consumer Healthcare Products Association - *CHPA is committed to promoting the increasingly vital role of over-the-counter medicines and nutritional supplements in America*

CVS/Caremark Corporation

Mallinckrodt Pharmaceuticals - *a $2.1 billion global pharmaceutical company specializing in generic and branded pharmaceuticals, medical imaging, nuclear medicine. Registered in Ireland*

MetLife Foundation

Pharmaceutical Research & Manufacturers of America - *also known as PhRMA, this is one of the largest and most influential lobbying organizations in Washington.*[1] *Representing 48 pharmaceutical companies, PhRMA has 20 registered lobbyists on staff and has contracted with dozens of lobby and PR firms including Akin, Gump, Strauss, Hauer & Feld,*[3] *Barbour Griffith & Rogers, DCI Group, and The Dutko Group to promote its members' interests. PhRMA has a record of hiding its lobbying and PR activities, often by paying other organizations to advocate industry-friendly policies. In 2010, PhRMA spent $21,740,000 on lobbying costs. It has 20 lobbyists on staff in 2011. PhRMA has lobbied for 51 bills in 2010*

Purdue Pharma L.P. - *makers of pain medicines such as hydromorphone, oxycodone, fentanyl, codeine, and hydrocodone. It is widely known for the production of drugs such as MS Contin, Oxycontin, and Ryzolt. As a result of the drugs that they made and how they carried, they are a high potential for abuse by drug abusers and people with a history of addiction. The most commonly abused medications that the company produces are MS Contin and OxyContin. Both can be abused by crushing, chewing, snorting, or injecting the dissolved product. This is a significant risk to the abuser because it can result in overdose and death. Drug-seeking tactics that addicts undergo to obtain the medication will include "doctor shopping," which is visiting a number of different physicians to obtain additional prescriptions, and refusal to follow up with appropriate examinations. Along with the high potential for abuse among people without prescriptions, there is also a risk for physical dependency and tolerance for patients that are prescribed them.*

Jazz Pharmaceuticals - *developing and commercializing products including: Xyrem, Erwinaze, Prialt, Fazaclo LD And HD, And Luvox CR.*

Siebel Foundation

**$100,000 - $249,999**

Endo Pharmaceuticals - *Endo Health Solutions Inc. is an American pharmaceutical company. It was created as a result of a management buyout from DuPont Merck in 1997. Makes several opioids. OPANA is an opioid.*

The Hershey Company

Thomas S. Murphy

Reckitt Benckiser Pharmaceuticals - *RBP is a specialist pharmaceutical company with a single minded focus on the needs of people suffering from the chronic diseases of addiction. Makes Suboxone, Subutex & Temgesic*

Allen G. Rosenshine
David S. Gottesman
The Meth Project Foundation

**$25,000 - $99,999**

A&E Television Networks
Actavis, Inc.-*Makes Oxycodone*
Aetna
American International Group, Inc.
Daryl and Frank H. Barker
BBDO Worldwide Inc.
Bryan Beller
Bloomberg LP
Merilee and Roy J. Bostock
Daniel B. Burke
Diane W. Burke
CBS Corporation
CIGNA Foundation
Clear Channel
Comcast Corporation
Delta Air Lines
Dial America Marketing
Joseph Drown Foundation
ESPN and ABC Sports
Expedia, Inc.
Flambeau, Inc.
Grey Group
GroupM

Grünenthal USA, Inc. - *Grünenthal became infamous through the development and sale of the drug Thalidomide. They make Tramadol an opioid that is sold under almost a hundred different names all over the world.*

Hill and Knowlton Strategies- *In 1953, members of the tobacco industry hired the firm to help counteract findings that suggested cigarette smoking led to lung cancer. H&K represented the Bank of Credit and Commerce International (BCCI) following its drug-money laundering indictment.*

Horizon Media, Inc.

HBO Horizon Media, Inc.

IAC/InterActiveCorp

J. Seward Johnson, Sr. 1963 Charitable Trust

Jazz Pharmaceuticals

Hearst Corporation

IAC/InterActiveCorp

J. Seward Johnson, Sr. 1963 Charitable Trust

Jazz Pharmaceuticals

Betty Wold Johnson

Johnson & Johnson

JPMorgan Chase & Co.

J. Walter Thompson

David A. Katz

F.M. Kirby Foundation, Inc.

Landor Legacy

Major League Baseball

Merck Partnership for Giving

Millward Brown, Inc.

Morgan Stanley

National Association of Chain Drug Stores Foundation

National Basketball Association

National Football League Inc.

National Hockey League
News Corp
The Nielsen Company
Ogilvy CommonHealth Worldwide
Ogilvy & Mather
Robert Wood Johnson Jr. Charitable Trust
Patricia F. Russo
Sony Corporation
TeamDetroit

Pfizer Inc. - *Makes many opiates. Development program for Remoxy® (oxycodone) around-the-clock opioid*

Teva Pharmaceutical Industries Ltd. - *Oxycodone, Oxymorphone. Teva holds a patent on multiple drugs including: Copaxone (for the treatment of multiple sclerosis), now the world's bestselling MS drug, and Azilect (sold as Agilect in some countries) for treatment of Parkinson's disease.*

Treatment Research Institute- *Products for drug treatment programs*

Wachtell, Lipton,Rosen & Katz

Wunderman - *The foundation is a 501(c)3, allowing tax-free donations but no lobbying; SOS is a 501(c)4 and it's allowed to lobby, according to Fay, who started two successful businesses before taking the nonprofit path.*

## Last Word on DFAF and SOS

Saving Our Society from Drugs, a St. Petersburg Group that fights marijuana legalization proposals across the country, blasted the Florida medical marijuana initiative in recently filed written testimony.

The group points to an imaginary study that says increased marijuana cultivation can have a negative environmental impact, the danger of "drugged driving," and that the Federal Drug Administration does not regulate marijuana.

"Simply put, crude marijuana does not meet the standards of modern medicine," read the testimony, which was written by Amy Ronshausen, the group's interim deputy director. She serves as the manager of Congressional and legislative affairs for the nonprofit Drug Free America Foundation and Interim Deputy Director Saving our Society from Drugs.

Her testimony was filed with the Office of Economic and Demographic Research, which is tasked with determining the proposed amendment's economic impact. Her paper had no references to economic impact. One official remarked that she probably didn't understand the purpose of the hearing.

But the manager of Congressional and legislative affairs for the nonprofit Drug Free America Foundation said decriminalization efforts often have unintended effects, like normalizing drug use.

"Once you start treating it like a traffic or speeding ticket, we've seen drug use start to go up," Ronshausen said. She also expressed concern that people issued tickets don't have the same chances to get drug treatment as those who go to court.

She feels compassion is not a good reason to pass medical marijuana. "The people that support and that are pushing for these ballot measures are working on these issues to play on people's compassion," she said.

## Who Is This Campaigner Against Compassion?

After a stint tending bar, she has lined her pockets at the Pinellas County Drug Court, forcing cannabis users into a useless and expensive rehab program at Operation PAR, Inc.

“Operation PAR, Inc. offers a full continuum of services for individuals with substance abuse and/or mental health disorders. Our services are provided on a sliding fee scale based on income. Insurance and Medicaid are accepted for most services. Operation PAR, Inc. serves more than 13,000 individuals a year in intervention and treatment services and another 40,000 participants are impacted annually by the agency's messages of substance abuse awareness, education, prevention, research and information and referral. Additionally, the Pinellas Juvenile Assessment Center (PJAC) admits more than 7,500 juveniles a year.”

Check out her FaceBook account: Amy Stahley Ronshausen. Amy, the anti-drug warrior, believes in “Starting the night off right!” with a drink.

## A Closer Look at Colorado

According to a press release, the Brookings Institution has taken a careful look at marijuana decriminalization in Colorado, which became the first state to allow recreational use amount of the substance. Despite the lies shared from high-power podiums about the dangers and the criminal risks, the report paints a much clearer and much more positive picture of the result of this experiment.

### Brookings Institution Report: Roll Out of Colorado Marijuana Legalization Successful

The Brookings Institution released a report today evaluating the initial implementation of marijuana legalization in Colorado and pronouncing it a success. The independent think tank praised the regulatory system in place, saying it addresses "key concerns such as diversion, shirking, communication breakdowns, illegal activity, and the financial challenges facing the marijuana industry" and cited good leadership, strong communication and cultural changes in government, interest groups and the public as having contributed to the favorable outcome.

"Today the Brookings Institution proved what many of us have known for a long time: that legalizing and regulating marijuana and other drugs can be done thoughtfully and responsibly to the benefit of our communities," said Major Neill Franklin (Ret.), executive director of Law Enforcement Against Prohibition. "As legalization spreads across the country, regulatory models will only continue to improve, crime continue to drop, and public understanding of drug addiction as a public health problem, not as a matter for law enforcement, continue to expand."

# Chapter 4: Black and White in the Marijuana Debate

According to the website of the Drug Policy Alliance, the nation's leading organization that promotes drug policies that are actually based on science, compassion, medical needs, and human rights, "The drug war has produced profoundly unequal outcomes across racial groups, manifested through racial discrimination by law enforcement and disproportionate drug war misery suffered by communities of color. Although rates of drug use and selling are comparable across racial lines, people of color are far more likely to be stopped, searched, arrested, prosecuted, convicted and incarcerated for drug law violations than are whites. Higher arrest and incarceration rates for African Americans and Latinos are not reflective of increased prevalence of drug use or sales in these communities, but rather of a law enforcement focus on urban areas, on lower-income communities and on communities of color as well as inequitable treatment by the criminal justice system. We believe that the mass criminalization of people of color, particularly young African American men, is as profound a system of racial control as the Jim Crow laws were in this country until the mid-1960s."

The DPA website continues, "The life-long penalties and exclusions that follow a drug conviction have created a permanent second-class status for millions of Americans, who may be prohibited from voting, being licensed, accessing public assistance and any number of other activities and opportunities. The drug war's racist enforcement means that all of these exclusions fall more heavily on people and communities of color. DPA is committed to ending these highly discriminatory policies and to combating the stigma attached to drug use and drug convictions."

The DPA has hit the nail on the head. While African-Americans make up approximately 14% of the drug-using population, they make up 37% of the arrests. This disproportionate number has an even greater impact on their communities following the outrageously unbalanced conviction rate. When blacks are targeted for marijuana offenses and locked away in forced labor pools, who stays behind in the communities and raises their children? Who serves as community leaders?

But a more important question is how the government plans to continue to get away with this once the public becomes more aware of it. The ACLU conducted an exhaustive study that examined the marijuana arrest and conviction rates by population for African-Americans and whites.

First, some of the most alarming news from the report: "The report finds that between 2001 and 2010, there were over 8 million marijuana arrests in the United States, 88% of which were for possession. Marijuana arrests have increased between 2001 and 2010 and now account for over half (52%) of all drug arrests in the United States, and marijuana possession arrests account for nearly half (46%) of all drug arrests. In 2010, there was one marijuana arrest every 37 seconds, and states spent combined over $3.6 billion enforcing marijuana possession laws."

Whether or not concerned citizens take any interest whatsoever in the reasons and the history of marijuana and cannabis criminalization, this single finding alone should be enough to spur the populace into action. Eight million marijuana arrests means taxpayer dollars were wasted on law enforcement and prosecution; if even a portion of those arrests resulted in no jail time—yet another astronomical cost to the country—there are financial costs associated with simply apprehending and charging those individuals. For the sake of playing devil's advocate we'll overlook the undue stress and emotional strain that is placed on a person when arrested since they are admittedly violating the law, however unjust and unjustified that law may be. But look at that figure again and really let it sink in...in one year alone, our country spent $3.6 billion enforcing the law regarding marijuana possession.

Nearly four billion dollars. While some of that money was surely spent on fighting foreign drug cartels, how much of that money went towards keeping cannabis out of the hands of a man dying from AIDS? How much was spent to ensure that an elderly glaucoma patient suffered as she went blind? How many young people were locked up with hardened criminals, some of the most evil people ever to walk the streets, all for possessing a personal amount of a drug that only became illegal so that Hearst and DuPont could ensure their power and wealth remained intact?

Unfortunately, that first bombshell wasn't even the worst thing about the report, which was actually implemented to uncover the racial inequality that rages on in America's war on cannabis. The report, "The War on Marijuana in Black and White," examined the very real, blatant, government-supported and government-instigated abuse of African-Americans in our legal system where marijuana is concerned.

Let's look at some of the highlights from this very telling report:

*Point #1: Blacks and whites use marijuana in approximately equal numbers for their communities.*

If a white community made up of 1,000 people has ten marijuana users, then a black community of 1,000 people has about ten marijuana users. With numbers only reaching through 2010, the African-American demographic has pulled slightly ahead each year in percentage of the overall population that uses marijuana, but that number for both blacks and whites is less than 15% of the total population using marijuana.

Interestingly, when the population of marijuana users is broken down by age group, the 18 to 25-year-old white demographic reports far greater marijuana use than among 18 to 25-year-old members of the black population. Black young adults use far less marijuana than white young adults...so why are they arrested more often than whites for it?

*Point #2: Blacks are far less likely to experiment with marijuana than whites.*

Interestingly, in every single year of the study from 2001 through 2010, more blacks than whites report that they've never used marijuana. Again...why are more blacks arrested for marijuana-related offenses than whites, when fewer blacks are using it in the long-term?

*Point #3: Then why are African-Americans more than three times as likely to be arrested for marijuana than whites?*

The real kick in the gut from the ACLU report was the arrest rate. At its highest point (2007), 192 out of every 100,000 white Americans were arrested for marijuana. Take a stab in the dark at how high you think the arrest rate for African-Americans was that year, strictly for marijuana-related offenses. Go ahead, guess.

716 out of every 100,000 black Americans.

Yes, roughly 200 whites and 750 blacks out of the same sample size were arrested for marijuana, and that's only in 2007. The numbers for both demographics have been slowly dropping each year since then, but they're still higher than 2001, and African-Americans are still arrested at incredibly disproportionate rates. In fact, taken around the country as a whole, blacks are between two and eight times more likely to be arrested for marijuana possession than whites.

In fact, Oregon, the US state with the lowest disparity between white and black arrest rates for marijuana possession, still had double the number of African-American marijuana arrests versus white arrests for the same charges. This number—563 black arrests to 271 white arrests (out of every 100K people)—is in spite of the fact that in 2013 Oregon's racial makeup was 88% white and only 2% black.

(SOURCE:http://quickfacts.census.gov/qfd/states/41000.html)

Why is that? It's simple math: there are more whites than blacks in the US, whites and blacks across the entire age spectrum report using marijuana in fairly even numbers, blacks are less likely than whites to ever touch marijuana...so why are they arrested in such outrageously skewed numbers?

*Point #4: If you're black in a major city, forget it.*

The numbers above—200 and 750 out of every 100,000—were based on the average around the entire country. But if you live in a major metropolitan area, things look a whole lot worse for you if you're black.

According to recent survey information, (SOURCE: http://en.wikipedia.org/wiki/Demographics_of_Chicago)

the city of Chicago is broken up like this: "the racial makeup of the city in 2010 was 32% black (including Hispanics), 45% white (31% non Hispanic white + 14% white Hispanics), 5% Asian (including Hispanics), and 3% from two or more races (including Hispanics). The ethnic makeup of the population is 28% Hispanic (of any race) and 72% belong to non Hispanic background (of any race). In 2000, 21.7% of the population was foreign born; of this, 56.3% came from Latin America, 23.1% from Europe, 18.0% from Asia and 2.6% from other parts of the world."

According to the ACLU's report, in 2010 there were 250 marijuana arrests of whites in Chicago for every 1,750 marijuana arrests of African-Americans. So if Chicago is 32% black and 45% white, why does this statistic stand?

But let's think like concerned taxpayers again. In 2010, in Cook County, Illinois (the county that holds Chicago), there were 33,000 marijuana possession arrests, or an average of 91 per day. *Ninety-one people per day* were arrested for possession; not trafficking, not cultivating, but simply owning enough marijuana on their physical person that the law could only charge them with possession. Where do police officers even house that many people for booking, let alone for serving any kind of sentence? Ninety-one people per day, thirty-three thousand people per year...and that is just for one major city.

# Chapter 5:
# The Money Trail

This is just one more example of how broken the criminal justice system has become and another indication that fascist principles have taken over rule of law. It's no surprise to see ALEC—the American Legislative Exchange Council that your Republican/Tea Party elected officials have sworn "loyalty oaths" to—legislators are among the list of perpetrators attempting to subvert the will and best interests of the voters.

## The Top Five Special Interest Groups Lobbying To Keep Marijuana Illegal

*From http://www.republicreport.org/2012/marijuana-lobby-illegal/*

Last year, over 850,000 people in America were arrested for marijuana-related crimes. Despite public opinion, the medical community, and human rights experts all moving in favor of relaxing marijuana prohibition laws, little has changed in terms of policy.

There have been many great books and articles detailing the history of the drug war. Part of America's fixation with keeping the leafy green plant illegal is rooted in cultural and political clashes from the past.

However, we at Republic Report think it's worth showing that there are entrenched interest groups that are spending large sums of money to keep our broken drug laws on the books:

1.) Police Unions: Police departments across the country have become dependent on federal drug war grants to finance their budget. In March, we published a story revealing that a police union lobbyist in California coordinated the effort to defeat Prop 19, a ballot measure in 2010 to legalize marijuana, while helping his police department clients collect tens of millions in federal marijuana-eradication grants. And it's not just in California. Federal lobbying disclosures show that other police union lobbyists have pushed for stiffer penalties for marijuana-related crimes nationwide.

2.) Private Prisons Corporations: Private prison corporations make millions by incarcerating people who have been imprisoned for drug crimes, including marijuana. As Republic Report's Matt Stoller noted last year, Corrections Corporation of America, one of the largest for-profit prison companies, revealed in a regulatory filing that continuing the drug war is part in parcel to their business strategy. Prison companies have spent millions bankrolling pro-drug war politicians and have used secretive front groups, like the American Legislative Exchange Council, to pass harsh sentencing requirements for drug crimes.

3.) Alcohol and Beer Companies: Fearing competition for the dollars Americans spend on leisure, alcohol and tobacco interests have lobbied to keep marijuana out of reach. For instance, the California Beer & Beverage Distributors contributed campaign contributions to a committee set up to prevent marijuana from being legalized and taxed.

4.) Pharmaceutical Corporations: Like the sin industries listed above, pharmaceutical interests would like to keep marijuana illegal so American don't have the option of cheap medical alternatives to their products. Howard Wooldridge, a retired police officer who now lobbies the government to relax marijuana prohibition laws, told Republic Report that next to police unions, the "second biggest opponent on Capitol Hill is big PhRMA" because marijuana can replace "everything from Advil to Vicodin and other expensive pills."

5.) Prison Guard Unions: Prison guard unions have a vested interest in keeping people behind bars just like for-profit prison companies. In 2008, the California Correctional Peace Officers Association spent a whopping $1 million to defeat a measure that would have "reduced sentences and parole times for nonviolent drug offenders while emphasizing drug treatment over prison."

### Why Can't You Smoke Pot? Because Lobbyists Are Getting Rich Off of the War on Drugs

SOURCE: http://www.republicreport.org/2012/exclusive-why-cant-you-smoke-pot-because-lobbyists-are-getting-rich-off-of-the-war-on-drugs/

Police Association Lobbyist John Lovell

John Lovell is a lobbyist who makes a lot of money from making sure you can't smoke a joint. That's his job. He's a lobbyist for the police associations in Sacramento, and he is a driving force behind grabbing Federal dollars to shut down the California marijuana industry. I'll get to the evidence on this important story in a bit, but first, some context.

At some point in the distant past, the war on drugs might have been popular. But not anymore — the polling is clear, but beyond that, the last three Presidents have used illegal drugs. So why do we still put hundreds of thousands of people in steel cages for pot-related offenses? Well, there are many reasons, but one of them is, of course, money in politics. Corruption. Whatever you want to call it, it's why you can't smoke a joint without committing a crime, though of course you can ingest any number of pills or drinks completely within the law.

Some of the groups who want to keep the drug illegal are police associations that want more members to pay more dues. One of the primary sources for cash for more policing activities are Federal grants for penalizing illegal drug use, which help pay for overtime, additional police officers, and equipment for the force. That's what Lovell does, he gets those grants. He also fights against democratic mechanisms to legalize drugs.

In 2010, California considered Prop 19, a measure to legalize marijuana and tax it as alcohol. The proposition gained more votes than Meg Whitman, the former eBay executive and Republican gubernatorial nominee that year, but failed to pass. Opponents of the initiative ran ads, organized rallies, and spread conspiracy theories about billionaire George Soros to confuse voters.

Lovell managed the opposition campaign against Prop 19. He told *Time Magazine* that he was pushing against the initiative because, "The last thing we need is yet another mind-altering substance to be legalized."

But *Republic Report* reviewed lobbying contracts during the Prop 19 fight, and found that Lovell's firm was paid over $386,350 from a wide array of police associations, including the California Police Chiefs Association.

While Lovell may contend that he sincerely opposes the idea of marijuana legalization, he has constructed an entire business model predicated on pot prohibition.

Shortly after President Obama's stimulus program passed, Lovell went to work channeling the taxpayer money for California into drug war programs. According to documents *Republic Report* obtained from the Police Chiefs Association, Lovell helped local departments apply for drug war money from the Federal government. Here's a copy of one letter sent to a police department in Lassen County, California:

THERE ARE A NUMBER OF IMPORTANT OPPORTUNITIES AVAILABLE TO POLICE AGENCIES ARISING OUT OF THE RECENTLY ADOPTED AMERICAN RECOVERY AND REINVESTMENT ACT OF 2009. PLEASE TAKE THE TIME TO READ THIS BULLETIN FROM THE US DEPARTMENT OF JUSTICE OFFICE OF JUSTICE PROGRAMS. JOHN LOVELL WILL BE ABLE TO PROVIDE FOLLOW-UP INFORMATION. HIS PHONE NUMBER IS 916-447-3820.

**OJP's Information Related to the American Recovery and Reinvestment Act of 2009**

---

There is big money in marijuana prohibition. Lovell represented a police association in a bid to steer some $2.2 million dollars into a "Marijuana Suppression Program." In 2009 and 2010, California police associations sought a $7,537,389 chunk of Federal money for police to conduct a "Campaign against Marijuana Planting" program. The anti-marijuana money went directly into the paychecks of many officers. For example, police departments in Shasta, Siskiyou, and Tehama Counties formed a "North California Eradication Team" to receive $550,000 in grants that helped pay for overtime, a new officer, and flight operations.

The total amount awarded was $550,000, to be split between Shasta, Siskiyou and Tehama counties, which make up the Northern California Marijuana Eradication Team (NorCal-MET). Broken down in the agenda worksheet, the sheriff's office is expecting to spend $20,000 on flight operations, $94,895 for the full-time deputy's salary and benefits, $16,788 for the administration assistant salary and benefits and $29,983 to cover up to 666.29 hours of overtime.

The Federal anti-marijuana honeypot might have dried up if Prop 19 had passed. Legalizing marijuana would have generated billions in tax revenue for the state of California, while also reducing victimless crime prosecutions. But for lobbyists like Lovell, legalization was a direct assault on hundreds of thousands of dollars in potential fees for helping to solicit taxpayer money for his clients.

Police associations also contributed about $100,500 to a campaign account used to coordinate opposition to Prop 19. Of the $386,350 in fees paid by police associations to Lovell through 2009 and 2010, status update reports reviewed by Republic Report reveal that Lovell worked on a number of issues, from advocacy against Prop 19 to channeling grants and monitoring legislation.

Of course, police associations aren't the only interest group with a stake in maintaining broken drug laws. The alcohol industry and prison guard interests also contributed money to help Lovell stop Prop 19. Howard Wooldridge, a retired police officer who now helps push for legalization as a citizen advocate, told Republic Report that drug company lobbyists also fight to keep marijuana illegal because they view pot as a low-cost form of competition.

**This post originally described Lovell as a police union lobbyist. It has been corrected to note that he represents law enforcement associations, not labor unions. We regret the error.*

## The Drug Warriors Cashing in on Pot Prohibition

SOURCE:
http://www.thefix.com/content/marijuana-legalization-drug-prohibition-lobbying-revolving-door8111?page=1

Former public servants, from DEA chiefs to cops, are using their clout to lobby for drug policies that enrich themselves—before it's too late.

When eight former DEA chiefs signed a letter to US Attorney General Eric Holder earlier this month demanding that the feds crack down on Washington and Colorado, the states which voted last November to legalize marijuana, there was more than just drug-war ideology at stake. There was money.

Two of the elder drug warriors, Peter Bensinger (DEA chief, 1976–1981) and Robert DuPont (White House drug chief, 1973–1977), run a corporate drug-testing business. Their employee-assistance company, Bensinger, DuPont & Associates, the sixth largest in the nation, holds the pee stick for some 10 million employees around the US. Their clients have included the biggest players in industry and government: Kraft Foods, American Airlines, Johnson & Johnson, the Federal Aviation Administration and even the Justice Department itself.

"These are not just old drug war architects pushing a drug war model they've pushed for 40 years," says Brian Vicente, a Denver lawyer and co-author of Colorado's Proposition 64, which legalized marijuana for recreational use. "These guys are asking Eric Holder to pursue prohibition policies that line their own pockets."

Bensinger and DuPont both deny money is their motive. "It's true we might benefit from keeping marijuana illegal," says DuPont. But he argues it's equally true that marijuana legalization could benefit his bottom line, putting forth the old drug-war line that legalization would create more users. "The more success legalization has, the better it is for our business because they are creating a problem for employers," he says. "That would be smart for us." DuPont also points out that only 15% of their business is made up of training employers to detect the warning signs of drug and alcohol abuse and supplying third-party testing. But both men are involved in industry-controlled lobbying groups like the Drug & Alcohol Industry Testing Association, which backed the Drug Testing Integrity Act of 2008, outlawing products that help people beat drug tests and keeping their business healthy.

By inserting themselves into the legal-pot debate, Bensinger, DuPont, and other drug warriors benefit by promoting their own legacies and bolstering their own business, lobbying, and consulting interests—even in the face of an increasingly skeptical public. A 2011 Gallup survey showed that half of Americans favor legalizing weed.

"This letter that they signed is their attempt to once again become relevant within the public policy debate that has largely turned its back on such archaic viewpoints," says Paul Armentano, deputy director of the pro-marijuana nonprofit, National Organization for the Reform of Marijuana Laws (NORML).

The time-honored revolving door between government and business swings fast and often. It can be straightforward, like the appointment of banking behemoth Goldman Sachs' alumni as economic policymakers by recent presidential administrations. But when it comes to the drug war, the family tree is more like a thicket of interests among law enforcement, federal and state prisons, pharmaceutical giants, drug testers, and drug treatment programs—all with an economic stake in keeping pot illegal.

Bensinger and DuPont are longtime allies of the marijuana prohibition group that sent the letter to Holder, Save Our Society from Drugs (SOS), which was founded by Mel Sembler, a Florida shopping-mall magnate, and his wife, Betty. The Semblers also founded Straight, Inc.—a drug-treatment program that used sleep deprivation, beatings, and psychological abuse to treat 10,000 teenage patients in nine states from 1976 to 1993, at $1,400 a month plus a $1,600 per patient evaluation fee, raking in millions. Straight was shut down after investigations in state after state corroborated the hundreds of complaints. But the Semblers, longtime major Republican Party fundraisers, retain their influence as behind-the-scenes bankrollers of the anti-drug faction.

The department of the White House drug czar, otherwise known as the Office of National Drug Control Policy (ONDCP), is another arm of the government's war on drugs that can be lucrative to incumbents. Andrea Barthwell, MD, former deputy drug czar during President George W. Bush's first term and his point person against medical marijuana, has earned a living both treating drug addicts and lobbying against policies that weaken marijuana laws—and cut into her own bottom line.

As a past president of the American Society of Addiction Medicine (ASAM)—a group that opposes medical marijuana, and whose members' business model could be threatened by legalized marijuana, since two-thirds of its clientele are court-ordered pot users trying to avoid jail time—Barthwell has been one of its fiercest attack dogs. In ASAM campaigns against Oregon and Illinois' medical marijuana initiatives, she called those who favor medical marijuana "cruel" and "snake oil salesman." She denounces this pain-relief and anti-nausea approach for patients with cancer and AIDS because, she claims, it is unregulated and unproven. (The Institute of Medicine declared medical marijuana useful in 2003, and since then many studies, and many more users, attest to its benefits.)

Yet Barthwell was happy to jump from the ONDCP to the payroll of GW Pharmaceutical in 2005, lobbying for the Canadian company's Sativex—a liquefied marijuana spray, extracted from whole plant cannabis, for the same pain benefits. Even as the American Medical Association and federal lawmakers maintain that pot has no medicinal value, Big Pharma is applying for dozens of cannabis-based new medicines in order to take hold of of the $1.8 billion medical marijuana industry, as NORML's Paul Armentano pointed out five years ago in the Huffington Post.

Barthwell, like Bensinger and DuPont, also has a financial stake in the prohibition treatment culture. She is founder and CEO of EMGlobal LLC, parent company of the Chicago-based Two Dreams Outer Banks drug treatment center, and is also a director of Catasys Inc., which provides substance abuse programs and behavioral health management services to companies, health plans and unions—a role for which she received $77,994 in compensation in 2011.

When it comes to the drug war, money rolls into whichever corporate pockets are willing to play ball, whether it's big-time lobbyists or broadcast TV networks. Barry McCaffrey—President Clinton's second-term drug czar and a former Army general, who also signed the recent letter to Holder—was in charge of the purse strings at ONDCP. He oversaw a money-soaked, ham-handed propaganda campaign: In 1999, his office hired PR giant Fleishman-Hillard (at $10 million a year), which encouraged TV networks to slip anti-drug messages into sitcoms and dramas in exchange for ad time worth millions. The secret effort allowed networks to avoid running PSAs, freeing up airtime for paid ads. Networks also gave the ONCDP advance copies of scripts to review. It's estimated that between 1998 and 2000, the networks received up to $25 million in benefits.

At the same time, McCaffrey was sharpening his stick for the battle against medical marijuana, flatly denying that patients in pain could receive relief from pot. After he left the drug czar's job, he went on the payroll of military contractors, promoting their interests in the Iraq war as a frequent talking head on national network TV, never disclosing his financial ties.

Lobbying your former employer—whether it's the government itself or taxpayers who foot the bill—is the No. 1 way one-time public servants can serve themselves. The same is true of current state-paid employees, like cops and other law enforcement personnel whose job it is to crack down on illegal weed smoking. As Armentano notes, federal grants that target illegal drug use are a major source of funding for local police coffers, paying for new hires, equipment and coveted overtime pay.

John Lovell, a lobbyist for police associations in Sacramento, California, not only obtains those grants, he is a front-line fighter on behalf of the cops to keep pot illegal. When California weighed Proposition 19 to legalize marijuana in 2010, Lovell helped manage the opposition campaign. During the fight, according to a review of lobbying contracts by Republic Report, Lovell's company received $386,350 from police groups, including the California Police Chiefs Association. The same report noted that Lovell helped local police departments apply for drug war money from President Obama's American Recovery and Reinvestment Act. In 2009 and 2010, state police groups sought some $75 million from the feds to conduct a Campaign Against Marijuana Planting. Lovell represented one such group.

The tangled money trail can seem at times like something from a smoke-filled Cheech and Chong plot.

Indeed, law enforcement agencies around the country could lose as much as $11 billion in taxpayer money if marijuana prohibition is repealed, according to Harvard economics professor Jeff Myron. Weed arrests account for half of all drugs arrests in the US. The tangled money trail can seem at times like something from a smoke-filled Cheech and Chong plot.

In 2009, the California Police Chiefs Association posted on their website a position paper against pot for pain, courtesy of a group called Friends of the DEA. "Requiring the DEA unequivocally to take a 'hands-off' approach, no matter how egregious the dispensary's practices, will not serve the best interests of patients. Uncontrolled proliferation of dispensaries will seriously undercut our FDA drug approval system and deprive patients of important regulatory protections," the group argued. What the paper didn't note was that Friends was a lobbying group headed by Michael Barnes, a former Bush appointee to the drug czar's office, as first pointed out by CounterPunch that year. The nine-page, heavily footnoted position paper was written by none other than Andrea Barthwell, MD, the promoter of Sativex, which is likely to receive FDA approval soon.

Among the biggest financial winners from the war on pot are private prisons and the army of DEA agents, local deputies and SWAT teams who help fill them up. Since 1980, federal prisons have ballooned some 790% because of the war on drugs, which began in earnest the previous decade. Private prison companies have seen their business soar. Corrections Corporation of America (CAA), the largest operator in the US, with 60 facilities and a 90,000-bed capacity, had $1.7 billion in taxpayer-funded revenue last year. The GEO Group, a worldwide player with 53,000 beds, pulled in $1.6 billion in government-funneled revenue.

In its 2010 annual report, CAA is fairly transparent about its stake in the anti-drug battle: "Any changes [in laws] with respect to drugs and controlled substances or illegal immigration could affect the number of persons arrested, convicted and sentenced, thereby potentially reducing demand for correctional facilities to house them." Last year, both companies stuffed millions of dollars into the pockets of Washington lobbyists to pressure lawmakers to maintain the status quo, as revealed in an investigation by Laura Carlsen in March's Counter Punch magazine.

"My most powerful adversity is the police-prison industry," says former cop–turned–drug policy specialist Howard Woolridge, who lobbies lawmakers for marijuana reform for Citizens Opposing Prohibition. "They can say, 'If you don't vote for more prohibition, we will tell people you are soft on drugs on and soft on crime.' The Fraternal Order of Police is looking out for their 326,000 members' paychecks. If they say you're soft on crime, they can move upward of 2% of the electorate. In a close election, that's victory and defeat."

Vincente doesn't doubt that the Bensingers, Bathwells and McCaffreys are fervent believers in their anti-pot mission, even as they earn their living on its front lines or flanks. The same people who wrote to Holder battled Vincente's initiative as well. "It's what they do—they get together and sign letters," he says. For the older fighters, says Paul Armentano of NORML, "Their motivation is the fact their failed policies have been proved wrong. All they have is the ability to try to intimidate a couple of high-ranking officials. Most of America has moved on."

*Kevin Gray is a New York-based journalist. He writes about business, crime, politics and celebrity. He has reported from the Congo, Libya, Lebanon, Colombia, China, and throughout the US. His work has appeared in the New York Times Magazine, New York, Details, People, Men's Journal and the Washington Post.*

## Greedy Bottom Feeders Are Everywhere

The following is a report prepared by my good friend **Chris Goldstein** for a hearing in N.J. that was looking into ethical misconduct and conflict of interest. The subject was a local assemblywoman, Mary Pat Angelini, the area's own homegrown version of Calvina Fay.

**Chris-Investigation-Mary Pat Angelini**

**Chris Goldstein** NOTES for hearing:

Assemblywoman Mary Pat Angelini has used federal, state, and municipal grants to pay herself a salary of almost $100,000 per year while pursuing a personal agenda against medical marijuana patients and overall access to state-legal medicinal cannabis by qualifying and even registered patients. Her approach may have violated a number of provisions in the New Jersey Code of Ethics for Legislators.

Angelini is the Executive Director of a non-profit organization called Prevention First whose mission is ostensibly to educate children and adults about substance abuse and substance treatment options for all drugs, including prescription pharmaceuticals. Angelini made $91,000 in 2011 alone and has been executive director for ten years.

Marijuana arrests in New Jersey comprise about half of all drug-related arrests in the state. Those arrested for marijuana are often given the option to complete a substance abuse treatment program, often at their own expense, as part of plea agreements with courts and prosecutors in exchange for lesser charges and reduced sentences and/or fines. Thus marijuana offenders are often required to seek out third party information about available treatment options to satisfy the court.

Assemblywoman Angelini proudly states that Prevention First is the overall substance abuse prevention and treatment information "hub" in Monmouth County, but the organization also works statewide.

Monmouth is in the top four counties in New Jersey for marijuana arrests. The ACLU recently released a report that indicated a racial disparity to those arrests in Monmouth County specifically.

In 2010, the New Jersey Compassionate Use Medical Marijuana Act was signed into law. Implementation of the extremely limited Medicinal Marijuana Program (MMP) has been significantly delayed. As a legislator, Angelini has voted against every effort to give seriously ill residents access to cannabis, often supporting her position with her title at Prevention First. Angelini even sponsored a superfluous bill to prevent any of the six Alternative Treatment Centers from obtaining preserved farmland for any part of their state regulated medicinal cannabis operations; all were required to be non-profit.

About 1,000 patients have registered with the MMP out of a patient population well over 300,000 statewide. The single Alternative Treatment Center open to those patients has now been closed for more than eight weeks. Many New Jersey residents with qualifying medical conditions use cannabis purchased in the underground marijuana market; sometimes they are arrested for it. Patients caught by police with underground marijuana (even those registered in the program with state-issued ID cards) are given no immunity by the police or the court system. They are prosecuted and treated like any other offender.

Assemblywoman Angelini has almost singular public voice of absolute opposition to the compassionate use law. She has written numerous opinion pieces in newspapers and submitted many letters to the editor. When addressing the issue of medical marijuana in public forums, Assemblywoman Angelini always uses her dual titles as an elected official and director of Prevention First.

Angelini's opposition to the medical marijuana law program and patients gaining access is a personal agenda because New Jersey recognizes cannabis as medicine in certain circumstances. Angelini's opposition is, according to her public statements, rooted solely in her efforts to attempt to prevent general drug addiction. Cannabis is, however, non-toxic and not addictive. When recommended or used as part of a medical therapy for serious illnessesm cannabis is not being used illicitly or in a behavior method that supports a habit. Thus medical marijuana use by seriously ill New Jersey residents should be outside of the concern of the chartered mission at the non-profit Prevention First.

Prevention First subsists on more than $1.8million dollars per year, mostly obtained through state and municipal grants earmarked for substance abuse education and prevention. Cash grants from the state of New Jersey, municipalities in New Jersey, and other government funds appear to be the sole sources of income for Prevention First. The organization lists collected fundraising and fundraising expenses as a financial wash in their most recent annual report.

Angelini's position as a legislator may have brought favor to Prevention First. We hope that a thorough inquiry will be performed into Assemblywoman Angelini's political operations to influence budgets, funds, or grants related to substance abuse treatment and prevention - made up of NJ tax dollars - that would eventually wind up in the bank account of Prevention First and the pockets of Mary Pat Angelini.

There are more than 20,000 marijuana possession arrests each year in New Jersey, more than for most other drugs combined. Some marijuana offenders, even if they are consuming cannabis medicinally, are now being forced into custodial substance abuse treatment programs under pilot programs approved under Senate Bill 881.

S881 has made than $1million tax dollars available in the just the pilot phase for "substance abuse treatment" at facilities approved by the NJ Department of Human Services. Angelini's non-profit, Prevention First, has worked under grants from the Dept. of Human Services to create directories of substance abuse treatment facilities. The law will require the state to contract with substance abuse treatment centers. Angeleni voted for the Assembly version A2883 and publicly lauded its passage into law by Governor Christie.

Sending medical marijuana patients into mandatory substance treatment is happening right now and will only get worse. These residents are getting scammed by the state of New Jersey. Told that marijuana is legal, the state has not provided access. Forced to get cannabis on the underground market, these individuals are used as an excuse to funnel tax dollars into the now state-funded substance treatment and "prevention" industry.

Assemblywoman Angelini and her non-profit, Prevention First, have moved millions of tax dollars into their bank accounts under the guise of substance abuse prevention, but they may be contributing to an expensive scheme that profits on the backs of NJ drug offenders, mainly marijuana consumers.

Mary Pat Angelini is entitled to her opinions. Her position at Prevention First, her longtime personal profit from her role there, and her potential influence for more favorable funding creates serious questions within the Code of Ethics.

Much of the information needed to fully examine these issues is not available to the public. We hope the committee will use all of its power to assure that New

Jersey taxpayers and medical marijuana patients are not being cheated.

*What follows is excerpts from an update to the hearing results:*

**Who Really Benefits from Illegal Marijuana in New Jersey?**

SOURCE:
http://www.philly.com/philly/columnists/philly420/Big_Bucks_In_New_Jerseys_Illegal_Marijuana_.html#2m0EjvXhEcpQtMCc.99

**Chris Goldstein**

Posted: Wednesday, July 24, 2013, 3:54 Pm

When a little known committee dismissed a complaint filed against a New Jersey Assemblywoman, it shined some rare sunlight on an industry raking in a healthy profit from marijuana prohibition: substance abuse prevention and treatment centers.

The Joint Committee for Ethical Standards at the New Jersey Legislature on Tuesday dismissed a complaint filed against Assemblywoman Mary Pat Angelini (R. Monmouth) who had been accused of appearing to benefit from Garden State's marijuana laws.

Angelini is the executive director of a non-profit called Prevention First, a company whose mission focuses on youth addiction and even violence issues. While Prevention First does not operate any substance treatment centers, they do provide the training and state certifications required for those who work within those facilities. Prevention First also facilitates directories of drug treatment facilities and options in Monmouth County.

The core issue in the complaint was if Assemblywoman Angelini was garnering a personal profit by voting against medical marijuana access, voting against decreasing penalties for adults caught with small amounts of cannabis and voting in favor of S881.

The Joint Committee entered into an interesting discussion, eventually acknowledging that substance abuse education, prevention and treatment were all part of the same "industry." They concluded that Angelini could express her opinion and vote on the bills because any benefit would be to her entire industry and not her non-profit specifically. The committee members compared it to a legislator who was a bank executive who sponsored and voted for bills favoring all financial institutions.

Because the committee opted to dismiss the complaint (based on the carefully crafted recommendation by their attorney) not even a cursory investigation took place that may have revealed a few more salient points.

The New Jersey Compassionate Use Medical Marijuana Act was signed into law back in 2010 but implementation of the extremely limited Medicinal Marijuana Program (MMP) has been significantly delayed. About 1,000 patients have registered with the MMP out of a patient population well over 300,000 statewide. The single Alternative Treatment Center allowed to start growing cannabis for those patients has now been closed for more than eight weeks.

Many residents with qualifying medical conditions use cannabis purchased in the underground marijuana market; sometimes they are arrested. Patients caught by police with underground marijuana in New Jersey (even those registered in the program with state-issued ID cards) are given no immunity by police or the court system. They are prosecuted and treated like any other offender.

Angelini is the singular public voice of absolute opposition to the compassionate use law. She has written numerous opinion pieces for newspapers and submitted many Letters to the Editor. When addressing the issue of medical cannabis in public forums, Angelini always uses her dual titles as an elected official and director of Prevention First.

Now some cannabis prohibition offenders (even if they are consuming it medicinally) can be remanded by judges into mandatory substance abuse treatment programs under Senate Bill 881.

SB 881 has also made more than $1 million in state money available (in the just the pilot phase) for "substance abuse" services at facilities certified and approved by the N.J. Department of Human Services.

*Philly420's Chris Goldstein smoked his first joint in 1994 and has been working to legalize marijuana ever since. He serves on the Board of Directors at PhillyNORML has been covering cannabis news for over a decade. Contact Goldstein at chris@freedomisgreen.com or on Twitter @freedomisgreen*

Just how deep does the corruption on the part of lawmakers and law enforcement go? Here's a look by Russ Belville of 420Radio.org and host / producer of The Russ Belville Show - The Independent Voice of the Marijuana Nation at http://radicalruss.com. In this article, Belville outlines the waste of taxpayer funding as law enforcement officers spend on-the-clock hours to solicit funds for an anti-marijuana "education" assembly just prior to the vote for Oregon's Measure 91. This, in light of the fact that a woman who called 911 to report an attacker at her home but was told there was no one working during the weekend because of budget cuts; she was beaten and raped by the intruder.

## Oregon Marijuana Election Shenanigans Part III: Public Resources Used to Fight Legalization

by Russ Belville September 7, 2014

*As Oregon gears up to pass a marijuana legalization initiative known as Measure 91, law enforcement officials throughout the state may have already been using taxpayer-funded offices, email accounts, facilities, and work hours illegally to campaign against the initiative. Check back on Part I and Part II of our report for more details.*

The original sponsor of the two-day "Oregon Marijuana, Alcohol & Other Drugs Summit" in Madras, Oregon pulled its $15,000 of federal grant funding, because of the event's political nature. The event, scheduled to take place as voters receive their ballots to vote on the marijuana legalization initiative, Measure 91, has been criticized by the Measure 91 campaign as a political event, not an educational one. Stepping up to fill the funding gap is a county district attorney and the Oregon State Sheriffs' Association, who may have violated the law by using public funds for electioneering purposes.

Jefferson County DA Steven Leriche, who "said he spent Friday morning on the phone trying to raise the $15,000 it would take to make sure the conference goes on. He said he's chipped in $500 personally and has raised $2,000 so far," according to the Oregonian. **If that was time spent on a county phone**, or a call made from a county office on county time, or he represented himself as "Jefferson County DA," or he was using contacts from a county or state database to fundraise from, he has already broken the law.

Leriche was aided recently by the Sheriffs' Association donation of $10,000 to keep the summit alive. (Funny how there's plenty of money for sheriffs to oppose marijuana legalization, but **not enough to send a sheriff out to respond to a 911 rape call**.)[i] Leriche tells KTVZ in Bend that the summit is merely "a much needed public education opportunity," but then goes on to complain that "big out-of-state money interests who just bought over $2 million of TV ads to promote **legalized marijuana ... seem compelled to shut down our small-town educational forum**," and that "Someone with a lot of influence doesn't want Oregonians hearing what Dr. Sabet has to say," which seem to indicate that Leriche also understands full well the political nature of these events.

Then there are the "Marijuana Educational Ads" presented by BestCare online in association with the summit, which explains, "Prevention staff in Jefferson, Grant, Deschutes, and Crook counties have partnered together with Dr. Kevin Sabet and Eric Martin to develop marijuana educational ads to be used to disseminate public health facts." For questions, BestCare directs folks to call Russ Comer at Grant County, Jessica Jacks at Deschutes County, and Brenda Comini at Crook County. While the ads may have been developed in 2012, **taking calls about them in conjunction with a political event scheduled in 2014 on county phone lines while on county time** is illegal and helping to put them on the BestCare summit website certainly qualifies as "posting material to an official website (and approving material to be posted to an official website)" which is forbidden by law.[ii]

Connie Raemakers is the head of Tigard Turns the Tide, which is a non-profit dedicated to fighting youth drug abuse. She is now coordinating the twelve-city tour and she insists "We are not out to tell voters how to vote," and says the local groups will not use public funds for their individual stops on the tour. However, a flyer for the event in Oregon City explains how Kevin Sabet, the head of anti-legalization Project SAM, will be there. **It explains how it is "made possible by your local Drug Free Communities Coalitions" (federal grant money) "and the Clackamas County Prevention Coalition" (state money).** It directs people to RSVP to Elizabeth Russell at an orecity.k12.or.us email address, which is the domain for the school district in Oregon City. Perhaps even the paper, ink, and printers necessary to make the flyer are state property as well as the contacts list used to determine recipients of the flyer.

---

[i] "I don't have anybody to send out there. You know, obviously, if he comes inside the residence and assaults you, can you ask him to go away?" – 911 operator, Josephine County, May 2014, to a woman who was then later choked and raped by her ex-boyfriend, because budget cuts prevented staffing the sheriff's office on the weekends.

[ii] Common activities that are always undertaken in an official capacity (regardless of time of day or location) and are therefore subject to the requirements or ORS 260.432 include – posting material to an official website (and approving material to be posted to an official website) [and] – drafting or distributing an official publication from the jurisdiction. — Oregon Secretary of State, "Restrictions on Political Campaigning by Public Employees ORS 260.432"

## Why Are Law Enforcement Agencies So Invested In Blocking Legalization?

It's been well established that marijuana is not the evil substance that many opponents to access would have the public believe. So if it's as harmless as advocates claim, wouldn't it seem logical that law enforcement organizations, agencies, and the officers themselves would want to see one less issue for their manpower to deal with? Since marijuana—certainly where medical cannabis use is concerned—isn't a criminal issue, why are agencies fighting so hard alongside anti-legalization proponents to keep the public under lock and key for its possession?

This article by Ray Strack, who worked 27 years as a U.S. Customs special agent and is now the principal Florida spokesperson for Law Enforcement Against Prohibition, may shed some light on the situation. According to his piece in the *Orlando Sentinel*, stopping citizens on suspicion of marijuana possession, even if no arrest is made, results in big business and hefty seizure payoffs for law enforcement.

"In the Broward County town of Sunrise, millions in soon-to-be-forfeited cash led narcotics officers to lure international drug buyers into suburban restaurants so the department could confiscate $6 million in just two years. Much of the money went for police overtime in coordinating the seizures, with one narcotics detective in 2012 bringing home a combined salary and overtime of $183,156 — more than his chief of police earned."

Of course, in that circumstance, we're not talking about an individual with a medical need for marijuana. This was international drug traffickers, after all. That makes it right, doesn't it? Unfortunately, no. The same situation happens to individuals with medically necessary cannabis all the time.

"Florida's Contraband Forfeiture Act lets the sheriffs and other local law-enforcement agencies keep 85 percent of the value of the property they seize, with the remainder given to charities — doubtless buying considerable good will for the elected sheriffs at campaign time."

As stated above, an arrest or conviction isn't even required for the police to seize property owned by free

American citizens. Someone pulled over who is found to be in possession of even a small amount of marijuana, regardless of its medical nature and oversight by a licensed physician, can have his car impounded and his property seized. If he had any amount of cash on him, the police can seize that money under pretenses that he must have earned it from selling drugs. (See article below about how prosecutors in one state worked with a dishonest crime lab chemist to ensure that the "amount" found weighed in at the correct legal amount to get a conviction.)

"According to Justice Department records, the Polk County [FL] Sheriff's Office took in more than $1.2 million from the federal Assets Forfeiture Fund just since 2007, part of the $230 million that all of Florida's law-enforcement agencies received from the fund during that period.

"The fund distributes the proceeds of property seized in law-enforcement asset forfeitures, primarily from those suspected of drug crimes. No arrest is even required, and the standard of proof is significantly less than in a criminal case, making it a favorite tool of police and prosecutors. Carrying excess cash? It can be confiscated if officials can convince a judge the funds came from drug trafficking. Caught driving with a marijuana cigarette? Your car can be hauled away.

"Between 1989 and 2010, U.S. attorneys seized at least $12.6 billion in assets, with the fund growing sixfold in just two decades, and from $2.9 billion to $4.4 billion in 2012 alone."

And there's still some question as to why law enforcement organizations are working so hard, even engaging in illegal fundraising activities themselves, to help ensure that their cash cow doesn't dry up?

## Philadelphia Police Vow to Continue Marijuana Crackdown Despite Policy Makers Decriminalizing It

You read that right. Philadelphia has voted to decriminalize marijuana possession up to 30 grams, yet the chief of police has declared that he and his officers will not stop detaining citizens for this amount. Why? Because there's money to be made in the war on drugs, and these good little soldiers aren't about to pass up the opportunity to make a buck.

According to an article by Craig R. McCoy, Nancy Phillips, and Dylan Purcell, Inquirer Staff Writers, for Philly.com, "People caught with 30 grams (a bit more than an ounce) or less of marijuana in Philadelphia will no longer be charged with criminal misdemeanors, but with civil summary offenses under a new policy that will go into effect later this month. Fines are expected to be in the $200 to $300 range. But while pot smokers won't face criminal charges, they will still be arrested, handcuffed, searched, detained, and fingerprinted. Then, their cases will be heard by a special "quality of life" court that is already in use for things like dealing with unruly Eagles fans and public drinking. "We're not going stop locking people up," Lt. Frank Vanore, a police spokesman, told the Philadelphia Inquirer. Marijuana possession remained illegal, he said. "We're going to stop people for it... Our officers are trained to do that. Whether or not they make it through the charging process... We can't control that. Until they legalize it, we're not going to stop."

In spite of the fact that local lawmakers have decided to treat certain amounts of marijuana possession in the same way they handle an irate football fan who had a little too much to drink and yelled at a stadium security officer, the sworn officials whose duty it is to protect the public from serious crime have declared that the war on drugs is far from over. And instead of using this measure as an opportunity to alleviate some of the caseload and pressure from his already stretched-thin police force, the Philadelphia police department has every intention of treating private-use marijuana possession in the same way they always have: with an iron fist.

The city first introduced and then passed this measure because the court dockets were bursting at the seams with cases both frivolous and serious. In an effort to lighten the load, the city's district attorney and several state Supreme Court justices worked to make these cases less of a big deal. This would mean that everyone with a court case pending would see speedier results, and that individuals with medically necessary cannabis would be treated somewhat better by the justice system.

But not if these cops have their way. Remember, there's money at stake. And they can't go letting that money slip from their greedy little grasp.

It's also very important to know that of the few thousand small-amount marijuana possession arrests last year in the city, 75% of those individuals were African-Americans. Again, another clear illustration that the police do, indeed, go looking the other way when it comes to marijuana. They are apparently quite capable of not arresting an individual with a minor amount of weed, since they so obviously pick and choose which individuals actually get arrested and taken in. Even when taking into consideration that African-Americans make up the majority demographic within Philadelphia, it's certainly not by 75%. In fact, in the last census, the city was only 44.3% black, and 36.6% white.

"We have to be smart on crime," District Attorney Seth Williams told the Inquirer. "We can't declare a war on drugs by going after the kid who's smoking a joint on 55th Street. We have to go after the large traffickers."

**Minnesota Lawmakers Squares Off with Law Enforcement over Medical Marijuana**
Article by Johnny Green for TheWeedBlog.com.

*Minnesota Representative Carly Melin has been trying to bring medical marijuana to her state. When she set out to achieve this goal, she assumed that there would be some tough negotiations and compromises along the way. Minnesota Governor Mark Dayton has insisted that any successful medical marijuana bill would require getting law enforcement on board. Unfortunately, it appears that members of Minnesota law enforcement are unwilling to compromise in any way.*

*"It's like negotiating with a brick wall. All along I have said that I am willing to amend the bill. But they won't move at all." said Carly Melin according to Politics In Minnesota. The article went on to describe how Representative Melin met with the Minnesota Law Enforcement Coalition to discuss her proposal. The Minnesota Law Enforcement Coalition includes the Minnesota Police and Peace Officers Association, Minnesota Chiefs of Police Association, Minnesota Sheriffs Association, Minnesota County Attorneys Association, and Minnesota State Association of Narcotics Investigators.*

*Ultimately the officers presented a 10 page bulleted outline of their absolute opposition to medical marijuana. One objection that was raised at the meeting, yet was absent in the report, was the truth – that officers are concerned about what the measure would do to police budgets which thrive due to asset forfeitures from marijuana investigations.*

*"According to Melin, Dennis Flaherty, the executive director of the MPPOA, explicitly told her that he was worried that legalization — in any form — could lead to*

*harmful reductions in the federal grants that are an important funding source for many police agencies." the Politics In Minnesota article stated.*

*This is a very common thing, and the importance of Representative Melin bringing attention to this area of public policy cannot be understated. From Minnesota to Oregon to every other state in the union, law enforcement uses the drug war to bolster their budgets. It's an area that doesn't get nearly enough attention because it's not flashy, and doesn't draw big headlines. However, if more people new about it, reform would come, and with it, positive change.*

*If cops didn't get a cut of what they take from marijuana arrests (cars, money, property, etc.), would they bust as many people for something that is harmless? Law enforcement groups oppose medical marijuana in Minnesota and beyond with everything they got. Patients go without the medicine they need, even though it's a safe, effective alternative to prescription drugs. Why is that? Obviously it's because these members of law enforcement care more about their budgets than they do suffering patients, which is a sad thing.*

## Government Chemist Tampered With 40,000 Cases, Locking Countless Innocent Americans in Prison 245

SOURCE: http://filmingcops.com/corrupt-government-chemist-tampered-with-40000-cases-locking-countless-innocent-americans-in-prison/

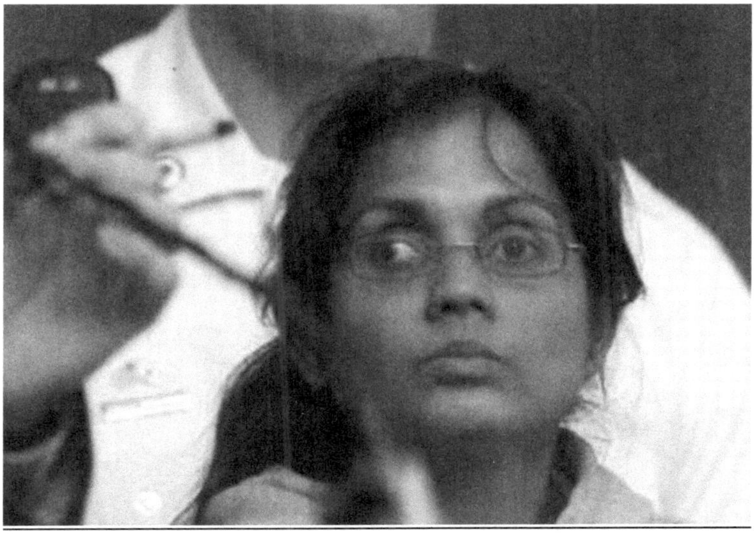

*MASSACHUSETTS — In a maddening scandal that is rocking the state of Massachusetts, a government crime lab chemist has been caught intentionally forging signatures and tampering with evidence in as many as* ***40,000 cases****, destroying the lives of countless innocent Americans.*

*Annie Dookhan worked as a chemist for the State of Massachusetts, and it turns out she had close relations with prosecutors.*

*These prosecutors were able to successfully convict innocent Americans because Dookhan would chemically taint the "evidence," resulting in career boosts for the prosecutors while innocent men and women were torn from their families and locked in cells.*

*Prosecutors praised Dookhan's work and depended on her to get the convictions they wanted.*

*Hundreds of "convicts" and defendants have already been released, and there are potentially thousands more waiting to be set free.*

*Norfolk County District Attorney Michael Morrissey is reviewing thousands of files to determine which cases must be thrown out or retried because of potentially tainted evidence. | Source: Tovia Smith/NPR*

*Dookhan used her position to forge results for nearly a decade. "I don't think anyone ever perceived that one person was capable of causing this much chaos," said Norfolk County District Attorney Michael Morrissey.*

*"You can see the entire walls full of boxes... in one of these cardboard boxes, there could be hundreds of cases ... in each box," said Morrissey.*

*Hundreds of defendants and "convicts" had been arguing that they were framed and claiming that the evidence used to convict them was mishandled. They were right.*

*In one recent case, a man was charged with "selling cocaine and heroin." His public defender, Julieann Hernon, believes that this man was a potential victim of Dookhan's fake evidence and ought to be released.*

*"[Dookhan] was mis-testing evidence, dry-labbing evidence, saying she had 'conducted tests' when she had not, deliberately tainting drugs," said Hernon.*

*"Certainly, I think, we have to presume a taint here when Annie Dookhan was the chemist in the case," said Hernon.*

*In another recent case, defense attorney William Sullivan was able to successfully reverse his client's prior "guilt" because Dookhan was the secondary chemist involved in the conviction.*

*"This is a lab that was pretty much wholly and fully contaminated by Ms. Annie Dookhan,"Sullivan told the judge. "She had full access to everyone's drugs."*

*While many have been set free, they will never get the lost years of their lives back.*

*"The tragedy is that my client already did four years on this," said Sullivan. "I mean, that is disturbing in itself."*

*Many other innocents have lost their careers, lost their children, and lost their marriages.*

*Michael Morrissey, Norfolk County District Attorney, is now sifting through thousands of files to find out which should be thrown out because of Dookhan's corruption and deceit.*

*In federal court, many innocents received even harsher sentences due to prior convictions based on Annie Dookhan's fake "evidence."*

*Several civil suits are getting started by those accused of crimes based on Dookhan's tampering, accusing Dookhan of trampling on their rights to fair trials.*

*"I screwed up big time. I messed up. I messed up bad. It's my fault. I don't want the lab to get in trouble," Dookhan was reported as saying.*

*Of course, Dookhan's "screw up" — a "screw up" that she intentionally committed for nearly a decade —*

*will never bring back the lives that have been destroyed.*

*In analyzing Dookhan's career, it was found that she also routinely invented fanciful job titles for herself. Examples include "special agent of operations" and "on-call terrorism supervisor." She would testify in court as an "expert."*

*She maintained her composure year after year as innocents were bound and forced into prison cages.*

*The relationships she had with prosecutors are also under scrutiny. Dookhan once told a prosecutor in an email that she couldn't use her expert testimony at a trial. The prosecutor replied, "No no no!!! I need you!!!"*

*Was the prosecutor intentionally depending on Dookhan's deception to score a conviction and a career boost?*

**Related: Number of US Prisoners Now Exceeds High School Teachers and Engineers**

*Many of the prosecutors became devoted fans of Dookhan and wanted to take her out for drinks, saying she was on their "dream team." The Boston Globe provided an email between Dookhan and a prosecutor with whom she had a particularly friendly relationship:*

*"Glad we are on the same team," he once wrote Dookhan — including one day in May 2010 when he told her he needed a marijuana sample to weigh at least 50 pounds so that he could charge the owners with drug trafficking.*

*"Any help would be greatly appreciated!" he wrote, punctuating each sentence with a long string of exclamation points. "Thank you!"*

*Two hours later, Dookhan responded: "OK . . . definitely Trafficking, over 80 lbs." Papachristos thanked her profusely.*

*Boston attorney David Meier found that in Dookhan's nine-year government position,**over 40,000 people** may have had their cases tainted by Dookhan.*

*But the devastation done to families is impossible to calculate.*

*Dookhan is now facing charges of her own. If she is convicted she will receive a relatively light sentence of three to five years, which has outraged citizens even more.*

***UPDATE (11/29/13):***

*Dookhan has pled guilty to all the counts brought against her. As expected, she was given a three to five year sentence.*

*"Sadly, the saga continues for the thousands of individuals who have borne the impact of Dookhan's misdeeds, and the lab's scandalous management," says Anthony Benedetti, chief counsel of the state public defender agency.*

*Dookhan showed no emotion as the impact of her actions was described in court, according to a report.*

*So far, more than 600 people have had their convictions deleted or set aside. More than 300 people have been released from captivity, with potentially thousands more still waiting to be set free.*

*Disturbingly, this scandal of sending innocents to prison on fake "evidence" may stretch far beyond Dookhan's case, who government officials describe as a rogue chemist acting alone. Many Americans question how Dookhan was able to do this for nearly a decade without being detected by anybody.*

*A writer to the Boston Globe asks, "Indeed, where were her supervisors and those responsible for checking and approving her work? Why were no red flags raised at the speed with which Dookhan completed tests and submitted reports?"*

*Martin W. Healy, general counsel for the Massachusetts Bar Association is conducting an ongoing investigation into the lab.*

*"This is one chapter in a continuing saga," Healy said. "The legal community and the general public still have a number of unanswered questions about what's gone on here. How deep was the problem? Is it really just isolated to Dookhan or does it go beyond that?'*

*Dookhan is currently in protective custody at the state women's prison in Framingham but will likely transition to the prison general population soon, according to her attorney.*

## Breaking: Another Government Chemist Accused Of Deception, Over 180,000 Cases Now Need Review 5

*BOSTON — The Annie Dookhan deception continues to unfold. Dookhan was a government chemist who tampered with thousands of cases, creating fake "evidence" that caused the imprisonment of countless innocent Americans.*

*These innocent men and women were rounded up and locked in prison cages while prosecutors scored successful "convictions" because of Dookhan's fake evidence.*

*Many lost their marriages, lost their children, and lost their careers. Many immigrants were also deported, losing the lives they had built when they traveled to the US.*

*Dookhan recently pleaded guilty to all counts brought against her.*

*However, many have been questioning the State's official story that one rogue chemist was responsible for all the catastrophic injustice.*

*Indeed we now have reports that a second "chemist" has been fired over doubts concerning her qualifications.*

*Kate Corbett, who worked in the same lab as Dookhan, claimed that she had a "chemistry degree" from Merrimack College.*

*That turns out to be a lie, as investigators determined that she took some chemistry classes in college but her degree is actually in sociology, according to a report.*

*Which is to say, a sociology major may well have worked in a lab that required high-level expertise in chemistry, a lab whose "evidence" determined the fate of thousands of human beings.*

*Corbett also may have testified as a chemistry "expert" in dozens of court cases leading to the conviction of Americans, which could add to the devastation that Dookhan has already caused.*

*Defense attorneys argue that there are now more than **180,000 cases that need to be reviewed**, cases connected to the work done by alleged chemists at the Hinton lab.*

*Meanwhile several questions remain unanswered.*

*Did Corbett also tamper with evidence alongside Dookhan? Are we really to believe that Dookhan's forgeries continued for almost a decade without anybody else participating?*

*A writer to the Boston Globe asks, "Where were Dookhan's supervisors and those responsible for checking and approving her work? Why were no red flags raised at the speed with which Dookhan completed tests and submitted reports?"*

*Corbett has not yet been accused of tampering with evidence.*

*Jonathan W. Blodgett, president of the Massachusetts District Attorneys Association, found out about the problems with Corbett last week.*

*He and other defense attorneys are now reviewing the cases she worked on to see whether she, like Dookhan, created any fake evidence.*

# Chapter 6:
# The Hidden History of ALEC and Prison Labor

Years after ALEC's Truth In Sentencing bills became the law of the land, its Prison Industries Act has quietly expanded prison labor across the country.
Mike Elk and Bob Sloan August 1, 2011

This article is part of a Nation series exposing the American Legislative Exchange Council, in collaboration with the Center For Media and Democracy. John Nichols introduces the series.

Bob Sloan is a former offender, Stop ALEC organizer, and blogger who has spent the past decade researching the PIE.

Mike Elk is a labor journalist and third-generation union organizer based in Washington, D.C.

*"The breaded chicken patty your child bites into at school may have been made by a worker earning twenty cents an hour, not in a faraway country, but by a member of an invisible American workforce: prisoners. At the Union Correctional Facility, a maximum security prison in Florida, inmates from a nearby lower-security prison manufacture tons of processed beef, chicken and pork for Prison Rehabilitative Industries and Diversified Enterprises (PRIDE), a privately held non-profit corporation that operates the state's forty-one work programs. In addition to processed food, PRIDE's website reveals an*

*array of products for sale through contracts with private companies, from eyeglasses to office furniture, to be shipped from a distribution center in Florida to businesses across the US. PRIDE boasts that its work programs are "designed to provide vocational training, to improve prison security, to reduce the cost of state government, and to promote the rehabilitation of the state inmates."*

*Although a wide variety of goods have long been produced by state and federal prisoners for the US government—license plates are the classic example, with more recent contracts including everything from guided missile parts to the solar panels powering government buildings—prison labor for the private sector was legally barred for years, to avoid unfair competition with private companies. But this has changed thanks to the American Legislative Exchange Council (ALEC), its Prison Industries Act, and a little-known federal program known as PIE (the Prison Industries Enhancement Certification Program). While much has been written about prison labor in the past several years, these forces, which have driven its expansion, remain largely unknown.*

*Somewhat more familiar is ALEC's instrumental role in the explosion of the US prison population in the past few decades. ALEC helped pioneer some of the toughest sentencing laws on the books today, like mandatory minimums for non-violent drug offenders, "three strikes" laws, and "truth in sentencing" laws. In 1995 alone, ALEC's Truth in Sentencing Act was signed into law in twenty-five states. (Then State Rep. Scott Walker was an ALEC member when he sponsored Wisconsin's truth-in-sentencing laws and, according to PR Watch, used its statistics to make the case for the law.) More recently, ALEC has proposed innovative "solutions" to the overcrowding it helped create, such as privatizing the parole process through "the proven success of the private bail bond industry," as it recommended in 2007. (The American Bail Coalition is an executive member of ALEC's Public Safety and Elections Task Force.) ALEC has also worked to pass state laws to create private for-profit prisons, a boon to two of its major corporate sponsors: Corrections Corporation of America and Geo Group (formerly Wackenhut Corrections), the largest private prison firms in the country. An In These Times investigation last summer revealed that ALEC arranged secret meetings between Arizona's state legislators and CCA to draft what became SB 1070, Arizona's notorious immigration law, to keep CCA prisons flush with immigrant detainees. ALEC has proven expertly capable of devising endless ways to help private corporations benefit from the country's massive prison population.*

*That mass incarceration would create a huge captive workforce was anticipated long before the US prison population reached its peak—and at a time when the concept of "rehabilitation" was still considered part of the mission of prisons. First created by Congress in 1979, the PIE program was designed "to encourage states and units of local government to establish employment opportunities for prisoners that approximate private sector work opportunities," according to PRIDE's website. The benefits to big corporations were clear—a "readily available workforce" for the private sector and "a cost-effective way to occupy a portion of the ever-growing offender/inmate population" for prison officials—yet from its founding until the mid-1990s, few states participated in the program.*

*This started to change in 1993, when Texas State Representative and ALEC member Ray Allen crafted the Texas Prison Industries Act, which aimed to expand the PIE program. After it passed in Texas, Allen advocated that it be duplicated across the country. In 1995, ALEC's Prison Industries Act was born.*

*This Prison Industries Act as printed in ALEC's 1995 state legislation sourcebook, "provides for the employment of inmate labor in state correctional institutions and in the private manufacturing of certain products under specific conditions." These conditions, defined by the PIE program, are supposed to include requirements that "inmates must be paid at the prevailing wage rate" and that the "any room and board deductions...are reasonable and are used to defray the costs of inmate incarceration." (Some states charge prisoners for room and board, ostensibly to offset the cost of prisons for taxpayers. In Florida, for example, prisoners are paid minimum wage for PIE-certified labor, but 40 percent is taken out of their accounts for this purpose.)*

*The Prison Industries Act sought to change this, inventing the "private sector prison industry expansion account," to absorb such deductions, and stipulating that the money should be used to, among other things: "construct work facilities, recruit corporations to participate as private sector industries programs, and pay costs of the authority and department in implementing [these programs]." Thus, money that was taken from inmate wages to offset the costs of incarceration would increasingly go to expanding prison industries. In 2000, Florida passed a law that mirrored the Prison Industries Act and created the Prison Industries Trust Fund, its own version of the private sector prison industry expansion account, deliberately designed to help expand prison labor for private industries.*

*The Prison Industries Act was also written to exploit a critical PIE loophole that seemed to suggest that its rules did not apply to prisoner-made goods that were not shipped across state lines. It allowed a third-party company to set up a local address in a state that makes prison goods, buy goods from a prison factory, sell those products locally or surreptitiously ship them across state borders. It helped that by 1995 oversight of the PIE program had been effectively squashed, transferred from the Department of Justice's Bureau of Justice Assistance to the National Correctional Industries Association (NCIA), a private trade organization that happened to be represented by Allen's lobbying firm, Service House, Inc. In 2003, Allen became the Texas House Chairman of the Corrections Committee and began peddling the Prison Industries Act and other legislation beneficial to CCA and Geo Group, like the Private Correctional Facilities Act. Soon thereafter he became Chairman of ALEC's Criminal Justice (now Public Safety and Elections) Task Force. He resigned from the state legislature in 2006 while under investigation for his unethical lobbying practices. He was hired soon after as a lobbyist for Geo Group.*

*Today's chair of ALEC's Public Safety and Elections Task force is state Representative Jerry Madden of Texas, where the Prison Industries Act originated eighteen years ago. According to a 2010 report from NCIA, as of last summer there were "thirty jurisdictions with active [PIE] operations." These included such states as Arizona, Arkansas, California, Colorado, Florida, Georgia, Hawaii, Idaho, Indiana, Iowa, Kansas, Louisiana, Maine, Maryland,*

*Minnesota, and twelve more. Four more states are now looking to get involved as well; Kentucky, Michigan and Pennsylvania have introduced legislation and New Hampshire is in the process of applying for PIE certification. Today these state's legislation are based upon an updated version of the Prison Industries Act, which ALEC amended in 2004.*

*Prison labor has already started to undercut the business of corporations that don't use it. In Florida, PRIDE has become one of the largest printing corporations in the state, its cheap labor having a significant impact upon smaller local printers. This scenario is playing out in states across the country. In addition to Florida's forty-one prison industries, California alone has sixty. Another 100 or so are scattered throughout other states. What's more, several states are looking to replace public sector workers with prison labor. In Wisconsin Governor Walker's recent assault on collective bargaining opened the door to the use of prisoners in public sector jobs in Racine, where inmates are now doing landscaping, painting, and other maintenance work. According to the Capitol Times, "inmates are not paid for their work, but receive time off their sentences." The same is occurring in Virginia, Ohio, New Jersey, Florida and Georgia, all states with GOP Assembly majorities and Republican governors. Much of ALEC's proposed labor legislation, implemented state by state is allowing replacement of public workers with prisoners.*

*"It's bad enough that our companies have to compete with exploited and forced labor in China," says Scott Paul Executive Director of the Alliance for American Manufacturing, a coalition of business and unions. "They shouldn't have to compete against prison labor here at home. The goal should be for other*

*nations to aspire to the quality of life that Americans enjoy, not to discard our efforts through a downward competitive spiral."*

*Alex Friedmann, associate editor of Prison Legal News, says prison labor is part of a "confluence of similar interests" among politicians and corporations, long referred to as the "prison industrial complex." As decades of model legislation reveals, ALEC has been at the center of this confluence. "This has been ongoing for decades, with prison privatization contributing to the escalation of incarceration rates in the US," Friedmann says. Just as mass incarceration has burdened American taxpayers in major prison states, so is the use of inmate labor contributing to lost jobs, unemployment and decreased wages among workers—while corporate profits soar."*

The following information is from a report on America's for-profit prison system that essentially creates a slave labor pool of non-violent offenders. Marijuana convicts are especially susceptible to falling victim to this system as they are not addicted to their drug of choice, tend to have little to no history of violence, and stand to gain from the system that pays these laborers in time off of their sentences instead of actual funding, whereas someone serving a life sentence for a violent crime cannot hope to earn this sentence reduction for his efforts and behavior.

SOURCE:
http://unitedstatesvmarijuana.blogspot.com/2011/10/dispatches-from-field-prisoners.html

**United States v. Marijuana**
**Dispatches from the Field: Prisoners -- America's New Cash Crop**
--Cynthia Johnston

A disciplined minority of totalitarians can use the instruments of democratic government to undermine democracy itself.~ Hannah Arendt

*Today, with for-profit prisons a burgeoning growth industry, the incarceration rate of people of color can be extrapolated to the population at large. Indeed, one out of every one hundred adults in America today is incarcerated, and one out of every thirty-two is somewhere in the system – either on probation, on parole, or behind bars. Put another way, the United States has five percent of the world's population and twenty-five percent of the world's prison population. And more than half of these arrests are for marijuana.*

*The FBI puts the number of marijuana arrests over the last decade alone at 7.9 million. This was not caused by the laws of supply-and-demand for weed. This was caused by the laws of supply-and-demand for prisoners and, hence, for profits. Since 1984, when privatization of prisons was made legal again, after having been stamped out in 1928 due to gross abuses against prisoners in the name of profit, the for-profit prison industry has moved quickly to expand into as many states as possible before enough resistance could be amassed to stop them. And with each new prison constructed, there is a need for more prisoners to fill it.*

*In the intervening years, lobbyists for the corporate, for-profit prison industry have spent millions of dollars per year writing laws and implementing strategies to put people in prison for as long as possible. The harsher the policies and the longer the sentences, the more money flows into these corporations from the government. And nothing grows the prison population better than the War on Drugs --*

*a war funded by taxpayers, some of whom are later fed into the machine, including those you've met, and others you will meet, in these pages.*

### *Big Money Machine*

*Back in my political days there was a running joke in Washington: the "building trade" unions would build their own prison camps for the jobs. Not so funny anymore, given that California's prison guard union -- the California Correctional Peace Officers Association, or CCPOA -- was a driving force behind California's "Three Strikes and You're Out" law, a law that requires a mandatory 25-years-to-life sentence for a third "similar" felony, even if that felony is shoplifting.*

*Three Strikes is one of a systematic web of laws designed to incarcerate the maximum number of people for the longest possible time; a web of laws that creates a self-perpetuating money machine for its creators – a cabal of corporations and lawmakers with the shared goal of growing America's prison population for profit; a web of laws written by special interests and introduced by the legislators they have bought with campaign contributions. Just one small example of the way our democratic system of government has been hijacked by the corporate thugs, greed-heads and fixers of America's sprawling prison cartel.*

*Former Navy journalist and "conservatarian" co-founder of All American Blogger Duane Lester reports that in only three decades CCPOA has become one of the most powerful political forces in California. In an article published by FreeRepublic.com, he wrote that the union has contributed millions of dollars to support Three Strikes and other laws that lengthen sentences and increase parole sanctions (the sentences imposed when a parolee violates the terms of parole). After then-governor Pete Wilson backed Three Strikes, the prison-guard union donated a cool million to his campaign.*

### *Don't Look for the Union Label*

*On a much more insidious scale, a right-wing lobby group, the American Legislative Exchange Council (ALEC), writes 'model bills' (legislation to be enacted in one state and replicated in others, also known as 'copy-cat laws') for corporate sponsors like Koch Industries, Exxon Mobile, BP, American Bail Coalition, R.J. Reynolds, Wal-Mart, Phillip Morris, Pfizer, AT&T, and Glaxo Smith Kline, to name a few – including bills specifically designed to exploit cheap prison labor on behalf of profit-making corporations.*

*Writing for thenation.com, labor journalist Mike Elk and blogger Bob Sloan detail ALEC's "instrumental role in the explosion of the US prison population in the past few decades," explaining how ALEC pioneered some of the toughest sentencing laws on the books today – mandatory minimums for nonviolent drug offenders, Three Strikes laws, and so-called truth-in-sentencing laws, which require violent offenders to serve 85% of their sentences before being considered for release. After ensuring that more prisoners would be incarcerated for longer and longer periods, ALEC then "paved the way for states and corporations to replace unionized workers with prison labor."*

*The "convict lease program," instituted in the South after the Civil War, was the precursor to today's for-profit prison industry. The then-governor of Mississippi imprisoned freed slaves and then leased them out to a private party who could work them to death, and often did, with no pay. It took churches, families, and civil libertarians sixty years to wipe these laws off the books and the Reagan Administration no time at all to bring them back.*

*Only a lobby funded by profit-driven corporations would replace preexisting laws with legislation like the Prison Industries Act, allowing "the employment of inmate labor in state correctional institutions and in the private manufacturing of certain products." A federal program called PIE (Prison Industries Enhancement Certification Program) conveniently certifies prison work programs for exemption from federal restrictions on prisoner-made goods in interstate commerce.*

*Prison labor for private profit was illegal before ALEC came along. Now the lobbyists have instituted two federal programs to regulate and certify prison labor. Just goes to show what money can buy.*

*In Florida, an outfit calling itself PRIDE (Prison Rehabilitative Industries and Diversified Enterprises) now runs forty work programs where inmates manufacture "tons of processed beef, chicken and pork," as well as office furniture and other commercial items – for twenty cents an hour.*

*Aside from the obvious slave labor issue, here's another concept for you: the intersection of processed meat with prison hygiene. I've heard the stories about prison conditions -- a hundred-and-twenty to two-hundred inmates in gym-sized rooms; fifty or more sharing a single filthy toilet, without privacy or sanitation. "Some guys just shit in the shower," said a friend who spent a few eye-opening nights at L.A.'s Twin Towers. And these guys are processing tons of meat that wind up, among other places, in school lunches.*

*Granted, prison laborers featured on a recent exposé on CNBC, entitled "Billions Behind Bars," worked in facilities outside the prison, and wore gloves. But that was a single example in Colorado – a 6,000-acre complex with fifty businesses, including a goat farm and a fish farm, staffed by inmates. Colorado Correctional Industries, a division of the state Department of Corrections, which runs the complex, is on "a mission to save taxpayers' money while helping to rehabilitate Colorado's inmates." Perhaps. They also happen to garner $56 million per year in revenue. But elsewhere, and for twenty cents an hour, how motivated could long-term prisoners be to maintain pristine job-site sanitation standards? Especially when they work under threat of punishment if they refuse to work?*

*In a 2007* letter *to prisonersolidarity.org, an inmate wrote that he and other prisoners at Ohio State Penitentiary had been trying for seventeen months to call attention to inhumane conditions such as "broken toilets that leak profusely, the urinals that overflow onto our feet, and the lack of ventilation that results in fumes and condensation that are unbearable at times." Even if they are transported elsewhere to work, how clean can they be? Yet, these are the living conditions many inmates endure. Conditions bad enough to cause one man to commit suicide at Dickens County Correctional Center in Spur, Texas – a prison run by the for-profit prison company, GEO Group, Inc.*

*How could GEO, or any corporation, justify making people live in such deplorable conditions? Because it's cheaper, according to the inmates' rights group Partnership for Safety and Justice in Portland, Oregon. In an msnbc.com* article *entitled "Suicide Reveals Squalid Prison Conditions," the organization's program director, Caylor Rolling stated, "they cut corners because the bottom line is making money."*

### *Corporate Corrections Companies*

*Meet some of the players in the new, for-profit prison industry. Correction Corps of America (CCA), headquartered in Nashville, Tennessee, touts itself as "America's Leader in Partnership Corrections." CCA designs, builds, manages and operates correctional facilities and detention centers for the Federal Bureau of Prisons (BOP), Immigration and Customs Enforcement (ICE), the U.S. Marshall Service, a couple dozen states, and nearly a dozen counties across the USA. CCA pocketed $2.9 billion in 2010.*

*Management Training Corporation (MTC), headquartered in Centerville, Utah, with branches in Texas, Georgia, and Washington, D.C., operates twenty correctional facilities in Arizona, California, Florida, Idaho, New Mexico, Ohio and Texas. They have the capacity to "secure and train 25,310 offenders and detainees at federal and state correctional facilities across the United States."*

*Formerly known as Wackenhut Corrections, GEO Group, Inc., of Boca Raton, Florida, manages and/or owns 116 correctional, detention and residential treatment facilities, boasting some 80,000 beds. GEO ran the Texas prison where the previously mentioned suicide took place. Among the many services GEO provides are Secure Prisoner Escort and Secure Detainee Transportation. Since its inception in 2008, GEO has transported over 200,000 prisoners and detainees by land and air.*

*Among the three of them, these for-profit prison companies own over two hundred facilities with*

*150,000 bed-spaces, cranking out a tidy five billion dollars a year in profit.*

*A perfect money machine, indeed -- but only if the system keeps them supplied with prisoners. And how does it do that, besides detaining defenseless immigrants? By feeding more and more marijuana and medical-marijuana users into their giant corporate maw.*

### War on (Wonder) Drugs

*It's worth repeating here that cannabis was only outlawed in the first place as an accommodation to corporate interests. There was no moral imperative to make it illegal, nor is there one today. It doesn't kill people, the way alcohol and tobacco do. According to Lester Grinspoon, M.D., Associate Professor Emeritus of Psychiatry at Harvard Medical School, who has studied it extensively, cannabis is safer than aspirin! To quote him directly, "Compared to aspirin, which people are free to purchase and use without the advice or prescription of a physician, cannabis is much safer: there are well over 1000 deaths annually from aspirin in this country alone, whereas there has never been a death anywhere from marijuana." He went on to say that "it will eventually be hailed as a 'wonder drug' just as penicillin was in the 1940s."*

*Yet the practice of jailing people for growing, transporting, buying, selling or possessing marijuana, and locking them up for longer and longer periods of time, continues. In Louisiana this year, 35-year-old Cornell Hood II was sentenced to prison for life for having been caught four times for possession and/or distribution of a substance more innocent than aspirin and with fewer side effects than any pharmaceutical painkiller on the market. In Oklahoma, Patricia*

*Spottedcrow, whose case we examine in an upcoming post, was sentenced to prison for ten years for having sold $31 worth of marijuana. Ten years. Second degree felony assault, in which a person bludgeons another person with a deadly weapon, causing severe bodily injury, carries five years. Yet you can sell a few "dime bags" of weed and get locked up for a decade, even when you have no prior arrests and four young children at home depending on you.*

*Just as the for-profit health-care industry relies on sick people for profits, and thus has an interest in keeping them sick, the for-profit prison industry relies on prisoners for profits, and thus has an interest in keeping them incarcerated. And though a recent Gallup poll shows that fully fifty percent of Americans favor legalizing marijuana and another seventy percent favor allowing doctors to prescribe it, the fight will really heat up when all those who profit from the War on Drugs mobilize their efforts against legalization.*

### How Marijuana's Criminal Status Has Been Determined by For-Profit Prisons

It hardly seems possible, but there's a thriving slave trade in the United States, funded by major corporations and special interest groups and furthered through the legislative system by lobbyists. Sadly, unbeknownst to many US citizens, this slave trade is not only already in place and requires its victims to produce goods that are sold throughout the US and international economies, but it also allows for every day citizens to be captured and put to work for little to no pay.

This government-approved slavery is happening at the hands of the for-profit prison system, and powerful groups like PRIDE and ALEC work very hard and line deep pockets to make sure that the crop of slave workers continues to grow to meet the demand for cheap labor.

Organizations like American Legislative Exchange Council (ALEC), Prison Rehabilitative Industries and Diversified Enterprises (PRIDE), and even the California Correctional Peace Officers Association, or CCPOA, have campaigned relentlessly and donated millions of dollars each to help ensure that America's tough-on-drugs laws remain intact, essentially providing an ever-growing pool of laborers who work for as little as twenty cents per hour—often paid out in the form of credits that can only be spent in the prison canteen, thus returning the money to the prison—in everything from office furniture manufacturing to the production of processed meats.

Yes, hardened criminals are producing the food that you eat and that you serve to your family for next to no pay. Even worse, citizens whose only crime is taking advantage of medically-required cannabis can also find themselves working on the virtual chain gang, thanks to mandatory sentencing laws for marijuana, Three Strikes Laws, and the after effects of the War on Drugs.

A part of our minds really wants to argue against this notion, stating that this kind of thing doesn't happen in America. But with FBI reports stating an approximation of eight million marijuana arrests over the last decade and the evidence of the thriving prison labor industry, what other possible correlation can there be?

In an article for TheNation.com, labor journalist Mike Elk and blogger Bob Sloan detail ALEC's "instrumental role in the explosion of the US prison population in the past few decades," which exposes how ALEC helped put in place some of the harshest sentencing laws on the books today. These laws go far beyond the Three Strikes Laws to include mandatory minimums for even first-time non-violent criminals and laws that require a minimum of 85% of a violent offender's sentence be served before he can be considered for parole, regardless of circumstances or the inmate's efforts at rehabilitation or prison behavior record. It wasn't enough to lock up individuals for marijuana possession, these organizations then had to make sure that their crop of slaves stayed put in order to provide a cheap source of goods for corporations. According to Elk and Sloan, ALEC "paved the way for states and corporations to replace unionized workers with prison labor."

Let's examine the many ways this is wrong and should not be tolerated by the American people. In addition to the forced incarceration of citizens to provide labor, especially citizens whose crimes are non-violent and victimless, these inmates are essentially taking jobs away from free individuals while also being housed, fed, clothed, and cared for by the taxpayers.

People are being locked away so they can work...the taxpayers pay for their care and then pay for the goods they produce...while "law-abiding" citizens go without work, which in turn creates a further burden on the taxpayers to provide unemployment insurance and welfare benefits to people who are actively seeking employment.

And we still think groups like PRIDE and ALEC have the best interests of the people at heart? The prison guard union of California is concerned with protecting citizens? Of course not. But it gets worse.

Enter into the equation the Prison Industries Enhancement Certification Program, or PIE program. It's a federal program that certifies for-profit prisons to use inmate labor to produce goods for outside corporations. There are

The so-called Prison Industries Act from ALEC's 1995 state legislation "provides for the employment of inmate labor in state correctional institutions and in the private manufacturing of certain products under specific conditions." Okay, we're good so far. But these conditions as they're spelled out by the PIE program are supposed to include requirements that "inmates must be paid at the prevailing wage rate" and that the "any room and board deductions...are reasonable and are used to defray the costs of inmate incarceration."

Yes, some states incarcerate non-violent offenders, give them jobs at third-world pay rates, then charge them room and board because they're working. One state, Florida, actually goes so far as to pay its prisoners the legal minimum wage for PIE-certified labor, but 40 percent of their pay is deducted from their wages for their room and board. Ask yourself this: if the inmates are working and paying for their own room and board, why are the taxpayers still being charged for their care? Because it's an "offset" amount, meaning that the company who benefits from their goods being produced by inmates doesn't actually pay the full amount and therefore doesn't pay the room and board to the state. They just skim the money off the top instead of giving it to the individuals who worked for it. Someone still has to pay for the actual care and housing of the inmates, so that's where the taxpayers come in.

But wait, there's more.

New laws and existing loopholes actually made it possible for the states to charge the inmates a portion of their wages and then use that money to (wait for it) expand the prisons and these prison labor programs. Yes, inmates got to enjoy the benefit of turning over a portion of their earnings so that states could lock up more people and increase the slave labor pool.

According to Elk and Sloan, "The Prison Industries Act sought to change this, inventing the 'private sector prison industry expansion account,' to absorb such deductions, and stipulating that the money should be used to, among other things: 'construct work facilities, recruit corporations to participate as private sector industries programs, and pay costs of the authority and department in implementing [these programs].' Thus, money that was taken from inmate wages to offset the costs of incarceration would increasingly go to expanding prison industries. In 2000, Florida passed a law that mirrored the Prison Industries Act and created the Prison Industries Trust Fund, its own version of the private sector prison industry expansion account, deliberately designed to help expand prison labor for private industries."

And according to the US Department of Justice's own document, the purpose of the PIE certification program lets prisons and the corporations that hire through them skirt the law: "The Prison Industry Enhancement Certification Program (PIECP) exempts certified state and local departments of corrections from normal restrictions on the sale of inmate-made goods in interstate commerce. In addition, the program lifts restrictions on these certified corrections departments, permitting them to sell inmate-made goods to the federal government in amounts exceeding the $10,000 maximum normally imposed on such transactions."

The document goes on to explain that the PIE program allows for fifty jurisdictions to have these exempt facilities, and as of 2011 there were already thirty jurisdictions with four more that had begun the application process.

Think we're done examining how the current for-profit laws are meant to exploit everyday citizens by ensuring that their convictions are overly punitive? Not by a long shot. There's one more piece of the puzzle, this one involving a loophole that allows corporations to setup "mailbox" offices in states where their goods are produced by inmates, which then lets them sell those goods with a number of tax benefits that everyday small business owners don't have. It's one more way that major corporations and lobbying groups have joined forces with the legal system and the correctional system to make themselves rich off the backs of people who have no business being in jail, while simultaneously screwing the competition into losing their shirts.

Now, none of this is to say that prison industries are not worthy endeavors. Inmates and honest correctional officers alike will tell you quite plainly that having a job to go to and a legitimate wage to earn have their benefits, such as on-the-job training, an increased likelihood that a released inmate will be able to secure employment, and simply giving the inmates something to look forward to that will make the days go by a little faster. But when non-violent, victimless offenders are locked up for decades in order to supply cheap grunt workers in order to avoid employing free citizens with a living wage, it's not hard to connect the dots.

Marijuana is illegal because it's too profitable for a handful of one percenters to let it become legal.

## The Vested Interest in Creating Felons

Profit isn't the only thing that the forces behind marijuana criminalization are concerned about. The legal system works against marijuana users in a wide variety of ways, not the least of which is to help ensure that the demographics of society who are most likely to support marijuana de-criminalization don't ever get the chance to voice that opinion.

One way they achieve that goal is to impose ridiculous legislation surrounding marijuana use that strips the offender of his civil rights, namely the right to vote, the right to run for public office, and the right to serve on a jury. By ensuring that a marijuana offender becomes a convicted felon, he cannot to enact decriminalization, he can't run for office and enact this type of change from within, and he cannot serve in a courtroom and vote to find another defendant not guilty of a marijuana-related offense.

So much for a government of the people, and a jury of your peers. The current laws and the people whose only goal is to keep marijuana in place as a cog in the punitive wheels of justice help prevent any chance that marijuana will become legal.

Fortunately, there's a little-known process that a convicted felon can undertake in order to have his civil rights reinstated following serving out his conviction. Be warned, the process is by no means simple and it can often prove to seem like a waste of time. Take a look at one state's process to get your rights reinstated following a conviction, and note that a marijuana conviction qualifies as a non-violent offense but can carry some extenuating circumstances if the arrest was made near a school, church, or minor children.

Here's an example of one state's lengthy and hit-or-miss process to trying to have your civil rights reinstated:

> In Florida, a past felony conviction usually means loss of civil rights, including the right to vote, even after completion of all the terms and conditions of the sentence. Loss of civil rights takes away not only the right to vote, but also the right to hold

public office, serve on a jury, and hold certain types of state job licenses.

A person with a past felony conviction loses those civil rights permanently until and unless he or she is granted restoration of civil rights by the Board of Executive Clemency. The Board of Executive Clemency is comprised of the Governor, Attorney General, Chief Financial Officer, and Commissioner of Agriculture and Consumer Services.

The right to restore civil rights is vested in the sole discretion of the Board of Executive Clemency. Rights are restored by an executive order signed by the Governor and two Cabinet members. Once your civil rights are restored, you will once again be able to vote, serve on a jury, hold public office, and apply for many state occupational licenses.

On April 5, 2007, the Florida Board of Executive Clemency adopted new Rules of Executive Clemency. Under these new rules, there are now three levels of approval for restoration of civil rights depending on the nature of the felony conviction.

UNDER ALL THREE LEVELS, INDIVIDUALS MUST:

Complete their sentence and supervision
Have no pending charges or detainers
Pay all victim restitution

Visit the Office of Executive Clemency website for the OEC's description of the new RCR process and for the OEC's answers to frequently asked questions.

The three levels created by the new Rules of Executive Clemency are summarized here. For a full description of the different levels, review the Rules of Executive Clemency.

LEVEL I Eligibility

No violent offenses (see Level 1 list)

Not declared a habitual violent felony offender, a 3-time violent felony offender, violent career criminal, prison releasee reoffender, sexual predator

Procedure

Rights are restored without a hearing

Ex-offenders in Level I are not required to apply for rights restoration but we recommend that they submit an application (Data Worksheet) form to update their contact information with the Office of Executive Clemency.

LEVEL II Eligibility

Convicted of offenses more severe than Level 1 offenses, except murder and sex offenses (See Level II list)

Not declared to be a sexual predator

Or

15 years arrest and crime free

Procedure

Rights may be restored without a hearing after a mid-level investigation. If civil rights are not restored without a hearing, then the case can be considered at a hearing after a full investigation, if you notify the Office of Executive Clemency that you want a hearing.

LEVEL III Eligibility

Convicted of murder or sex offenses, sexual predators and those not approved in Level I or II

Procedure

Full investigation and hearing

If you are in Level II or Level III, you should follow the steps outlined below to complete your application for restoration of your civil rights (RCR). For additional information about the RCR process, you may also visit the Florida Clemency website.

Members of the Florida Rights Restoration Coalition are available to assist you with this process, free of charge. We can help you complete your application, put together your portfolio, and prepare for your hearing, if your case requires one. You may contact the FRRC at info@restorerights.org, or 786-363-2731.

You do not need an attorney to apply for RCR.

Step 1: When Do I Need to Have My Civil Rights Restored?

You lost your civil rights (right to vote, right to sit on a jury, right to hold public office), and the ability to apply for certain state-issued occupational licenses if:

You have a federal or state felony conviction and you were a resident of the State of Florida when the offense and conviction occurred

You have federal or state felony conviction outside of Florida and your rights have not been restored before you became a Florida resident

Only an adjudication of guilt results in a loss of civil rights ? a withholding of adjudication that does not result in a felony conviction does not result in loss of voting and other civil rights

Step 2: Am I Eligible for Restoration of Civil Rights?

You are eligible to apply for restoration of your civil rights if:

You have completed your sentence and all conditions of supervision, such as probation, parole

You have satisfied any obligation to pay restitution
You have no outstanding arrests/detainers

Step 3: What Should I Consider Before I Apply for Restoration of My Civil Rights?

Before you submit your application, ask yourself the following questions:

Have I put forward every reasonable effort to be a productive and lawful member of society?

Have I documented my progress in society with regards to my employment, community activities, involvement in church and other social programs etc.?

Have I cultivated any ties in the community that would be useful to my future progress? Am I still maintaining open communication with these constituents; and keeping them informed of the ways that I am contributing to my community?

Am I staying abreast of all events, which are related to my case, situation, and needs?

Am I prepared to take full responsibility for getting my civil rights restored?

If you're satisfied with your answers to these questions, you're ready to apply for restoration of your civil rights.

Remember: If you are in Level I, you are no longer required to apply for rights restoration. However, we recommend that you submit an application (Data Worksheet) form to the Office of Executive Clemency to update your contact information. If you move, or if your contact information changes before your civil rights are restored, be sure to provide your up-to-date contact information to the Office of Executive Clemency.

Step 4: How Do I Apply for Restoration of My Civil Rights in Florida?

To start your restoration of right process, you must complete a Restoration of Civil Rights Data Worksheet and submit it to the Office of Executive Clemency. You can also apply by submitting an online Civil Rights Restoration Request Form; however, it is suggested that you submit a written application rather than submitting your application online; this would allow you to copy your application and have proof that you completed and mailed your application to the Office of Executive Clemency.

Step 5 : Should I Submit Additional Information Supporting My Application?

YES, you are more likely to achieve a successful outcome in the RCR application process if you submit additional information in support of your application. Remember, if you are in Level 1, you do not need to submit additional information supporting your application.

In deciding what to submit, think about how to make the most of your activities, community contacts, and your own attitude will help you advance not only in the RCR process, but possibly also in other life endeavors. You should:

1. Engage in an honest assessment of yourself: Have you done anything that would incline others to want to help you or make an extraordinary recommendation on your behalf? Have you done something that would cause them NOT to want to assist you? If so, what can you do about it?

2. Invite Feedback From Others. Ask family members, church leaders, employers, and community leaders that you respect and trust. Make yourself accountable to some individuals of your own choosing. It may not be easy to open yourself up, but you can often get valuable feedback when you do.

3. Ask for Assistance. If you want others to support your efforts for RCR, ask them. It will be your responsibility to keep them abreast of all events relating to your case/situation. Employment, community activities, and group or organization

affiliations, etc. are all important to you. THEY ARE EQUALLY AS IMPORTANT TO THOSE DESIRING TO HELP!

Step 6: How Should I Put Together My Supporting Information?

Now that you have considered how the people and activities in your life (not to mention your own positive attitude) can help you in the RCR process, you're ready to start collecting supporting information for your portfolio. We encourage you to use the checklist below as a guide for the types of letters that you can get to support your application. This checklist is not all inclusive. Don't limit yourself to the above list. You may be able to think of other persons from whom you could request a letter of support.

Remember, if you are in Level I, you do not need to submit additional information supporting your application.

Letters of Support:

Letter(s) from present and/or former employer(s);

Letter(s) from church or religious affiliation(s);

Letters from representatives of social organizations in which you participate, such as the Jaycees, Toastmaster, Fraternal Order, etc.;

Letters from community-based organizations with which you have had contact;

Letter from the victim or victim's family, if applicable for your conviction. While this may be difficult, if it is possible to get such a letter, it can be extremely helpful to your RCR application;

If you choose to include letters from family members, please note that they carry little weight

You may think of additional items such as press clippings from a community event in which you were involved that you would like to include in your portfolio

Personal Letter:

You may want to write your own letter expressing your remorse for the actions that resulted in your felony conviction, and a desire to be restored as a full member of society. (These reasons are more persuasive to the Clemency Board than your desire to get an occupational license. So, you may want to mention your employment goals, but the other reasons are more important.)

In addition to sending the letter to the Clemency Board Coordinator, you should also send the letter to the members of the Board of Executive Clemency and to their Clemency Aides.

Step 7: Where should I send my application and supporting documents?

Mail all documents to: Coordinator
Office of Executive Clemency
2601 Blair Stone Road, Building C
Room 244
Tallahassee, Florida 32399-2450

If you are in Level I, you only need to submit your updated contact information.

If you are in Level II or Level III, your complete package should include:

Cover letter to Clemency Board Coordinator

Personal Letter, including a Statement of the relief you are requesting (restoration of civil rights)

Letters of Support in the order of importance

You can always send in additional materials while your application is pending.

BE SURE TO KEEP A COPY OF EVERY DOCUMENT THAT YOU SEND TO THE OFFICE OF EXECUTIVE CLEMENCY.

Step 8: Should I Do Anything After I Submit My Application and Portfolio?

Yes. After you send in your application and portfolio, you should follow up to make sure all documents have been received. The following checklist will help you make sure to take the proper steps to monitor the progress of your application.

1. Once your package has been mailed, wait 2 weeks, and then call Office of Executive Clemency to verify receipt of your package.

If you are eligible for restoration of civil rights without a hearing, your process iscomplete. You need only wait for a certificate of restoration to be mailed to you. (To see if you will require a hearing, see the Rules of Executive Clemency Rule 9)

If your case requires a hearing, you can expect to receive notice from the Parole Commission informing you of an investigation that will likely be conducted by a local Parole and Probation field officer (Parole Examiner).

2. If you submit additional documents, call the Office of Executive Clemency to make sure the documents have been received.

3. Always inform the Office of Executive Clemency if you change your address and/or telephone number.

Bear in mind that the RCR process from start to finish may take as long as 1 year to 2 years to be completed. Once the interviewing Parole Examiner completes their investigation of your case, a full report will then be forwarded to the Parole Commission in Tallahassee, as well as to the Executive Clemency Board. A notice of a hearing date will be sent to you if it is determined that your case requires a full review by the Executive Clemency Board.

Step 9: Should I attend the hearing of my case?

Yes! If you case requires a hearing, you should make every effort to attend the hearing at which the Board of Executive

Clemency will consider your case. This will increase the chances of a favorable outcome.

The Office of Executive Clemency is required to mail you advance notice of the date on which your case will be heard. The Board of Executive Clemency meets four times each year.

At the hearing, you will have an opportunity to address the Clemency Board directly. Also, you may have others address the Clemency Board on your behalf. In addition, if there was a victim of your crime, the victim may also address the Clemency Board.

Note that your case may not require a hearing:

If you are in Level I, your civil rights will be granted without a hearing.

If you are in Level II, your civil rights also may be granted without a hearing. You will be notified if your civil rights are not granted within 30 days after the Office of Executive Clemency supplies your information to the Clemency Board. You should then file an application and supporting documents and attend your hearing.

Closing Thoughts on the RCR Process

Congratulations on going the extra mile to make sure that your RCR application is the best it can be! Applying for RCR and/or other forms of clemency can be a real "close encounter" with your community contacts, with yourself, and maybe even with the Governor. As you go through this process, and as you begin new endeavors in your life, keep in mind these final "Do"s:

1. Maintain your sense of hope and unbending motivation. Motivation is the fire that makes you GO!

2. Develop and stick to a realistic plan with achievable goals. This will sustain your motivation.

3. Further your education and expand your job skills.

4. Pursue opportunities to give back to your community.

5. Seek the support you need from loved ones and community resources (emotional, social, etc.).

This is the laundry list of work that is required to have your rights reinstated following a felony marijuana conviction, even if no jail time is served. It's easy to see why many citizens never bother with the process, as the work involved is time consuming and can open the person up to having others scrutinize their behavior.

It's also easy to see why rampant prosecution of individuals for marijuana possession can help determine the outcome of elections and prosecutions by keeping a "certain element" from participating in the voting and jury processes. There's a vested interest in barring citizens of the United States from having all of their rights, and our current marijuana laws make it all too easy to strip citizens of these rights.

# Chapter 7: Medical Cannabis and Its Enemies

## Why Does the Medical Community Fight So Hard Against Cannabis?

We can argue the merits of decriminalization versus the alleged concerns of anti-marijuana lobbyists all day long. We can highlight the racial disparity that takes place in our justice system over marijuana-related crimes, and we can open up lengthy discourse about the harmlessness of indulging in recreational marijuana use.

But the purpose of this book is to help the public understand that there is a conspiracy against marijuana and its benefits to severely ill citizens. This book isn't intended to be a manifesto on how good it feels to get high or a work of revisionist history that claims our founding fathers sat around passing joints while they drafted the Constitution. This is a serious look at the intentional withholding of viable medication from desperately sick people.

The fact of the matter is people are dying, and even cannabis has the power to stop death. But there is evidence that—used in conjunction with approved courses of treatment—it may have the power to help sick people fight their illnesses in ways that traditional pharmaceuticals have not. Basically, it has been proven to not be harmful and has countless sources of anecdotal evidence to support the claim that it can actually help a number of diagnosed medical conditions; so why is it still being relegated to "voodoo medicine" if it has a long history of medicinal uses and is widely recognized even among members of the medical community as a potentially valid drug protocol?

## Fear of Losing Money

According to an article for AlterNet, big pharmaceuticals took in an astounding—and even heartbreaking—amount of money last year: "Thanks to America's for-profit health insurance industry, prescription drugs are a big business. In fact, in 2012, the *top 11 global drug companies made nearly $85 billion in net profits*. (emphasis the author's)

"They made these profits by slapping extraordinary price tags on the prescription drugs and health treatments that Americans are forced to rely on in order to survive devastating diseases like cancer. But while drug companies have been largely able to get away with robbing Americans left and right for the past several decades, more and more people are speaking up about the outrageous costs of lifesaving treatments."

It's no longer even newsworthy that Americans are being given the shaft when it comes to pharmaceuticals. Not only are most drugs cheaper in other countries by a wide margin, the US government (with the help of pharmaceutical industry lobbyists) has helped ensure that it's illegal for patients to secure their drugs from other countries.

Let's examine the thought process here:

1. Your cousin in Canada cannot mail you your refills. That's illegal.

2. If your cousin in Canada had a copy of your prescription for your cow, he could mail you your prescription.

Why? Because the US agriculture industry buys its drugs from foreign countries all the time. That's how they save a buck and pretend to pass that savings on to the American consumer. So your cow can ingest medication that was manufactured and sold overseas, but you cannot.

3. The drugs you were prescribed by a US doctor and bought in a US pharmacy and swallowed while standing in your US kitchen were manufactured overseas.

Conspiracy theory? Not by a long shot. According to NaturalNews, "Issued by the US Government Accountability Office, the new report says up to 40 percent of all pharmaceuticals sold in the US are actually manufactured overseas in countries like India and China. A whopping 80 percent of all ingredients used to manufacture drugs, including those manufactured in the US, reportedly come from overseas as well. And the FDA has inspected a mere 11 percent of all foreign drug manufacturing facilities, as opposed to the 40 percent it has inspected domestically.

"As of 2007, there were an estimated 152 registered drug manufacturing facilities in Canada, 299 in Indian, and 566 in China, which together total 1,017 facilities. However, FDA has only conducted 368 inspections among these countries and their drug manufacturing facilities, which means 649 facilities have never received an inspection. And if these 368 inspections include multiple inspections at the same facility, then that number is even lower.

"For years, drug companies have been shutting down domestic drug manufacturing facilities and moving production overseas. A 2009 report in *The New York Times* explains that most of the ingredients used for manufacturing critical drugs like antibiotics, allergy medicines, diabetes medications, and high blood pressure medications, are now almost exclusively produced in either China or India.

(SOURCE: http://www.nytimes.com/2009/01/20/health/policy/20drug.html)."

So you can't buy your prescription medication in the country that actually produces it because—as the consumer health advocates swear—it's not safe and there's no way to know what's actually in it, yet the pharmaceutical companies are producing the drugs in factories in those countries. Are we to believe that the markup on drug prices is somehow due to shipping costs?

Of course not. The key difference is the governments in those countries would never hear of allowing a pharmaceutical company letting patients die because they could not afford their government-approved drug protocols. But how much of a price difference are we talking about?

"In 2009, Americans spent $7,960 per person on health care," states Ezra Klein in an article for the *Washington Post.* "Our neighbors in Canada spent $4,808. The Germans spent $4,218. The French, $3,978. If we had the per-person costs of any of those countries, America's deficits would vanish. Workers would have much more money in their pockets. Our economy would grow more quickly, as our exports would be more competitive.

"There are many possible explanations for why Americans pay so much more. It could be that we're sicker. Or that we go to the doctor more frequently. But health researchers have largely discarded these theories. As Gerard Anderson, Uwe Reinhardt, Peter Hussey and Varduhi Petrosyan put it in the title of their influential 2003 study on international health-care costs, 'it's the prices, stupid.'"

The authors of the report Klein mentioned concluded, "The United States spends more on health care than any of the other OECD countries spend, without providing more services than the other countries do. This suggests that the difference in spending is mostly attributable to higher prices of goods and services."

But why do we pay more for our healthcare? Because we're powerless to stop it. We let lobbyists pull the puppet strings on our lawmakers by dangling cash incentives in front of them in exchange for legislation that prevents us from securing pharmaceutical care elsewhere. We believe the lies they hype that medical care in other industrialized nations is sub-standard, that American hospitals and doctors are the only way to go despite the fact that we actively encourage doctors from foreign countries to practice in the US.

There's an even more alarming risk in government-mandated overpaying for pharmaceuticals and other healthcare services. Klein explains that the government is also in on the spending and is paying artifically inflated prices, simply because the industry corporations can require it. All of that is money that we're not spending on other vital needs.

"And others point out that you also need to account for the innovations and investments that our spending on health care is squeezing out. 'There are opportunity costs,' says Reinhardt, an economist at Princeton. 'The money we spend on health care is money we don't spend educating our children, or investing in infrastructure, scientific research and defense spending. So if what this means is we ultimately have overmedicalized, poorly educated Americans competing with China, that's not a very good investment.'"

But future worries be damned, as long as they get their money today, right? Who cares that our schools are underfunded and that our civil engineering needs updating, as long as the company bonuses at the executive level have enough zeros behind the dollar sign?

More importantly, who cares that an HIV patient cannot afford the mandated protocol? They should just get a better job with better health benefits, right? Take a look at the chart below and see if even your job covers this:

| COST PER MONTH (estimates) | |
|---|---|
| Agenerase | $772 |
| Aptivus | $1117.50 |
| Combivir | $752.64 |
| Crixivan | $570.96 |
| Emtriva | $347.11 |
| Epivir 300mg | $347.11 |
| Epzicom | $813.55 |
| Fortovase | $263.35 |
| Fuzeon | $2315.40 |
| Hivid | $273.00 |
| Invirase | $748.50 |
| Kaletra | $796.26 |
| Lexiva | $658.99 |
| Norvir | $321.46 |
| Rescriptor | $316.35 |

| Retrovir | $405.59 |
|---|---|
| Reyataz | $892.91 |
| Sustiva 600mg | $499.43 |
| Trizivir | $1164.35 |
| Truvada | $867.99 |
| Videx EC 400mg | $346.04 |
| Viramune | $442.45 |
| Zerit | $385.88 |
| Ziagen | $466.44 |

*Source: Test Positive Aware Network;*

*"Annual HIV Drug Guide"; 2006.*

But not everyone has HIV, right? And after all, just like conservatives have told us in the past and continue to spout today, HIV is one of those diseases you could have prevented if...you know...you'd just been more *responsible*.

So let's see what the latest news from one of those "unpreventable" diseases like cancer can cost you. According to an article for the *Wall Street Journal*, there's an amazing new cancer drug, a real bargain at only $143,000 per patient. (Yes, read that again...the drug, not the entire process of having and battling cancer, just the drug.)

"The first of a promising new class of cancer drugs went on sale in Japan this week at an average annual cost of $143,000 a patient, a harbinger of hefty prices the new drugs are expected to command in the U.S. and Europe in coming months.

"The drug Opdivo, from Ono Pharmaceutical Co. and Bristol-Myers Squibb Co., is a so-called PD-1 inhibitor, a new type of drug that harnesses the body's immune system to fight tumors, including melanoma. Several other pharmaceutical companies are also developing PD-1 targeting drugs.

"High prices for the treatments come as concerns mount about the affordability of new drugs. Debate about pricing reached a peak this year with the launch of an expensive new drug for hepatitis C.

"Government health officials, private insurers and some members of Congress expressed concern that the $84,000-per-patient drug—Sovaldi from Gilead Sciences Inc.—was straining health budgets. Some prisons and state Medicaid programs said they couldn't afford to give the drug to every patient who qualified for it medically. Gilead said the drug has a high cure rate and can stave off more costly health interventions if the disease is left untreated."

Please go back and read that last sentence again. Yes, the reason the drug costs so much is because think of how much money you're going to save now that our wonder drug can do it all! You won't need expensive treatments since we're going to save you so much money with this one little pill!

The cost of the drug is artificially high because the manufacturer has to make up the difference on what it would have made if you'd suffered through the old-fashioned treatment. It's mind boggling to look at the sheer evil selfishness of blatantly admitting that this drug should cost more than many people pay for a house, simply because it's somewhat cheaper than what the treatment used to cost. The entire point of research and innovation, especially in a field like medicine where prestigious honors are awarded for lifesaving techniques and treatments, is to make society better, not to withhold medical treatment until you find a way to pay for it.

But as for this specific cancer drug, the one that costs more than the average annual household income for 96% of the country, there's even better news on the horizon: its manufacturer doesn't even know how much it will charge at this point, implying that the cost could be even higher than the current market price in Japan, a country that already pays 18% less for pharmaceuticals than US consumers.

"Bristol-Myers, which plans to market nivolumab in the U.S. if the FDA clears it for sale, declined to say how much it will charge. A spokeswoman said the company prices its medicines based on 'the value they deliver to patients and society, the scientific innovation they represent and the investment required to support' drug research-and-development. Prices for patented, brand-name drugs in Japan are typically at least 18% lower than in the U.S., according to the U.S. Department of Commerce. Japan imposes price cuts every two years, while manufacturers are free to raise prices in the U.S."

## How Does this Relate to Cannabis?

Here's the unthinkable dilemma: how does this have anything to do with marijuana? Cannabis is proving to be a legitimate treatment for cancer and HIV as well as helping to alleviate the harmful side effects of several other drugs and the accompanying conditions of other ailments. Could this be why the medical community as a whole shuns cannabis? Is it fear that there's even more to its benefits than we originally thought? Or is it a fear that consumers won't need all of the life savings-draining co-prescriptions that go along with key drugs?

If the pharmaceutical industry can dangle these veritable miracle drugs in front of patients, drugs that are so costly for the very reason that they're practically guaranteed to work, why do they care so much about a little weed? It makes you wonder if the research has proven there may be more to marijuana than we thought.

### Possibly the Stupidest Argument against Medical Marijuana

There is one surefire way to tell if you're being swindled: figure out if the person speaking sounds like he has an agenda to push. Sure, you thought there was going to be more to this foolproof method than that, but sometimes simple works best, especially when you're dealing with faulty logic.

According to the *Miami-Herald*, who ran a piece on how the medical community was fighting back against the so-called benefits of medical marijuana, there's one really important reason that cannabis should not be thought of as a viable medical treatment for any illness. Ready?

Because once a patient has a prescription for marijuana, he can stay on it forever.

Yes, according to Dr. Rafael Miguel, director of the Sarasota Memorial Institute for Advanced Medicine's Pain Medicine Program, once a doctor writes that little piece of paper for legally-approved and medically controlled cannabis, there's nothing in place to stop the patient from buying marijuana with his state-issued card for the rest of his life.

Oh, like...a prescription?

What currently stops patients from indulging in a lifetime of penicillin abuse? What prevents years and years of addiction to blood pressure medication? That's right, a prescription, a valid piece of paper that states a doctor thinks it is in the bearer's best interest to consume the item listed on the controlled document. Prescriptions are so tightly monitored, in fact, that even stealing a blank prescription pad from a doctor's office is a criminal offense, and using one to write your own prescription carries additional and more severe charges.

So why should we believe that a prescription for marijuana equates to a lifetime free-for-all of rampant drug use? Yet that is Dr. Miguel's claim, according to an article by Joshua Gillin.

"Miguel offered several reasons why the medical establishment did not like the constitutional amendment. He said there was an unreasonable focus on smoking marijuana in order to obtain psychoactive effects, and added that the process by which doctors help patients get cannabis flies in the face of the prescription model of doling out drugs. Miguel focused on how 'recommendations' to use marijuana are not prescriptions, and that they don't allow doctors to control the amount and dosage patients consume, or for how long they consume it.

"'You don't get refills — you get it forever,' Miguel said. 'There's no regulation on consumption.'"

So failure on the part of lawmakers to accurately address the terms and understanding of marijuana decriminalization and legal medical access to cannabis is supposed to result in no one ever being allowed to receive its potential health benefits? No. But currently, doctors don't issue prescriptions for marijuana, they review patient information and sign the appropriate documentation that cannabis is recommended for that patient, which then allows the individual to apply for a state-approved card. The documentation and card in the states that follow this system are required for making the purchase at a licensed dispensary.

"Doctors in states that allow medical marijuana don't prescribe the drug — that could potentially lead to federal sanctions, since the U.S. government classifies marijuana as a Schedule I drug. Inclusion on that list means, legally, that marijuana has no known medical benefits, even though that claim is much disputed," continued Gillin. "Instead, in states that allow medical marijuana, doctors recommend pot for people who suffer from certain approved conditions — typically diseases such as cancer, Parkinson's disease, ALS or other conditions causing chronic pain."

The International Federation of Pharmaceutical Manufacturers & Associations conducts its own statistical data gathering and releases its own report, called The Pharmaceutical Industry and Global Health Facts and Figures. According to their own report (2012):

- By 2016, the US pharmaceutical market will be a $1.2 trillion industry.
- It costs an average of USD 1.38 billion to develop a single drug.*
- In 2010, R&D spending by the pharmaceuticals and biotechnology sector grew by 6.2%, strengthening its position as the top R&D investing sector.
- In 2011, 5 of the 10 leading global R&D firms were pharmaceutical companies.

• The research-based pharmaceutical industry currently spends over USD 135 billion on R&D per year.

* (That's an awfully small number considering an August 2013 article in *Forbes* magazine that claims the average cost of developing a new drug is now $5 billion.)

Why such high numbers? As the report continues by bold-facedly stating, "Innovation cannot happen without a number of enabling conditions, such as access to world-class researchers, political and financial stability, and a regulatory framework that protects and rewards innovation."

Let's see..."political stability" in the form of paid-for politicians? Check. "Protecting innovation" by making sure US citizens pay more for drugs than anyone else in the world and are barred from buying their medications across borders or online? Check. "Rewarding innovation" where a handful of companies will eventually control a $1.2 trillion market? Check. "Preventing access to a natural medication through hysteria and criminal consequences, thus ensuring that the poor do without lifesaving medication in the form of cannabis?" CHECK.

## Marijuana's Enemies: No Level Too Low

There are political parties, government organizations, and lobbying groups with a great deal of money, all working to keep marijuana illegal. It serves their selfish interests. Here is a list of individuals who are working around the clock to spread lies, waste tax dollars, and support the criminal mindset that frightens voters into accepting their lies. We've already examined names like Calvin Fay and Mel and Betty Sembler, but they're far from alone in the damage they are doing to marijuana's reputation as a viable medical treatment.

## Marijuana's Public Enemy #1: Dr. Kevin Sabet

What does every person who relies on fear mongering in public speaking events need? A book, of course! Sadly, Kevin Sabet, who ranks high on our list of enemies to medical marijuana, has written a book, *Reefer Sanity: Seven Great Myths About Marijuana*. Reviewer comments indicate that the quality of the writing and the grammatical correctness are not all that they should be, but of course, that's not the half of it.

Sabet's book refers to the seven myths of marijuana use, a popular title that he also uses for his paid speaking engagements. The fact that Sabet does not cite many sources is troublesome, especially when his stated intent is to debunk the myths that the pro-cannabis and pro-medical proponents use in advocating for ending cannabis prohibition.

In the interest of disclosure, here are the seven myths that Sabet peddles as truth in his many paid appearances and speaking engagements:

### 7 Myths about Marijuana and Your Health

- I can't become addicted to marijuana
- Today's marijuana is the same old Woodstock weed my parents used
- Smoking marijuana once in a while won't harm me as a teen
- Marijuana is not tobacco – it won't harm my lungs
- I can't die from marijuana use
- Marijuana is medicine
- Marijuana will make me a more focused and better driver

Each of these myths has not only been refuted in this book with citations as to the study that disproved it, medical science has also found these myths to be just that. In fact, agencies like DARE are already removing mention of some of this faulty information from their documentation due to the flaws in the science behind them and the proven ineffectiveness of supporting this information.

Luckily, individuals speaking with the scientific data behind their arguments are not shy about firing back at this intentional dissemination of misinformation to concerned citizens. Here is a portion of one of the most insightful reviews of Sabet's book, posted by a voice of reason in the debate who goes by the user name Empathetic_Ent. He ranks the myths in the order that they appear in Sabet's farce:

*1) Cannabis is safer than virtually every single prescription drug, as it is nontoxic. In 2008, prescription drugs killed over 20,000 people in the US and cannabis killed zero. In a RAND study, they found fewer than 200 total patients were admitted to California hospitals in 2008 for "marijuana abuse or dependence," and an estimated 73,000 annual hospitalizations in California related to the use of alcohol. Schizophrenia has remained at a steady 0.5% of the population while cannabis use has increased exponentially. Schizophrenia is primarily genetic, and claims that there is a connection between cannabis usage and acquiring the disorder are controversial.*

*2) Marinol and Sativex have proven to be less effective and less safe than even smoked cannabis (the most harmful method of in-taking cannabis as it temporarily paralyzes the cilia but does NOT cause emphysema, black lung, or cancer), with Marinol actually directly killing people (something cannabis has never done).*

*3) In order for people to smoke cannabis, people need to grow and sell it as well. It costs American taxpayers over $1 Billion every year to incarcerate these "drug offenders." Organized crime grows in direct response to drug prohibition and with their growth comes gang warfare. This causes the incarceration rate to rise a bit bigger than the supposed 0.3 percent of all prison inmates that Sabet puts forth. Legalizing cannabis is the answer because it is wrong to imprison people for nonviolently using/growing/selling a plant that does far more good than harm.*

*4) Sabet accuses those who call for cannabis to be regulated as alcohol and tobacco of assuming America's policy on them is worth modeling. This is not the case, rather it merely points out that if alcohol and tobacco are legal then there is no justification in having cannabis (a demonstrably safer alternative) be illegal with such damaging punishment.*

*5) Right now it costs states around $3.6 billion a year to enforce laws and at least another $1 billion to imprison cannabis offenders, with a projected $8.7 billion in revenue if states were to legalize it. That is a surplus of around $13.3 Billion, money we could spend on education reform (which we desperately need). As cannabis is safer than alcohol and studies have shown that it reduces alcohol abuse, a normalization of cannabis will only help society.*

*6) This point by Sabet is a deliberate misrepresentation of his opponents' view, also known as a "straw man." Portugal and the Netherlands DECRIMINALIZED cannabis, and the only reason that officials have previously attempted to scale back their cannabis non-enforcement policy in the Netherlands is because of pressure from the US government. They returned to their open coffee-shop sales after the people of the Netherlands gave a stanch outcry against their officials.*

*7) Tens of millions of American citizens use cannabis regularly, and 6,000 Americans try cannabis for the first time every day. Cannabis is far healthier and safer than even moderate to sparse alcohol or tobacco use. It should be encouraged over the two, as they have high costs on their users and society. The efforts to stop cannabis use do not work and have never worked. Multiple studies have shown community programs such as D.A.R.E. actually cause a rise in cannabis use. D.A.R.E. even recognized these studies and removed cannabis from their curriculum.*

## Marijuana's Public Enemy #2: Andrea Barthwell, M.D.

Who is Andrea Barthwell, and why does she have an agenda against marijuana? It does seem odd that someone voted "The Best Doctor in America" in addiction medicine by her peers is unaware that the scientific data shows marijuana is not addictive, and yet she headed two different drug treatment centers:

"Andrea Grubb Barthwell, M.D., worked in the White House under President of the United States George W. Bush as Deputy Director for Demand Reduction at the Office of National Drug Control Policy.

"After entering the medical profession, Barthwell became President of the Illinois Society of Addiction Medicine and then President of the American Society of Addiction Medicine, an area of medicine that has been one of her specialties. She served as President of the Encounter Medical Group, an Oak Park, Illinois, professional consortium that also focused on addiction health care. *In nearby Chicago, Barthwell also has headed two drug treatment organizations: BRASS Foundation, a provider of addiction treatment services, and Interventions* (emphasis added to illustrate Barthwell's vested interest in keeping marijuana illegal).

"Barthwell founded and is CEO of the global health care and consulting firm EMGlobal LLC."

Unfortunately, Barthwell doesn't stop at simply promoting criminalization in order to serve her own interests. As the following article shows, Barthwell has a decades-long history of using whatever tactics she needs to serve her own interest, even if it means fraudulently claiming high-level support.

This article explains more of the concern associated with placing public trust in Barthwell:

**Andrea Barthwell, caught red-handed**
Pete Guither, DrugWarRant.com (2/13/05)

*Not only has Andrea Barthwell been touring Illinois misleading people about the facts about medical marijuana, she has also been claiming that her Illinois Marijuana Lectures were sponsored by Great Lakes Addiction Technology Transfer Center (GLATTC), an organization that "promotes state-of-the-art addiction science" and is funded through federal taxpayer dollars (through SAMHSA) and partners with such agencies as the Illinois Department of Human Services.*

***Well, that sponsorship turned out not to be true, either.***

*You can understand her desire to have such a group associated with the lecture series — it appears to lend scientific credence to what she's saying.*

*But I was curious as to the appropriateness of using federal tax dollars to lobby against a medical marijuana bill in the state legislature (particularly on the heels of recent GAO findings that the Drug Czar's office had engaged in illegal public relations activities), so I did some checking.*

*GLATTC is administered by the Jane Addams School of Social Work, which is part of the University of Illinois, Chicago. Here's the response I got from the University of Illinois Legal Counsel's office.*

***"Thank you for your interest, Mr. Guither. Your inquiry has been passed to me for review. The Great Lakes ATTC's name was used in connection with the lectures without UIC's permission, and the persons involved with the lectures have been so notified."***

*[Note: I have not included here the name of the University Counsel or others I contacted at GLATTC, UIC, or elsewhere, because I didn't think it was necessary. Quite frankly, the University is the one who was wronged here (along with the public), and they were quite forthcoming and prompt in responding to my inquiries. If there are members of the press who need a name to verify this information, please feel free to contact me directly.]*

*Now, before you say, "Oh, so she mistakenly added an extra name to her list of sponsors on her web site – that could be an honest mistake."*

*No. In fact, other than Andrea Barthwell and Judy Kreamer (the lecture presenters) there's only one co-sponsor: GLATTC. Check out the screen shot of the sponsor page (the web page itself should have GLATTC removed, but as of the time of this posting it had not).*

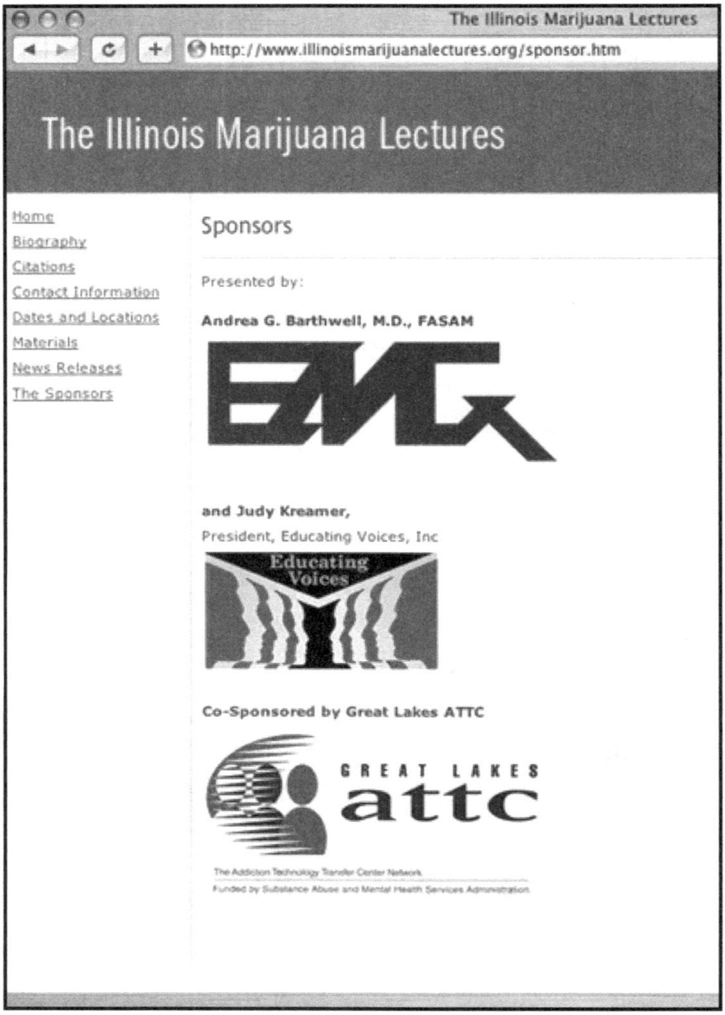


*And on the brochure/flyer: Note how GLATTC is shown as the sponsor both in text and in logo, and right near the text that talks about how the Illinois Marijuana Lectures is including lobbying efforts.*

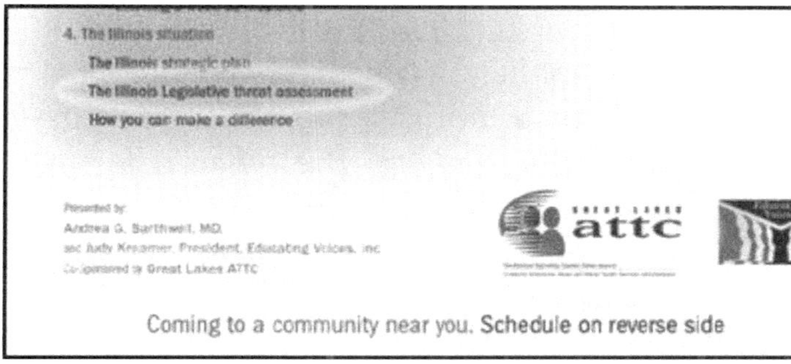


*Download the flyer at IllinoisMarijuanaLectures.com (pdf). If the first one has been corrected, you can download the original version of the flyer here (pdf)*

***A History of Deception***

*Andrea Barthwell is a former Deputy Director of the Office of National Drug Control Policy, where her job was to oppose medical marijuana, regardless of the facts. The function of the ONDCP as charged by Congress was one of propaganda. In fact, the GAO said as much (pdf) in a reply to Representative Ron Paul who was complaining about incorrect information being disseminated by another Deputy Director:*

*"... while the Deputy Director's statements pertaining to marijuana may be disputed by some with different viewpoints, they were made within the context of ONDCP's statutory responsibilities, which include taking such actions as necessary to oppose efforts to legalize certain controlled substances such as marijuana. ... Given this role, we do not see a need to examine the accuracy of the Deputy Director's individual statements in detail."*

*In other words, the ONDCP's purpose includes lying. Not a good background for the credibility of Dr. Barthwell.*

*Clearly, I'm not the only one appalled by Dr. Barthwell's deceptions. Today's Sun Times has a letter from Representative Larry McKeon, sponsor of the Illinois medical marijuana bill.*

*As a legislator, I am used to political disagreements, and I enjoy a healthy debate. But when a former White House official crisscrosses our state, deliberately spreading misinformation about a proposal toprotect some of our most vulnerable citizens, that's where I draw the line.*

*I welcome an honest debate about my medical marijuana bill, but let's base that debate on facts, not spin. Illinoisans deserve better than Andrea Barthwell's travelling con job.*

*And that's what it is, folks — Andrea Barthwell's travelling con job.*

*Representative McKeon also noted that Dr. Barthwell used "cruel hoax" to refer to medical marijuana. This is a phrase she uses all the time, and yet she is the one who is pushing the cruel hoax: by denying the tons of data supporting the medical benefits of marijuana, and trying to prevent sick and dying patients from following the recommendations of their doctor. And if that wasn't cruel enough, she wants those sick people put in jail for daring to want to relieve their pain or nausea.*

*In addition to lying about the evidence regarding the efficacy of medical marijuana, Andrea Barthwell adds further deceptions about marijuana and its use. One of her favorite claims is that today's pot is so much more potent it's creating problems of addiction and dependency.*

*"She is just not living in the real world on this issue," [Bruce Mirken of the Washington, D.C.-based Marijuana Policy Project said]. "A lot of things she talks about are blatantly not true, especially when it comes to medical marijuana. There is precisely zero medical evidence that higher THC levels in marijuana causes more dependence. As far as potency goes, there is an average of 7 percent*

*THC potency in medical marijuana in the United States. That's less than half the minimum potency standards set by the government in the Netherlands for medical marijuana sold in pharmacies in the Netherlands."*

She also talks about higher levels of youth in treatment for marijuana and infers that this is an indication of marijuana dangers — something the government's own numbers refute.

Unfortunately, Andrea Barthwell is often assumed to be a qualified expert due to her medical background and her background in government service. Certainly, she is entitled to give her opinion. But it should be clear by now that she cannot be considered credible or an expert in this subject.

**Marijuana's Public Enemy #3: Michele Leonhart**

This article by Pete Guither of DrugWarRant.com exposes Michele Leonhart, the current Administrator of the DEA, and outlines her long history of abuse of power. One of the most powerful law enforcement officers in the country has knowingly aligned herself with a convicted perjurer, a man who has influenced countless courtroom verdicts while agents and prosecutors are fully aware of his lies.

## DEA Bad Girl Michele Leonhart

by Pete Guither – Drug WarRant.com

*The Bush administration wants to head up the Drug Enforcement Agency with two women for the first time in the history of the agency.*

*The Senate has already confirmed Karen Tandy as DEA administrator by unanimous consent in a late-night session last Thursday. As Jason Vest reported in A New Hard-Liner at the DEA, Tandy has a history of "prosecutorial overzealousness" and "ignorance of key drug policy studies."*

*Now President Bush has announced his intention to nominate Michele M. Leonhart, Special Agent in Charge of DEA's Los Angeles Division, for the position of Deputy Administrator.*

*Leonhart has already established herself as another hard-liner who will not be popular in the drug reform community.*

*In June of 2001, she blasted ecstasy use at raves with her statement that "some of the dances in the desert are no longer just dances, they're like violent crack houses set to music."*

*She has also been a visible part of the DEA's attacks on California's medical marijuana laws. On January 9, 1998, when U.S. Attorney Michael Yamaguchi announced in a press conference that the government would take action against California medical marijuana clubs (arguably the start of the DEA's current war against the sick), Leonhart was standing at his side.*

*In some ways, Michele Leonhart's rise to her current position is a law enforcement Cinderella story. Richard Cole of the Associate Press talked to Leonhart in 1998 about her impetus for getting into crime fighting. Apparently when she was in fourth grade in White Bear Lake, Minnesota, her bicycle was stolen. She refused to give up on it, and found it several weeks later.*

*"I started thinking I was a bit of an investigator trying to locate my blue Huffy," she said three decades later.*

*She became enamored of the idea of fighting crime, and eventually decided on a career in law enforcement. After being turned down by academies in several cities for being too short (at 5'4"), she was accepted at Baltimore*

*Police Academy where she was first in her class, and earned the nickname "Mighty Mike" while patrolling.*

*But she wasn't satisfied.*

*"It would take me years to become a detective and get to the point where I could investigate cases, and these DEA agents were doing it every day," she remembered thinking. So she signed up with the DEA and almost immediately entered the world of undercover work in Minneapolis, playing all kinds of roles, from diplomat's daughter to troubled young woman.*

*She loved the action.*

*"One day I would go in as the head of my own organization — I'm in charge, I want to buy drugs," she said. "The next day I could be some flunky, dumb girlfriend who would just sit there and make phone calls. It was fun."*

*After five years of undercover work, she moved to St. Louis, where she became Group Supervisor for some very high profile cases, and earned a special DEA Administrator's Award. Shortly after leaving the Midwest, she moved to the west coast for a meteoric rise to Special Agent in Charge of the Los Angeles Field Division, commanding DEA offices and enforcement operations in Los Angeles, Nevada, Hawaii, Guam, and Saipan. And now she prepares for her nomination to the 2nd highest drug enforcement position in the country. A Cinderella story, indeed.*

*When DEA agents are not working undercover themselves, they rely on a special category of "employee" — snitches (also known as informants). These individuals often receive a cut of seized assets as payment for their services, so convictions can become profitable. When Michele Leonhart moved to St. Louis, she hooked up with the most prolific snitch of all time — Andrew Chambers.*

*The details of Andrew Chambers' career as a super-snitch are mostly hidden (partly to protect him, and partly to protect the DEA). Much of what we know about Chambers comes from an excellent investigative report by Michael D. Sorkin And Phyllis Brasch Librach for the St. Louis Post-Dispatch on January 16, 2000 and several follow-up reports later that year.*

*Here are some of the facts:*

*Chambers' career as a snitch spanned an amazing 16 years, from 1984 until 2000, and he was credited with 291 investigations, including 76 the DEA considers "significant."*

*He traveled all over the world for the DEA, but his home was St. Louis, and his second home Los Angeles.*

*For his snitch work with the DEA, he was paid over $2.2 million. DEA regulations limit informants to a career total of $200,000, but those regulations can be waived. The DEA says its second-highest paid informant has received about $500,000.*

*Since he also worked for the FBI, U.S. Customs Service, U.S. postal inspectors, Internal Revenue Service, Secret Service and state and local police, his total take may have been much more.*

*He lied. He lied under oath on the stand. He lied on the stand repeatedly, beginning the year after his recruitment in 1984.*

*For years, some prosecutors and many defense attorneys had expressed concerns about Chambers' perjury. In 1993 in California, a 9th Circuit U.S. Court of Appeals ruling agreed that Chambers lied on the stand. In 1995, the 8th U.S. Court of Appeals in St. Louis added its voice: "The record, however, clearly demonstrates that Chambers did in fact perjure himself . . ."*

*The DEA protected Chambers repeatedly, and avoided notifying prosecutors and defense attorneys about Chambers' past. At one point, the Drug Enforcement Agency and Justice Department lawyers stonewalled for 17 months, fighting a public defender who was trying to examine the contents of DEA's background check on Chambers.*

*Later, Assistant U.S. Attorney Stephen Wolf stated that it was clear that the drug agents never put any damaging reports into Chambers' file — even though DEA regulations require it.*

*Finally, the DEA conducted an internal review of Chambers' career, and although there was some talk of reprimanding DEA supervisors, the report was never made completely public, and the DEA refused to agree to stop using Chambers. Janet Reno finally intervened in 2000 and Chambers was deactivated as an informant.*

*During all this time, Chambers' biggest fan was Michele Leonhart.*

*At one point, she was asked whether it was time to stop using Chambers given all the problems with his credibility. "That would be a sad day for DEA," she said. "And a sad day for anybody in the law enforcement world... He's one in a million. In my career, I'll probably never come across another Andrew."*

*Clearly there were close ties. Chambers started as a snitch in St. Louis in 1984. Leonhart transferred to St. Louis in 1986 and started working with him then (close to the time that reports say Chambers began lying under oath). In 1989, Chambers was involved in a case in Minneapolis (near Leonhart's previous post). Chambers was moved around a lot by the DEA and spent time in both St. Louis and Los Angeles, but it seems clear that he mostly focused on St. Louis until around 1996, when he shifted his base to the Los Angeles area. This was about a year after Leonhart transferred to Los Angeles.*

*There's no published information regarding the extent that Leonhart was involved in DEA cover-ups or stonewalling regarding Chambers, or the omission of damaging reports from Chambers' file. However, given Leonhart's position and connection to Chambers, it is unlikely that any of it was done without her knowledge.*

*The most startling statement in the St. Louis Post-Dispatch investigation of Andrew Chambers was from Michele Leonhart:*

*"The only criticism (of Chambers) I've ever heard is what defense attorneys will characterize as perjury or a lie on the stand."*

*She continued by saying that once prosecutors check him out, they'll agree with his admirers in DEA that he's "an outstanding testifier."*

*That's the key. To an agent like Leonhart, getting the bust and getting the conviction is all that matters. The testimony is good if it leads to a successful conclusion (from her perspective). Why nitpick about the truth?*

*The Senate Judiciary Committee must, at the very least, investigate Leonhart's connection to Andrew Chambers. The fact that she apparently has no objection to the use of perjury in attaining a conviction should be an automatic disqualifier. Based on past experience, however, it is likely that Leonhart will be confirmed without discussion or recorded vote.*

*The DEA, possibly the most oppressive agency in the U.S., will now be led by the dynamic duo: Overzealous Prosecutor and her sidekick Rabid Agent. Nothing will interfere with their goals — not even truth or justice.*

But that's not the worst of Leonhart's crimes against cannabis and the patients who so desperately need it. According to multiple compiled sources, here is a look at her track record of effectiveness in her role.

According to an article by Alex Pareene for Salon.com: Pareene, Alex (April 15, 2011) DEA head: A thousand dead children means we're winning war on drugs, *Salon.com*

> "In 2011, the *Washington Post* reported that '994 people younger than 18 were killed in drug-related violence between late 2006 and late 2010' and that '[i]n 2009, the last year for which there is data, 1,180 children were killed, half in shootings.' In response to these statistics, Leonhart declared that while it 'may seem contradictory, the unfortunate level of violence is a sign of success in the fight against drugs.'"

Because according to Leonhart, children gunned down in record numbers are a clear indication that the war on drugs is effective.

According to this article by Eric Dolan for RawStory.com: Dolan, Eric. "Top DEA agent won't admit heroin more harmful, or caused more deaths, than marijuana". rawstory.com. Retrieved June 21, 2012.
SOURCE:
http://safeaccessnow.org/blog/blog/tag/michele-leonhart/

> "In 2012, Leonhart testified before Congress and refused to say that cannabis is less addictive or harmful than methamphetamine, heroin, or crack-cocaine. However, at one point she agreed with Rep. Steve Cohen (D-TN) that the right to use medical cannabis should be 'between [a patient] and his doctor.' Representative Cohen quickly criticized her statement as inconsistent with the actions of her agency."

Again, this is the head of the drug enforcement authorities in this country who claims there is no difference between marijuana and drugs like heroin or meth, at least as far as their harmfulness and their addictive nature are concerned.

According to these articles in *Weekly Standard* and *US News*:
SOURCE: http://www.weeklystandard.com/blogs/report-dea-chief-rips-obamas-pot-remarks_775420.html

SOURCE:
http://www.usnews.com/news/articles/2014/01/29/congressmen-dea-administrator-completely-incompetent-should-assume-a-japanese-posture-and-resign

> "In 2014, Leonhart openly criticized President Barack Obama's stance on cannabis at a meeting of the National Sheriffs' Association. Marijuana activists and two congressmen have called for her resignation due to her stance on cannabis while some law enforcement leaders have defended her position. She also proposed that dog owners should oppose marijuana legalization since edible products could kill animals, notwithstanding that the marijuana itself is not particularly toxic to dogs."

# CHAPTER 8:
# Kevin Sabet and the SAM Scam

## "Oregon Drug Abuse Officials Wanted To Pay Legalization Opponent Over $40,000 With Public Money"

8 October 3, 2014 by Russ Belville

I've concluded my last of seven stops following Kevin Sabet around Oregon as he performed a so-called "educational" tour two weeks prior to the mailing of ballots in Oregon that include marijuana legalization. It appears more than ever that county drug prevention staff and district attorneys were trying to secure over $40,000 in federal anti-drug education grant money to pay Kevin Sabet for what was clearly a political event to lobby voters against Measure 91.

This is an email and an attachment dated June 12, 2014 that I have uncovered with the help of Jennifer Alexander as part of my records requests to Clatsop County District Attorney Josh Marquis. It is from BestCare Prevention's Mandi Puckett, who is now on a leave of absence to act as director of the No on Measure 91 campaign.

In it, we learn that for every stop Kevin Sabet made on the Marijuana and our Youth "education" tour, he was paid $3,000 plus hotels, meals, and travel.

That's $21,000 for three days in Oregon at seven cities. Plus (working to confirm all these) three flights (from his home in Florida to Portland, from Medford to Boise for the Day Two/Three leg to Ontario*, and Portland back to Florida), two rental cars (he had one for Portland to Grants

Pass, would have had to turn it in at Medford, then would have had to pick up another one in Boise for the trip back through Ontario to Portland, and hotels in at least Roseburg, Boise, and Portland, and per diem for three days.

2014 Tour VictoriesNow, keep in mind that BestCare is Mandi Puckett's employer, whose director pulled out their $15,000 when I and others focused scrutiny on their use of federal grant funds. Before we did so, the tour was to be thirteen cities, which would have been $39,000 plus four more days of rental cars and hotels and meals expensed. Also recall: they did run this same summit and tour in 2012 with Kevin Sabet and made no attempt to either pull their federal money from funding it or to conceal its clear anti-Measure 80 messaging (and some of the materials created there were distributed at the Hood River event). (Oddly, there was no "annual" October summit and tour in 2013, when legalization was not on the ballot.)

And that would have been paid for partially or perhaps mostly by federal drug education grant money. It is also notable the BestCare is listed as the "Oregon SAM affiliate" – Project SAM is Kevin Sabet's national anti-legalization think-tank that uses brochures from CADCA (Community Anti-Drug Coalitions of America) to teach local drug educators how they can best lobby against legalization without running afoul of the laws prohibiting lobbying with government money.

OK, maybe that's just unwise spending, but is it actionable? Wait until you see the video I unpack from these events where it could not be clearer that it is an event meant to depress support for Measure 91 and sell Kevin Sabet's book. It includes me being threatened with expulsion and getting towed if I didn't remove my Yes on 91 banner from my car, me being shouted at by the Malheur DA in Ontario when I dared to calmly express some facts from Colorado's legalization that weren't being mentioned by Sabet, and mostly-empty auditoriums where audiences were about 30 to 60 people, and that's if I include the law enforcement, district attorneys, and professional rehab people in the audience.

Meanwhile, for comparison's sake, at five of the seven events was Eric Martin, who is a drug and alcohol addiction expert from the state of Oregon who teaches at U of O. He's also the current Policy & Legislative Liaison (and former executive director) of the Addiction Counselor Certification Board of Oregon (ACCBO). ACCBO is the state organization that provides certification services to addiction professionals in Oregon**. His expense was $200 per event. He's also a self-described thirty-year recovering marijuana addict.

So... an Oregon former pot addict / UO professor / drug expert is worth 15 times less for an "educational" forum on marijuana than a Floridian former adviser to the Drug Czar who heads the nation's anti-legalization strategy think tank and colludes with local drug prevention staff to secure drug education grant money to pay himself $7,000 per day plus expenses? Their spending priorities seem to indicate the political nature of the event to me.

But at least maybe 300 attendees statewide (if I include uniformed law enforcement, district attorneys, and rehab pros) got to enjoy an extremely disjointed PowerPoint chock full of:

- cherry-picked data (e.g., Colorado drivers in fatal wrecks with THC in blood have tripled, but no mention of overall traffic fatalities falling, mentions of increased daily use by teens without mentioning decreased monthly teen usage overall),
- correlation-not-causation (look how the more people smoked pot, the lower income, educational, employment attainment, and life satisfaction they had... that couldn't be because getting caught for pot

means the end of your job or scholarship and potential incarceration, could it?),

- non-sequiturs (how many people in the audience regularly attend the national conference of the American Medical Association?),
- tortured metaphors (People say marijuana's safer than alcohol, but drinking, smoking, and marijuana are all bad; it's like asking should I jump from the 10th floor, the 7th floor, or the 3rd floor... When people defend the THC chocolate bar the kid gets into by saying, 'vodka looks like water and a kid could into that if you left it out', that's like saying because my taillight is broken, I should go break my headlight, too.), self-contradiction (I really don't like comparing one drug to another... then rattles off statistics on alcohol and tobacco use to dissuade marijuana legalization. I don't really have a problem with a fifty-year-old guy who wants to smoke and grow pot in his basement... so he remains punishable by the law),
- No True Scotsmen (I believe marijuana has medicinal properties, but why can't we treat it like we treat all other medicines, with standardized doses and consistency – like how the aspirin you buy in Hawaii's the same as the aspirin in Connecticut.),
- Strawmen (People say that marijuana is harmless and non-addictive...), and plain old whoppers (chart showing average marijuana THC potency 1960-1980 ranging from 0.2% to 1.0%, when THC wasn't even discovered until 1964... saying "the industry" in Colorado reacted to Levi Thamba's tragic death by saying "he should have cut the bar into sixteen pieces", when, in fact, the industry worked quickly and decisively with the state regulators to craft stricter dosage and labeling regulations, as well as a high-profile educational campaign on edible

moderation... talking about teenagers who supposedly tell him they're better drivers when high because they drive 30MPH in a 65MPH freeway... saying Cheech & Chong could have never imagined the hash oil of today... so many...)

They also got these fantastic educational materials:

*"Pot probably doesn't cause lung cancer, but you might smoke cigarettes, too, and they do cause cancer!"*

*"Medical Marijuana has only 'healed' over one million sick and disabled people."*

*"Now brickweed is 'natural' marijuana of 1% THC and indoor marijuana is 'man-made' marijuana of 37% THC."*

*"Quitting marijuana is like quitting cigarettes, it's so addictive."*

* Sabet told me this when I asked about the drive from Grants Pass to Ontario, since I had to do that drive.

** Thanks to Doug McVay of Drug Policy Facts for this info.

## "Oregon Marijuana "Education" Only Occurs When Marijuana's on the Ballot"

September 11, 2014 by Russ Belville

*"Help us fight the use of public funds to defeat marijuana legalization in Oregon – donate to http://www.gofundme.com/fightsabet today!"*

My colleague Jennifer Alexander has been doing incredible work digging through the internet archives to expose so-called community education on marijuana for what is – blatant political propaganda funded by taxpayers to defeat marijuana legalization.

First, Jennifer uncovered the calendar of events for BestCare Treatment Services dating back to 2010. Rick Treleaven of BestCare was quoted in The Oregonian as saying, "the summit has been held for several years in October" and never received any complaints. This prompted me to investigate the 2012 Summit, as marijuana legalization was on the ballot in the form of Measure 80.

*BestCare Events Calendar "marijuana" events only – from Internet Archive, dated August 2014:*

*July 20, 2014*
*SAM Summit 8:30-4:30*
*Hilton Orlando Bonnet Creek*
*(Preceding CADCA's midyear training) Registration $200.00*

*July 19, 2014*
*SAM (Smart Approaches to Marijuana) Action Summit*
*7pm Dance & Reception*
*Florida*

*April 16, 2014*
*Marijuana Summit*
*Resort @ the Mountain*

*April 15, 2014*
*Marijuana Summit*
*Resort @ the Mountain*

*Oct 18, 2012 Time TBA*
*Statewide Marijuana Summit*
*Living Hope Christian Center*
*24 NE A Street*
*Madras, Oregon*

*Apr 17 & 18, 2012*
*Oregon Marijuana Summit*
*Welches, Oregon*

*Aug 17, 2010*
*Marijuana Training with Eric Martin*
*Location: Living Hope Christian Center*
*Click here for flyer*

The funny thing is there was no 2013 Summit. There wasn't a 2011 Summit, either. Back when Measure 74, our failed marijuana dispensaries initiative was on the ballot in 2010, there was "marijuana training". Searching for "marijuana" among the calendar of events BestCare had posted up until mid-August and including the scheduled October 2014 Summit, we find:

*2014: Legalization on ballot = two Oregon marijuana summits, one national summit;*
*2013: Nothing on ballot = nothing on marijuana;*
*2012: Legalization on ballot = two Oregon marijuana summits;*
*2011: Nothing on ballot = nothing on marijuana;*
*2010: Dispensaries on ballot = one Oregon marijuana training.*

We've already shown that the 2014 Summit features speakers Kevin Sabet and Eric Martin, the same speakers who were clearly urging no votes on legalization at the 2012 Summit. Sabet went so far as to say to the Summit audience, “Is the right to get high and buy legal pot worth the risk to kids in the form of greater addiction and learning deficits, the risk to society to have another legal entity advertising an addictive substance, and the risk to our economy in the form of greater safety and health costs (like car crashes, the cost to health care, and the costs of a newly regulated system)?”

But now we have evidence that the official spokesperson for the No on 91 campaign, Mandi Puckett, has been using her position as a substance abuse prevention counselor for Descutes County, Oregon, to campaign against the current legalization initiative and the initiative that failed in 2012. She has been coordinating and promoting the supposedly “educational” Summit on taxpayer time while simultaneously working as the No on 91 spokesperson and, apparently, the spokesperson for the Oregon chapter of Kevin Sabet’s Project SAM – a national anti-legalization propaganda organization.

In an official response to Rep. Blumenauer’s call for federal investigation into Oregon Marijuana Election Shenanigans, Puckett explained, “My job was to help apply for State and Federal grants and work with the local coalition to use that money to educate people about the dangers of using addictive substances,” apparently only in the years when marijuana legalization is on the ballot.

The document further explains, “On August 21st, Puckett took a leave of absence from her substance abuse prevention job to work on the No on 91 campaign,” telling us that perhaps she understands she’s not supposed to be campaigning on the taxpayers’ time. But Puckett was working hard to promote the No on 91 agenda well prior to stepping down at Deschutes County.

On May 28, 2014, the meeting agenda for the Jefferson County Prevention Task Force, held during normal working hours, showed the following entries:

*Prevention website services needed – Mandi*
*SAM Affiliate report – Mandi*
*Planning Committee for Fall conference in Madras & Oregon Education Tour – Mandi*
*Save the Date for October 1 & 2, 2014 – Mandi*

Puckett and No on 91 make no attempt to camouflage that involvement. "This educational summit in Madras, the accompanying tour of Oregon cities, including the timing of the events, has been in planning stages for nearly two years (Fall of 2012 to Spring of 2014 to be exact), long before Measure 91 was on the ballot."

So if the event is merely "educational", why did the planning that began in Fall 2012, following the previous Summit that was openly lobbying against legalization, not aim for 2013 and instead aimed for 2014? Claiming they planned "long before Measure 91 was on the ballot" is disingenuous when after the defeat of Measure 80 in November 2012, ABC News was reporting that Measure 80 proponent "Paul Stanford, for his part, has vowed to push the law again in 2014, unless the state legislature passes it first." In March of 2013, The Oregonian reported "[Anthony] Johnson said the coalition would seek to place an initiative on the November 2014 ballot."

On July 19-20, 2014, Sabet's Project SAM held a national summit in Florida that was being promoted by Puckett and BestCare. We are investigating whether Puckett and other state prevention staff were in attendance, where Kevin Sabet's opening plenary detailed:

*What are our messages in 2014?*

*Where are we with Alaska and Oregon, and beyond?*

*What are the 3 key issues you need to know this year?*

*What should every affiliate be doing in 2014?*

The SAM Summit also featured representatives of the Colorado and Washington SAM Chapters who are also listed as presenters at the 2014 Oregon Summit. Those representatives at the SAM Summit explained the "Overall picture in Colorado and how you can use this in your community" and "the status of legalization in Washington and what lessons can be brought to your community." Those presentations were followed by "How You Can Put a Group Together to Counter Marijuana Ballot and Legislative Measures" that was delivered by "Reps from Oregon, Alaska, SAM Affiliates and Board". We will find out who those Oregon reps were.

If one of those reps was Mandi Puckett, they must have informed her to be very careful about the appearance of electioneering at the Summit. As Puckett explained, "Later when it was announced the measure would be on the November ballot, we took extra steps to include in our work plan and advise presenters to not speak about the ballot measure."

Rep. John Huffman of The Dalles, Oregon, also tried to paint the Summit as merely educational. "These summits have been held over the years to help educate about the harm that marijuana, drugs and alcohol can have on youth. I went to one or two in Jefferson County a couple of years ago, long before a ballot measure proposing to legalize recreational marijuana was created." But that "couple of years ago" was 2012, when a "measure proposing to legalize recreational marijuana" was already on the ballot! One of my listeners, an attorney from Bend, Oregon, attended the 2012 Summit and told me the whole thing was "incredibly political" and that speakers routinely exhorted the audience to vote no on Measure 80 and to spread that message to their friends and family.

## "In 2012, Oregon Marijuana Education Summit Was Definitely Political" (UPDATED)

September 9, 2014 by Russ Belville

I have been reporting on the so-called Oregon Marijuana Education Summit & Tour starring anti-legalization leader Kevin Sabet or Project SAM. With assistance from Jennifer Alexander and others, I have discovered that by multiple indications, the people promoting the Summit & Tour know full well it is a political event designed to oppose the Measure 91 marijuana legalization initiative. Unfortunately for them, it appears as if they may have used taxpayer money and resources to promote and produce fliers for the event, violating the terms of their grants and state and federal election laws.

Their defense is that these events are merely to educate the public about the dangers of marijuana. The fact that every invited speaker whose opinion is known is an outspoken critic of marijuana legalization is just coincidence. The timing of the events in the week before Oregonians receive their ballots is simply happenstance. After all, Rick Treleaven of BestCare Prevention, one of the prime sponsors, "has noted that the summit has been held for several years in October" and never received any complaints.

Oh, really? Like, say, 2012, when Oregon was voting on a marijuana legalization initiative called Measure 80?

As the ballots for Measure 80 were being mailed out, BestCare Treatment Services was sending out "Save the

Date" fliers for the October 18, 2012 "Statewide Marijuana Summit", also to be held in Madras, Oregon, just like the current Summit. Kevin Sabet was slated to be a featured speaker (though he wasn't listed on the flier), just like the current summit. Eric Martin was listed as a featured speaker, just like the current summit. Shirley Morgan was listed as a speaker; her bio from a 2013 anti-legalization conference sponsored by the Coalition for a Drug-Free California and the Drug Free America Foundation explains her bona fides:

"Ms. Morgan is also the founder for the Oregonian's [sic] Against Legalization of Marijuana, a grassroots community group that was successful in November of 2004 and 2010 in Oregon defeating measures that would have required local government agencies to open pot dispensaries, and then again in November of 2012 defeating a measure that would have legalized marijuana."

This year, Rick Treleaven of BestCare explained that they pulled their $15,000 of government-grant money for the Summit because he "could see from an outside perspective that it could look like a conflict." If it's a conflict now, with the speakers telling folks the Summit won't be discussing Measure 91 a week before ballot mailing, why was it not a conflict in 2012 with Shirley Morgan and Kevin Sabet openly opposing Measure 80 at the Summit the week of ballot mailing?

Did $15,000 or more in federal grant money get used to promote and produce the 2012 Summit? The flier indicates it is "Full day training (It's Free!)". Does that indicate that in 2012, like this year, law enforcement professionals can earn their continuing education credits for attending? The flier also adds, "Provided at Summit: FOOD, PRIZES, CHILDCARE, SPANISH TRANSLATION," which certainly somebody paid for.

BestCare also worked with county drug prevention staff in Deschutes County to produce advertisements based on the education that was presented at the 2012 Summit. The public was called upon to contact county staff on their county email addresses and phone lines to acquire radio and internet ads they could use to "provide factual information so that citizens can make informed health-related decisions based on credible data."

"The information learned [at the Summit] became a catalyst" for the production of an educational brochure on marijuana facts that made no attempt to hide its anti-legalization political nature. Included in the 4-page brochure:

"2012 Oregon Summit - Kevin SabetWhat about marijuana legalization? Advocates of marijuana claim legalizing it will result in economic revenue and reduced drug trafficking cartels. Research shows if legalized, marijuana use will go up resulting in more social costs to society.

"Ultimately the question is this: 'Is the right to get high and buy legal pot worth the risk to kids in the form of greater addiction and learning deficits, the risk to society to have another legal entity advertising an addictive substance, and the risk to our economy in the form of greater safety and health costs (like car crashes, the cost to health care, and the costs of a newly regulated system)?' [footnoted: Sabet, Kevin, Ph.D., 18 October 2012. Oregon Statewide Marijuana Summit.]

"2012 Oregon Summit - Eric MartinWhat states have marijuana legalization ballot measures in 2012? According to polls, of the three states with marijuana legalization ballot measures, Oregon is least likely to pass. [includes table of Oregon's Measure 80, Washington's I-502, and

Colorado's Amendment 64 legalization proposals provided by Eric Martin]

"How does the Oregon Medical Marijuana Program work? Marijuana itself is not an approved medicine under the FDA's scientific review process, yet 16 states & the District of Columbia have permitted marijuana to be sold as 'medicine' for various conditions."

So Kevin Sabet was openly discussing what he imagined the pitfalls of marijuana legalization would be, Eric Martin was comparing and contrasting the three 2012 legalization proposals, and Shirley Morgan was leading Oregonians Against Legal Marijuana while speaking at the 2012 Summit, and BestCare and Jefferson County were sponsoring it, presumably with taxpayer money. Only in 2014, when a better-funded and more-politically-savvy campaign complained about it, did Oregon officials recognize the Summit's clear political intent, and only then did BestCare and others begin withdrawing their support.

Shall we look back to 2010 when Oregon had Measure 74, a medical marijuana dispensary initiative, on the ballot?

UPDATE: As KTVZ reported on the day of the Summit in their story entitled "Measure 80 focus at Madras Marijuana Summit" and subtitled as "Police, addiction specialists urge vote against legalized pot":

"Hundreds of people packed Living Hope Christian Church in Madras Thursday for the Statewide Marijuana Summit. Several speakers offered insight on Ballot Measure 80, which would legalize marijuana in Oregon.

"'There may be 500 votes that decide if Oregon has a bright future or a cloudy future,' Umitilla [sic] County Sheriff John Trumbo said. 'Everyone needs to go vote, and they need to vote no.'"

Every public official who used taxpayer time and resources and every speaker who collected honorariums from taxpayer dollars is personally liable under Oregon law for the value of their contribution to illegal campaigning against Measure 80.

# Chapter 9:
# Marijuana as a Preventive and Cancer Fighter

Since you're reading right now, you're probably sitting down. Otherwise, I'd have to tell you to sit down for this. (If you're still standing, you were warned.)

Not-so-new evidence has shown that not only does marijuana help alleviate the pain and harmful side effects of treatment for a wide variety of chronic illnesses, there are even accepted studies from reputable sources that show marijuana itself can actually shrink tumors and prevent tumors from forming.

According to a report on the Cancer.gov website:

"One study in mice and rats suggested that cannabinoids may have a protective effect against the development of certain types of tumors. During this 2-year study, groups of mice and rats were given various doses of THC by gavage. A dose-related decrease in the incidence of hepatic adenoma tumors and hepatocellular carcinoma (HCC) was observed in the mice. Decreased incidences of benign tumors (polyps and adenomas) in other organs (mammary gland, uterus, pituitary, testis, and pancreas) were also noted in the rats. In another study, delta-9-THC, delta-8-THC, and cannabinol were found to inhibit the growth of Lewis lung adenocarcinoma cells in vitro and in vivo. In addition, other tumors have been shown to be sensitive to cannabinoid-induced growth inhibition.

"Cannabinoids may cause antitumor effects by various mechanisms, including induction of cell death, inhibition of cell growth, and inhibition of tumor angiogenesis invasion and metastasis. Two reviews summarize the molecular mechanisms of action of cannabinoids as antitumor agents. Cannabinoids appear to kill tumor cells but do not affect their nontransformed counterparts and may even protect them from cell death. These compounds have been shown to induce apoptosis in glioma cells in culture and induce regression of glioma tumors in mice and rats. Cannabinoids protect normal glial cells of astroglial and oligodendroglial lineages from apoptosis mediated by the CB1 receptor."

Of course we're not done:

"No clinical trials of Cannabis as a treatment for cancer in humans were identified in a PubMed search; however, a single, small study of intratumoral injection of delta-9-THC in patients with recurrent glioblastoma multiforme reported potential antitumoral activity."

Did you like how they threw that in there at the end after a lot of medical jargon? *Potential antitumoral activity?* But yet, we're not going to study this in humans when there are already millions of reported humans giving it a try?

But wait, of course the pharmaceutical industry has to make its money. So they've developed prescription drugs from cannabis sources that are supposed to help patients fight nausea:

"Despite advances in pharmacologic and nonpharmacologic management, nausea and vomiting (N/V) remain distressing side effects for cancer patients and their families. Dronabinol, a synthetically produced delta-9-THC, was approved in the United States in 1986 as an antiemetic to be used in cancer chemotherapy. Nabilone, a synthetic derivative of delta-9-THC, was first approved in Canada in 1982 and is now also available in the United States.[16] Both dronabinol and nabilone have been approved by the U.S. Food and Drug Administration for the treatment of N/V associated with cancer chemotherapy in patients who have failed to respond to conventional antiemetic therapy. Numerous clinical trials and meta-analyses have shown that dronabinol and nabilone are effective in the treatment of N/V induced by chemotherapy.[17-20] The National Comprehensive Cancer Network Guidelines Exit Disclaimer recommend cannabinoids as breakthrough treatment for chemotherapy-related N/V."

So smoking your own bag of marijuana—or using cannabis oil, expressed butters, or edibles, for those who don't want to inhale it—is unacceptable, but the pharmaceutical industry can express out the potent chemical, grind it into a pill, and charge you for it?

According to DrugBnk.ca, a legitimate Canadian pharmacology site (as opposed to a site that actually sells drugs on the internet), Nabilone comes in two strengths at a cost of "Cesamet 0.5 mg 3.49USD, Cesamet 1 mg 13.99USD." Let's ignore for the moment the fact that Nabilone bombed as a viable option after the dogs in the trial convulsed and died.

In fact, let's take a look at what EverydayHealth.com tells patients about Nabilone, even as it supports the drug as a viable treatment to combat the side effects of chemotherapy:

### "What is the most important information I should know about Nabilone?"

"Nabilone may be habit-forming and should be used only by the person it was prescribed for. Nabilone should never be given to another person, especially someone who has a history of drug abuse or habitual marijuana use. Keep the medication in a secure place where others cannot get to it. Do not use nabilone if you have ever had an allergic reaction to natural or man-made marijuana.

“Before taking nabilone, tell your doctor if you have high blood pressure, heart disease, a history of mental illness or drug addiction, or if you are also using other medicines that can affect your central nervous system, such as a tranquilizer, sleep medicine, or anti-psychotic medications. Use this medication exactly as it was prescribed for you. Do not use it in larger amounts or for longer than recommended by your doctor.

“Avoid using other medicines that affect the central nervous system (such as stimulants, diet pills, cold medicine, pain medication, muscle relaxers, and medicine for seizures, depression, anxiety, mental illness, or Parkinson's disease). These other drugs can add to the effects of nabilone.

“Nabilone causes effects that will impair your thinking or reactions. Do not drive or do anything that requires you to be awake and alert until the effects of nabilone wear off. There are many other medicines that can add to the side effects of nabilone. Tell your doctor about all the prescription and over-the-counter medications you use. This includes vitamins, minerals, herbal products, and drugs prescribed by other doctors. Do not start using a new medication without telling your doctor.”

So should you decide to ingest a synthetic, expensive drug that causes death by convulsion in animals, be sure to tell your doctor about any other problems or medications you might be taking. Oh, and be sure to watch out for the fact that—unlike actual marijuana—*it may be habit forming*.

But let’s take a look at the monthly cost of 30 capsules of this habit forming, dog-killing, synthetic drug that you can take in order to avoid a) being a lawbreaker and b) dying from starvation while fighting the effects of chemo:

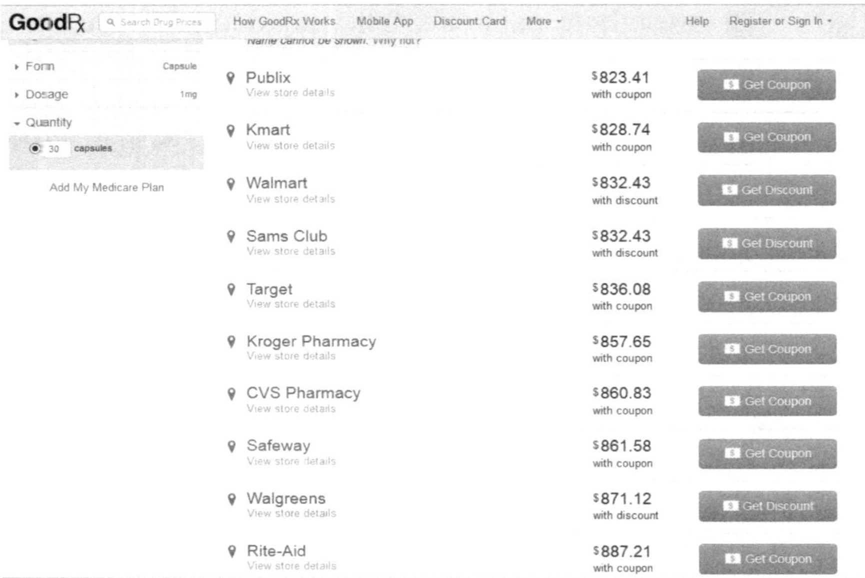



| | | |
|---|---|---|
| Publix | $823.41 with coupon | Get Coupon |
| Kmart | $828.74 with coupon | Get Coupon |
| Walmart | $832.43 with discount | Get Discount |
| Sams Club | $832.43 with discount | Get Discount |
| Target | $836.08 with coupon | Get Coupon |
| Kroger Pharmacy | $857.65 with coupon | Get Coupon |
| CVS Pharmacy | $860.83 with coupon | Get Coupon |
| Safeway | $861.58 with coupon | Get Coupon |
| Walgreens | $871.12 with discount | Get Discount |
| Rite-Aid | $887.21 with coupon | Get Coupon |

But even that wasn't enough to convince the medical establishment that synthetic and expensive pills weren't better than getting the derivatives directly from the source. Then this occurred:

"One systematic review studied 30 randomized comparisons of delta-9-THC preparations with placebo or other antiemetics from which data on efficacy and harm were available.[21] Oral nabilone, oral dronabinol, and intramuscular levonantradol (a synthetic analog of dronabinol) were tested. Inhaled Cannabis trials were not included. Among all 1,366 patients included in the review, cannabinoids were found to be more effective than the conventional antiemetics prochlorperazine, metoclopramide, chlorpromazine, thiethylperazine, haloperidol, domperidone, and alizapride."

But that still wasn't enough to convince the powers that be. All told, this one document on the government's cancer website cites 39 different studies that proved the effectiveness of cannabis in treating cancer and actively shrinking tumors, as well as preventing new tumor growth.

But the government doesn't care. Talk about your inconvenient truth.

Even worse is the news that this restorative and preventative effect of marijuana is not new. One study reported as early 1984 on the benefits of marijuana as a medical treatment, but of course the public wasn't well-informed about it.

"Three trials have evaluated the efficacy of inhaled marijuana in chemotherapy-induced N/V. In two of the studies, inhaled Cannabis was made available only after dronabinol failure. In the first trial, no antiemetic effect was achieved with marijuana in patients receiving cyclophosphamide or doxorubicin, but in the second trial, a statistically significant superior antiemetic effect of inhaled Cannabis versus placebo was found among patients receiving high-dose methotrexate. The third trial was a randomized, double-blind, placebo-controlled, cross-over trial involving 20 adults in which both inhaled marijuana and oral THC were evaluated. One-quarter of the patients reported a favorable antiemetic response to the cannabinoid therapies. This latter study *was reported in abstract form in 1984* (emphasis added later). A full report, detailing the methods and outcomes apparently has not been published, which limits a thorough interpretation of the significance of these findings."

The rest of the Cancer.gov report explores other health impediments associated with cancer, like inflammation, pain, anxiety, sleep deprivation, and more. The report goes into great detail in outlining how various forms of consuming cannabis, such as oral, oromucosal, or inhaled, produced beneficial results.

This is followed up here with an article from High Times that details anecdotal experiences with these so-called synthetic replacements for natural cannabis.

**Marinol: The Little Synthetic That Couldn't** by Elsa Scott
<u>High Times,</u> July 1994, pp. 18-21

*After dogs on Nabilone started having convulsions and dropping dead, the first attempts at producing synthetic THC were scrapped. Enter Marinol, a drug never intended for human use and one with many dangerous side effects.*

*Sam Skipper is a handsome man with black hair, blue eyes and a theatrical style that is well known in La Mesa, California. But in 1991, two years after the freelance gardener was diagnosed with HIV, his famous energy began to wane. "From August to December, I lost nineteen pounds," says Skipper. "When I went to the doctor, he said, 'It's obvious you're suffering from wasting syndrome.'"*

*Wasting syndrome, or anorexia-cachexia, afflicts 70 to 90 percent of AIDS patients, robbing them of their appetite. The resulting malnutrition can be more deadly than the virus itself. But there is only one drug that is commonly prescribed for the treatment of wasting syndrome: Marinol, the synthetic form of THC, the most psychoactive component of marijuana.*

*When Skipper tried a friend's Marinol, it passed through him without any effect. "But marijuana is wonderful," says Skipper. "It relaxes me, it takes away my pain. It makes me hungry and thirsty, so I eat and drink more, and that builds up my immune system."*

*After watching his lover suffer through AZT treatment, Skipper refused synthetic medication altogether. "I took it on myself to eat," he says - with the help of some homegrown sinsemilla. He liked to eat the buds fresh, or blend them into "peanut-butter balls" for breakfast, or cook them down into what he calls "cannabis tar." "You take a little bit of that on your finger and chase it with milk," he says.*

*The pot made Skipper hungry, and he started to gain back his weight. Blood tests taken last fall show that he has a high T-cell count (1210, which is 400 above normal), and also carries the antibodies to Hepatitis A, B, and C. "My immune system functions quite well," he declares. At 164 pounds, he feels fat.*

*But the US government isn't interested in Skipper's weight gain - only his criminality. In the spring of 1993, a local narcotics task force raided his home twice, seizing crops of about 40 plants each. He was charged with possession and cultivation, and went to trial in San Diego Superior Court last October. In a landmark decision, the jury accepted his medical-necessity defense. Skipper was free until January, when the judge threw him in jail for violating an earlier probation. There he was knifed and lost eight pounds before his release on March 3. His case is now on appeal.*

*After one look at this man, the San Diego jury understood something the US government cannot bring itself to admit: that it is more important to help AIDS patients eat than it is to punish them for smoking marijuana.*

*Today, millions of Americans suffer from medical conditions that can be alleviated by marijuana. Doctors have witnessed that smoking marijuana, among other things, promotes weight gain for AIDS patients and reduces vomiting for cancer patients undergoing chemotherapy.*

*But for cancer and AIDS patients, the US government has one answer: Marinol, or THC in a gel cap. Marinol has been approved by the FDA as a treatment for nausea and wasting syndrome, and the government claims it is superior to the "crude drug" marijuana. But the ban on marijuana isn't really driven by concerns over public health. Instead, it serves the interests of business and pharmacology.*

*Unlike marijuana, which can be grown cheaply by the masses, Marinol is produced by pharmaceutical companies that manufacture and distribute it for profit. And unlike hemp seeds, which reproduce in the presence of light, water and a green thumb, Marinol is hatched in a lab, the product of chemicals and machines.*

*The story begins in 1985, when Unimed, now located in Buffalo, IL, bought the patent for Marinol from the National Cancer Institute. In order to produce the artificial cannabinoid THC, Unimed purchases a raw material known as termpene olivitol from Hoffmann-LaRoche, and sends it to a laboratory in Southern California. There, the crude oil is treated by a process known as liquid chromatography. If you push enough termpene olivitol through a silica gel column, you get 99 percent THC.*

*Another lab takes that THC and mixes it with sesame oil, then seals it in gel caps, in doses of 2.5, 5 and 10 milligrams. These caps are shipped to Roxane Laboratories in Columbus, Ohio, where they are packaged and distributed to your local drug store. A month's prescription costs between $150 and $180.*

*The only problem is that the pill, which looks like a vitamin cap, isn't all that popular in the sick wards. There are three main objections. First, vomiting patients have trouble swallowing a pill. Then, if a patient does swallow the pill, the good effects don't kick in for hours. And when the pill finally starts to work - buckle up. "A 2.5 milligram Marinol pill absolutely knocked me out," reports one man with AIDS. "I wound up lying on the sofa for days, just totally drugged and unproductive."*

*Marinol has unpleasant side effects - as can be expected from a pill that is 99 percent THC. An April 1986 product insert from Roxane warned that Marinol elicits "disturbing psychiatric symptoms," and that even patients on low doses might experience "a full-blown picture of psychosis." The latter phrase has disappeared from recent product inserts, but experts say nothing has changed.*

*"It's way too psychoactive," says Robert Randall, the glaucoma patient who was the first American to obtain marijuana legally from the government. "When I took Marinol, I found it anxiety-provoking and intense, like I had wandered into a short story by Flannery O'Connor."*

*It's not unusual for AIDS patients who start smoking marijuana to gain 20 or 30 pounds. And many of them told Randall that Marinol didn't even make them hungry. Randall's informal poll is backed up by Dr. Robert Gorter of San Francisco, who has studied AIDS patients extensively. Writing in the journal of the Physicians Association for AIDS Care in 1992, Gorter stated, "Again and again patients have testified that they preferred marijuana above dronabinol [the scientific name for Marinol] for its appetite-stimulating effect."*

*Naturally, Roxane Labs has done studies that prove Marinol is effective as an appetite stimulant. "We went to a lot of trouble," says Dr. Kirk Shepard, Roxane's director of medical affairs. "It's very difficult to do clinical trials for patients who are very ill. But we did properly controlled, randomized studies over the past few years and have proved that, statistically, there was a benefit for the majority of patients."*

*Dr. Shepard is willing to admit that marijuana can be an effective treatment for cancer and glaucoma. "With chemotherapy, I would say yes, there are some studies that show that marijuana is effective," he says. But for*

*AIDS patients with a loss of appetite, he says, "there's just no data" to show that marijuana can be safe and effective.*

*Most doctors leave it to the patients to decide whether or not a drug works. But the DEA doesn't trust patients' judgment. In the government's 1992 decision to ban medical marijuana, a DEA administrator wrote, "Sick people are not objective, scientific observers, especially when it comes to their own health." The decision was backed by Robert Bonner, the head of the Public Health Service under George Bush, who declared, "There is not a shred of evidence that smoking marijuana assists a person with AIDS."*

*Some advocates of medical marijuana believe the best strategy for getting marijuana to AIDS patients is to conduct studies that will definitively prove its effectiveness. Randall scoffs at the need for such studies. Recalling the late Kenny and Barbra Jenks, the Florida AIDS patients who received legal government marijuana, he says, "What's to prove? Two people have AIDS. They smoke pot, they gain weight. End of story."*

*Advocates of clinical trials say the US government should supply the natural marijuana - and it's not as if Uncle Sam doesn't know how. Since 1969, a team of white coats has been cultivating the flowering tops of female cannabis plants in Oxford, MS. The notorious "pot farm," hidden on five acres of bottomland, is funded by the National Institute on Drug Abuse (NIDA) and run by the University of Mississippi. It continues to produce a limited quantity of low-grade marijuana each year.*

*After the plants are analyzed for THC content, they're shipped in barrels to the Research Triangle Institute in North Carolina, where the dried leaves are rolled at a cost of $2 per joint. The joints are stored and frozen, pending delivery.*

*Back in the 1970s, these machine-rolled cigarettes were considered the best way to give THC to cancer patients who needed it. But there was concern about whether it was advisable from a political point of view. On May 9, 1978, a group of doctors met at the National Cancer Institute to discuss whether the THC cigarette merited further study. At the time, there was a THC pill available for research, but no pill had passed the tests needed for FDA approval.*

*According to minutes of the NCI meeting, Dr. Monroe Wall of the Research Triangle Institute said that his THC cigarette "is now highly standardized and is a reliable and reproducible method of administering the drug."*

*Several doctors at the meeting noted that absorption of the THC pill was "erratic" and "unpredictable," They agreed that "all in all, the cigarette may be the best means of administering the drug."*

*Meanwhile, the news was spreading that marijuana could provide relief for cancer patients. In 1978, New Mexico passed the first state law recognizing the medical value of marijuana. Over the next few years, more than 30 states passed similar legislation. "By the summer of 1980," says Bob Randall, "there was building pressure on the federal government to provide marijuana through an experimental program." California requested one million joints.*

*The burgeoning demand for THC put the government in a pinch. But the bureaucrats rejected the obvious solution, which would be to increase production on the "pot farm." The idea that NIDA could grow enough marijuana to accommodate the needs of sick people is what the drug warriors call an "imponderable" - meaning simply that they refuse to think about it. And so the search began for a pharmaceutical substitute.*

*In the late 1970s, says Bob Randall, "Everyone had decided that nabilone was the great white drug" that would replace marijuana. Nabilone is manufactured by Eli Lilly under the trade name Cesamet; its active ingredient is hexahydro-cannabinol. By 1978, the drug was being tested on cancer patients, and Lilly officials were predicting FDA approval within a year. "They had it on double-tracking with humans and animals," Randall says, "until suddenly, dogs on nabilone started having convulsions and dropping dead."*

*Enter Marinol. Tested on rats and other animals in the 1970s, it was never meant for human consumption. But after Cesamet bombed, the bureaucrats decided to give it a chance. In October 1980, the NCI began distributing Marinol free of charge to 20,000 patients at 800 hospitals. One of the 2,600 doctors who participated in the program was Dr. Ivan Silverberg, an oncologist in San Francisco.*

*Silverberg, one of the first doctors to use chemotherapy on lymphoma patients, had been an early champion of medical marijuana. Nevertheless, he entered the NCI program, and began prescribing THC to his cancer patients. After a year, Randall says, "One of Ivan's patients walked into his office and threw the bottle at him, accusing him of trying to poison her." He subsequently dropped out of the program.*

*During the early '80s, studies were conducted in six states, offering smokeable marijuana to cancer patients who had not responded to traditional antivomiting medication. And while thousands of patients found marijuana consistently safer and more effective than synthetic THC, the government rejected the studies. They had already found a foster home for Marinol.*

*Back when Ronald Reagan was elected, Unimed was just a fledgling company in Somerville, NJ. Its executives didn't have the money to develop pharmaceuticals on their own, so they developed a strategy to purchase experimental drugs from university and government studies, then market the drugs for a profit.*

*In 1981, the government agreed to sell the Marinol patent to Unimed, and Unimed applied to the FDA for permission to market the pill as a treatment for nausea. In November 1984, the FDA rejected Unimed's application because clinical tests that had been done on the drug were deficient. But Unimed hustled up some more data, and by June 1985, the FDA delivered its approval. A year later, the DEA gave it a green light.*

*In 1987, two years after Unimed bought the Marinol patent from the NCI, the little company was flush with profits from the pill: $1.5 million in one year alone. In 1990, Unimed executives said they were anticipating a potential windfall of $80 million a year from the poor saps with cancer, and up to $1 billion a year from victims of the HIV virus. Marinol sales have never reached expectations. In fact, the company's annual revenues have never topped $3 million.*

*In 1992, soon after the FDA approved Marinol for wasting syndrome, Roxane's publicity department went into overdrive, printing out glossy pamphlets for AIDS patients. The pamphlets offer advice on weight gain ("Enjoy an ice cream sundae frequently!") and dining enjoyment ("Use a tablecloth and china; invite a friend to share your meal"). But the most bizarre tip involves marijuana: "Do not smoke marijuana while using Marinol. This can cause an overdose."*

*It's simply ludicrous to suggest that a patient who is taking gel caps of 99 percent THC is going to overdose by smoking a cigarette averaging 5 to 10 percent THC. The product insert for Marinol dated December 1992 makes no mention of interactions between Marinol and smoked marijuana.*

*Besides, you can't overdose to death on pot. According to pharmacologist Andrew Weil, researchers have tried to kill dogs with an overdose of marijuana, and the dogs simply won't die. You might die if you ate 40 aspirins or 10 raw potatoes, but not if you ate 10 pounds of pot.*

*Synthetic THC is another story: swallowing a handful of pills can leave a patient unconscious. The 1992 product insert offers this advice for treating a Marinol overdose: "A potentially serious oral ingestion, if recent, should be managed with gut decontamination. In unconscious patients with a secure airway, instill activated charcoal via a nasogastric tube. A saline cathartic or sorbitol may be added to the first dose of activated charcoal."*

*Does that sound risky? Let's move on to the potential for developing a habit. According to the December 1992 product insert, Marinol can be "habit-forming" - in other words, a patient who stops taking it abruptly may go through four days of withdrawal. Typical symptoms include irritability, insomnia, anorexia, hiccups and diarrhea. Sleep disturbances may last for weeks.*

Scott's article goes on to question the often-disseminated concern that medical cannabis is aking to fighting cancer with a drug that anti-legalization advocates claim is linked to cancer through inhaling. While studies have proven that marijuana is not only not connected to tumor growth or cancer, it has also been shown to reduce tumors and prevent new tumors from forming. Can the same be said of Marinol?

*You would think, with all the government-funded tests to see if marijuana can be linked to cancer, the same would be done for Marinol. But no one seems to care.*

*According to the 1992 product insert, "Carcinogenicity studies have not been performed with dronabinol."*

*Aside from lung cancer, smoking marijuana poses another potential risk for people with compromised immune systems. The government has long been telling pot-smokers that they risk "salmonella and fungal spore contamination." And a recent study conducted at Johns Hopkins School of Public Health found that smoking marijuana, crack, or other drugs is "significantly associated" with bacterial pneumonia among patients with HIV.*

*The government has not produced a single case of a pneumonia or lung cancer contracted from smoking marijuana.*

*Finally, it's worth reviewing the side effects of marijuana and Marinol. While there are numerous side effects from smoking marijuana (euphoria, laughter, anxiety, dry mouth, red eyes, sleepiness, clumsiness, the munchies), countless patients who have used marijuana in a medical setting have testified that they experienced no adverse side effects.*

*People who take Marinol, on the other hand, frequently complain about the "disturbing psychiatric symptoms" that are common side effects of the drug. According to a 1985 edition of The Medical Letter, the side effects of Marinol are "disorientation, depression, paranoia, hallucinations and manic psychosis."*

*The 1992 product insert for Marinol scatters these symptoms throughout the section marked ADVERSE REACTIONS but saves psychosis for a passing reference in the section called OVERDOSAGE: "Patients experiencing depressive, hallucinatory or psychotic reactions should be placed in a quiet area and offered reassurance."*

[Author's note: Robert Randal, quoted in this article passed away in 2001, after it appeared in print.]

**Marinol Sales Have Never Reached Expectations. In Fact, The Company's Annual Revenues Have Never Topped $3 Million.**

*The label from a bottle of Marinol reads:*
NDC 0054-2602-11
25 Capsules
5 mg
MARINOL ®
(DRONABINOL)
(Warning: May be habit
forming)
See Package Insert for
Complete Prescribing
Information
Keep Tightly Closed
Store in a Cool Place
DEA ORDER FORM REQUIRED

*The side effects of marijuana pale beside those of other drugs commonly prescribed by doctors in the US. The standard drugs used in chemotherapy can cause deafness, kidney failure, and cancer; those used to treat nausea can cause ulcers, secondary infections and psychosis; the eye drops and pills used to treat glaucoma can cause depression, heart failure, numbness and kidney stones; and the medications commonly given to paraplegics can cause kidney failure, hepatitis and seizures.*

*In 1987, after reviewing the evidence, DEA administrative law judge Francis Young declared, "Marijuana, in its natural form, is one of the safest therapeutically active substances known to man." But don't ask why the government is so afraid of medical marijuana. Even Bob Randall doesn't have an answer. "I think it's odd we've got a government that's willing to secretly give you plutonium," he says, "but it won't give you marijuana when you want it. That seems a little twisted to me."*

*Fortunately, the sick people who need marijuana are not alone in their struggle. In the last few years, cancer and AIDS doctors have begun to speak out, asserting a physician's right to prescribe any drug that might work. Last spring, the Lymphoma Foundation and the Physicians Association for AIDS Care joined a lawsuit on behalf of medical marijuana. The 1,000 members of PAAC, which is based in Chicago, treat nearly 250,000 people with HIV, so they have firsthand experience with marijuana as a treatment for wasting syndrome.*

*"First," says PAAC's executive director Gordon Nary, "physicians should try the drugs that have been FDA-approved." Of course, not all drugs work for all patients. Before suggesting marijuana, he says, doctors should "alert patients who have a compromised immune system to the risks" of fungal infection. But when you're treating someone whose life is at stake, Nary sighs, "It's simply a matter of appropriate medicine and human decency to allow compassionate use of any drug, experimental or on somebody's blackballed list."*

*Portland NORML notes: Roxane Laboratories, Inc. set up a Web site for Marinol in 1998 at http://www.marinol.com/.*

The really painful part of this information is that it is not new, not by a longshot. The government has known about many of these studies since the early 1980s, and some of them are even older. Throughout the raging debate about decriminalization, the War on Drugs, the teen rehabilitation centers, and the for-profit prisons, the government has known that marijuana not only helps sick patients endure their treatment protocols, it has actually been shown to be effective in fighting some of the actual diseases. It's not just something to enjoy while you suffer from chemo, for example, it can actually work with the chemo to be even more effective.

So why aren't these studies more widely discussed? Why aren't more research dollars being poured into marijuana as a cure?

Because the pharmaceutical industry can't charge thousands of dollars a month for a drug that is so readily available and so inexpensive. There is a very real fear that a cultivatable drug that can be grown and sold locally would cause a serious dent in their bottom lines, so the best way to protect their financial interests is to squash any hint—let alone actual evidence—that marijuana is a viable treatment option.

Fortunately, the internet age has made access to these studies possible. Find them, read them, and make your own informed decisions for your health and your vote.

# Chapter 10:
# It's All about the Taxes

One of the more common myths about marijuana legalization involves taxation. Spend some time doing a street corner poll about marijuana reform and you'll undoubtedly hear, "The government will never legalize it, man, because they can't tax it." Let's back up and explain the thinking behind that myth.

A few things come into play in the tax issue, and some of them involve our history. This view actually refers to the grow-your-own mindset, and it's a misguided look at Prohibition. They're referring to the issues we faced as a nation when yes, taxation became a major factor in the capture of notorious crime boss and bootlegger (among other things) Al Capone. But that wasn't the worst of it.

Those who believe marijuana can't be taxed are operating under the perception that it grows from the ground and therefore the government cannot regulate it and tax it. Unfortunately, yes it grows from the ground, but the government has made a billion-dollar industry out of regulating it and punishing the offenders instead of reaping the benefits to our economy and our national security by altering those regulations and taxing cannabis.

Of course, the faulty logic involved applies to other situations. Corn grows from the ground and the government certainly taxes that...ask any mid-western farmer. In fact, the government not only taxes the farmer's final sale of the corn where it leaves his hands (for which he pay income tax), it taxes every step leading up to the production of the corn, like the purchase, repair, and annual licensing in some places of the farmer's tractor, the seed he bought to grow it in the first place, the utilities he pays in order to irrigate his fields, the pesticide he uses to protect his crop...the list goes on. Again, ask any farmer how the government taxes him, and you'll get quite an education on the topic.

Then there are the taxes to be made at the end of the line, too. The government taxes the consumer who purchased the corn, but before they reach that point they've taxed the corporation who took it from the farmer and put it in cans or frozen food packaging. They taxed the company who shipped the corn in trucks to retail stores. They taxed the retailers for owning a company, using electricity, and having employees, *then* they taxed the consumer for purchasing it.

But this isn't a diatribe on what's wrong with government taxation; it's a scratching of the surface of how much money the government is losing out on because a comparative handful of people with an agenda don't want sick people to have access to cannabis.

Unfortunately, the "they can't tax it" argument isn't true, but it's widespread enough that people are getting this misinformation somewhere. In fact, the government has already proved how adept it is at taxing cannabis, although "inept" might be a better word.

### It's Not Legal, But We'll Tax You Anyway

In one of the most interesting legal twists in recent history, the federal government is taxing a product that is still illegal to grow, buy, sell, or own. Recent state-by-state decriminalization efforts have made little change to the federal mandate about marijuana, yet the US and state governments are reaping the benefits. You can still be charged with a crime under certain circumstances, but you're going to pay for the privilege of breaking the law.

Those who remember the 1969 Leary v. US lawsuit, heard by the Supreme Court, may remember that Leary's case was that a 1937 tax still imposed on the fully illegal marijuana was a violation of a person's Fifth Amendment right to not incriminate himself. Basically, paying taxes on marijuana was akin to announcing, "I just bought marijuana." The Supreme Court heard the arguments and agreed with Leary, thereby striking down the Marihuana Tax Act.

It was a tricky lawsuit, but it was actually based solidly on common sense. You can't charge people taxes for something that you still spend billions of dollars to punish people for. Either stand up and admit that marijuana is a viable crop and a valuable source of tax revenue that deserves to be treated with the same legal protocols we provide to all medications, or stop taxing it while slapping the handcuffs on citizens. It simply doesn't work both ways.

On February 5, 2013, Rep. Jared Polis (CO) introduced Ending Federal Marijuana Prohibition Act of 2013 (H.R. 499; 113th Congress), a bill that "Amends such Act to: (1) provide that schedules I, II, III, IV, and V shall consist of the drugs and other substances that are set forth in the respective schedules in part 1308 of title 21 of the Code of Federal Regulations; (2) exempt marijuana from such Act except as provided in this Act; (3) revise the definition of 'felony drug offense' to exclude conduct relating to marijuana; and (4) eliminate marijuana from provisions setting forth penalties applicable to prohibited conduct under such Act." Congress has yet to get to work on this.

## Colorado Citizens Found Out It DOES Work Both Ways

When Colorado voters first made the landmark decision to decriminalize medical marijuana, it paved the way for even more states to look at the example the state sets and use their experiment as a proving ground for further widespread decriminalization. But the current tax rates on marijuana in Colorado have some advocates not just scratching their heads, but actually crying foul.

Colorado has imposed not only a sales tax on marijuana, but a 15% excise tax as well. It does help explain the "millions" of dollars that the state has collected in taxes in just the first six months of recreational decriminalization. One Colorado attorney, Rob Correy, who was one of the powerhouses behind Colorado's current legal standing for cannabis when he helped draft Amendment 64, is leading the way in demanding tax reform that will keep marijuana affordable for its citizens.

According to an article by Michael Roberts for the Denver Westword Blogs, Correy has a number of issues with the current tax structure.

"The primary cause of action is based on the Timothy Leary case before the U.S. Supreme Court," he says, referring to 1969's Leary v. U.S. "That case struck down the Marihuana Tax Act of 1937 after Leary successfully argued to the court that payment of a marijuana tax was a violation of the Fifth Amendment right to avoid self-incrimination.

"The second claim is based on the public-policy argument that state and local governments cannot collect taxes expressly on activity that is federally illegal," he continues. "So the taxes are illegal.

"Our third claim," he goes on, "has to do with Amendment 64 itself. The purpose of Amendment 64 was to tax marijuana like alcohol -- and there's also a component in Amendment 64 that prohibits any regulation that is 'unreasonably impracticable.' And this is that. The taxes are so high that it makes it impracticable to run a reasonable business.

"Amendment 64 set out to end prohibition, the black-market trade in Colorado, and transform it from an unregulated, underground market into a regulated, legitimate, tax-paying market. But if you set taxes too high, you empower an underground market. So high taxation is 'prohibition lite.' And even as the state government has made it a criminal offense not to pay marijuana taxes, the federal government has made it a crime to pay the taxes. That puts individuals between a rock and a hard place."

**How Does This Affect Medical Use Patients?**

According to the Marijuana Policy Project, Washington, DC, the taxes that affect medical use patients who rely on cannabis strictly as a treatment for life-threatening and excruciatingly painful medical conditions are unjust as denying them medication in the first place. In fact, with current tax structures in place and the fact that most health insurance still won't cover medical marijuana, the taxes on cannabis amount to prohibition.

"Many patients believe medical marijuana should not be subject to sales tax because paying taxes on medicine can pose a hardship, particularly because medical marijuana is also not covered by insurance. While sales taxes generally include exceptions for prescription medications, most states' sales taxes apply to marijuana because it cannot be prescribed due to federal law. Instead, it is recommended or patients receive 'certifications.' In addition to medical marijuana sales generating tax revenue, in most or all states with regulated dispensaries, the application and registration fees levied on medical marijuana businesses cover the costs of regulating them. Nonrefundable fees for dispensary applications generally range from $1,000 to $5,000, with registration or annual fees typically between $5,000 and $20,000. While medical marijuana dispensary fees should not be so low that they encourage frivolous applications, it is important that they are not prohibitively high since costs may be passed on to patients, and medical marijuana businesses are generally unable to get bank loans due to concerns about federal law."

The chart below indicates some of the costs associated with running a dispensary in a state that even allows for medical sales of cannabis. The right-hand column lists only some of the fees associated with sales tax, not including excise taxes or the so-called vice tax that some states are considering.

| State | Application and/or Registration Fee | Taxes |
|---|---|---|
| Arizona | $5,000 application fee, $1,000 for renewal | 5.6% sales tax |
| California | Varies, all licensing is local | 7.5% state sales tax, also local taxes |
| Colorado | Applications: $7,500 to $18,000 for medical marijuana centers, $1,200 for infused product manufacturers and cultivators; Registrations: $3,750 to $14,000 for centers, $2,750 for infused product manufacturers and cultivators | 2.9% state sales tax, also local taxes |
| Connecticut | Fees proposed by the regulatory agency: $1,000 dispensary facility application fee; $5,000/year fee for dispensary facility; $25,000 application fee for producers; $75,000/year fee for producers | 6.35% state sales tax applies |
| Delaware | Will be determined by department rule | Gross receipts tax if above $1.2 million in revenue |
| Illinois | Fees will be determined by the department by rule, must cover costs | 7% excise tax at wholesale level and 1% sales tax |
| Maine | $15,000 application fee, $14,000 refunded to applicants that aren't chosen | 5% sales tax and 7% meals and rooms tax on edible products |
| Massachusetts | The health department proposed a $50,000 annual fee for dispensaries and $31,500 in fees for a two-stage application process | Likely not taxed |
| Nevada | Will be determined by department rule; maximum fees for initial registrations range from $3,000 for a cultivation facility to $30,000 for a dispensary; maximum renewal fees range from $1,000 to $3,000 | 6.85% to 8.1% state and local sales tax likely applies |

| State | Application and/or Registration Fee | Taxes |
|---|---|---|
| New Hampshire | Fees will be set by the health department; they must cover costs | New Hampshire does not have a sales tax |
| New Jersey | $20,000 dispensary fee each year, $2,000 for unsuccessful applicants | 7% sales tax |
| New Mexico | $1,000 application fee for producers, annual producer fee from $5,000-$30,000 | Gross receipts tax (5.125% to 8.8675% depending on location in state) |
| Oregon | Fees will be determined by Health Authority rule | Oregon does not have a sales tax |
| Rhode Island | $250 application fee, $5,000 registration fee | Compassion center surcharge of 4%; 7% state sales tax |
| Vermont | $2,500 application fee, $20,000 or $30,000 annual fee | Likely not taxed |
| Washington, D.C. | $5,000 application fee for dispensaries and cultivators, $3,000/year renewal fee; $10,000/year fee for dispensaries; $5,000/year fee for cultivators | 6% sales tax, revenue unknown |

If patients were taking any other drug for their medical conditions, they wouldn't even have to worry about paying a sales tax. According to the Federation of Tax Administrators' January 2014 document, only one state in the entire country charges a sales tax on prescription medications, and that's Illinois, which charges a 1% sales tax on prescribed drugs. No other state collects sales tax on prescription medications, while fourteen states and DC don't even tax over-the-counter medications; in addition, Illinois still charges that 1% tax on OTC medications, but doesn't tax either prescription or OTC at the usual 6.25% sales tax that is charged in that state on general items.

That means that 49 states and the District of Columbia do not tax prescriptions at all, one state reduces the sales tax on prescribed and OTC drugs to one-sixth the tax, and only fourteen states collect the usual sales tax percentage on ibuprofen, for example.

And yet, medically necessary cannabis that is recommended as a course of treatment by a licensed physician is not only taxed at the standard tax rate, some states are even considering something along the lines of a luxury tax.

**STATE SALES TAX RATES AND FOOD & DRUG EXEMPTIONS** (As of January 1, 2014)

| **STATE** | **Tax Rate (percentage)** | **Food (1)** | **Rx Drug** | **Non-Rx Drug** |
|---|---|---|---|---|
| ALABAMA | 4 | | * | |
| ALASKA | none 5.6 | | | |
| ARIZONA | | * | * | |
| ARKANSAS | 6.5 | 1.5% (4) | * | |
| CALIFORNIA(3) | 7.5 | * | * | |
| COLORADO | 2.9 | * | * | |
| CONNECTICUT | 6.35 | * | * | |
| DELAWARE | none | | | |
| FLORIDA | 6 | * | * | * |
| GEORGIA | 4 | * (4) | * | |
| HAWAII | 4 | | * | |
| IDAHO | 6 | | * | |
| ILLINOIS | 6.25 | 1% | 1% | 1% |
| INDIANA | 7 | * | * | |
| IOWA | 6 | * | * | |
| KANSAS | 6.15 | | * | |
| KENTUCKY | 6 | * | * | |
| LOUISIANA | 4 | * (4) | * | |
| MAINE | 5.5 | * | * | |
| MARYLAND | 6 | * | * | * |
| MASSACHUSETTS | 6.25 | * | * | |
| MICHIGAN | 6 | * | * | |
| MINNESOTA | 6.875 | * | * | * |
| MISSISSIPPI | 7 | | * | |
| MISSOURI | 4.225 | 1.225% | * | |
| MONTANA | none | | * | |
| NEBRASKA | 5.5 | * | * | |
| NEVADA(5) | 6.85 (5) | * | * | |
| NEW HAMPSHIRE | none 7 | | | |
| NEW JERSEY | | * | * | * |
| NEW MEXICO | 5.125 | * | * | |

| | | | | |
|---|---|---|---|---|
| NEW YORK | 4 | * | * | * |
| NORTH CAROLINA | 4.75 | * (4) | * | |
| NORTH DAKOTA | 5 | * | * | |
| OHIO | 5.75 | * | * | |
| OKLAHOMA | 4.5 | | * | |
| OREGON | none 6 | | | |
| PENNSYLVANIA | | * | * | * |
| RHODE ISLAND | 7 | * | * | |
| SOUTH CAROLINA | 6 | * | * | |
| SOUTH DAKOTA | 4 | | * | |
| TENNESSEE | 7 | 5.0% | * | |
| TEXAS | 6.25 | * | * | * |
| UTAH | 5.95 (4) | 1.75% (4) | * | |
| VERMONT | 6 | * | * | * |
| VIRGINIA | 5.3 (2) | 2.5% (2) | * | * |
| WASHINGTON | 6.5 | * | * | |
| WESTVIRGINIA | 6 | * | * | |
| WISCONSIN | 5 | * | * | |
| WYOMING | 4 | * | * | |
| DIST. OF COLUMBIA | 5.75 | * | * | * |

** -- indicates exempt from tax, blank indicates subject to general sales tax rate.*
*Source: Compiled by FTA from various sources.*
**Some state tax food, but allow a rebate or income tax credit to compensate poor households. They are: HI, ID, KS, OK, and SD.*
***Includes statewide 1.0% tax levied by local governments in Virginia.*
****Tax rate may be adjusted annually according to a formula based on balances in the unappropriated general fund and the school foundation fund.*
*****Food sales subject to local taxes. Includes a statewide 1.25% tax levied by local governments in Utah.*
******Nevada sales tax rate scheduled to decrease to 6.5% on July 1, 2015.*

FEDERATION OF TAX ADMINISTRATORS -- JANUARY 2014

Where does this leave patients? Those who are fortunate enough to live in an area that is progressively allowing medical marijuana sales are still taxing cannabis at a nearly prohibitive rate. Doctors aren't legally prescribing cannabis due to the current federal legislation banning its sale and possession. Therefore, health insurance companies—in spite of the overwhelming research into the medical benefits of cannabis and the oversight of its use by a licensed physician, as well as the fact that it's less expensive than most pharmaceuticals designed to treat illnesses that marijuana addresses—aren't covering the drug under most benefits plans.

That's why it's not enough to decriminalize marijuana at the state level. Certainly states have been correct in allowing their citizens to have a say in the legalization of cannabis; after all, the everyday citizens have been made aware of its benefits and been educated on the lies that have been spread to slander marijuana, so it's only right that average individuals have a say in how their state governments address the criminal issue. But it's not enough to say that each state should be allowed to mandate this type of medical need.

Until the federal government does its part and legalizes medical cannabis, patients will continue to be at the mercy of the health insurance industry, Big Pharma, and the punitive overtaxation of this "cash cow." Black market marijuana dealers and the related criminality will continue to foster in areas where the tax rate on marijuana makes it prohibitively expensive, especially for those patients who use it in conjunction with expensive pharmaceutical protocols. It's not enough to say that marijuana is beneficial or to take steps to make it semi-available...it must be accessible, which it cannot be if it's taxed at a "luxury" price.

But there's even more hope on the horizon. According to a press release from LEAP, a recent measure will allow banks to alleviate some of the financial strain on legitimate businesses that are licensed to sell cannabis to individuals with the proper medical authorization:

## HOUSE VOTES TO ALLOW BANKS TO WORK WITH MARIJUANA BUSINESSES

### Bill Amendment Would Remove Treasury Funding for Penalties of State-Legal Businesses

WASHINGTON DC—Today the US House of Representatives voted 231-192 to pass a bipartisan bill amendment introduced by Representatives Denny Heck (D-WA), Ed Perlmutter (D-CO), Barbara Lee (D-CA) and Dana Rohrabacher (R-CA) that would prevent the Treasury Department from using federal funds to penalize banks and other financial institutions providing services to state-legal marijuana businesses.

Banking has been a major sticking point for marijuana businesses trying to operate legally, since though the Treasury Department issued banks guidelines on how to properly report transactions with marijuana businesses in February, many financial institutions feared they might be charged with money laundering if they worked with businesses dealing with a substance still illegal under federal law. As a result, many marijuana businesses were forced to conduct transactions in cash, creating huge logistical and public safety issues.

"Though this isn't as flashy a win as some other drug policy reforms of recent years, banking regulations have been one of the most significant obstacles to creating a well-run legal marketplace," said Law Enforcement Against Prohibition's executive director Major Neill Franklin (Ret.). "This is a huge victory for those who care about the smart regulation and control of marijuana."

For supporters, the vote was an echo of a similar bill amendment that passed the House in May eliminating funding for DEA raids on state-licensed medical marijuana businesses and patients. That amendment passed 219-189 in another bipartisan vote.

"What we're seeing is not just that one of the most gridlocked Congresses in history is able to pass marijuana reforms, we're seeing that both Democrats and Republicans think of these reforms as smart, politically viable options to a failed drug war," added Franklin.

# Chapter 11:
# The Secret Weapon That Can Get Marijuana Legalized Nationwide

It often feels as though medical marijuana access is something we all know should happen, but yet, never does. When cities or states worked towards better access to lifesaving cannabis for sick and impoverished patients, the best they come up with is "decriminalization," which means it's still a crime but the punishment has been altered to be slightly less punitive.

Why is that? Why do voters not take the necessary steps when the evidence is right in front of them? For many, it's lack of access to quality, trustworthy information. For others, it's simply not being informed about the issue, again due to a lack of access to reliable statistics and information.

That's where The Silver Tour comes in. Robert Platshorn, a longtime advocate for medical marijuana, has made it his mission to ensure that senior citizens—arguably the demographic with the highest ratio of pharmaceutical expense to income, and the highest demographic of registered and active voters—have access to accurate information about medical marijuana, including its benefit-to-harm ratio and genuine information on what cannabis will treat and what it will not.

"Marijuana is much safer, more effective and less costly than many alternatives currently in use. The Drug Enforcement Administration's own top administrative law judge, Francis L. Young, dismissed the drug warriors' untrue propaganda when he ruled in 1988 that, 'Marijuana, in its natural form, is one of the safest therapeutically active substances known to man.'"

That's why the members and supporters of the Silver Tour have made it their goal to "educate and inform seniors on the benefits and exciting discoveries in the medical cannabis field. To encourage activism for legalization and create demand for safe access. Seniors vote and they talk to their representatives."

"In 2010, when Prop 19 was defeated in California, I was curious as to why," explained Robert Platshorn in an interview with High Times, speaking about reaching different demographics of voters, along with the need for better education and awareness about the medical applications of marijuana. "And I went and looked at the exit polls. Seniors made up 70 to 90% in every precinct in California. So I started the Silver Tour to teach them about marijuana, that it's good for more than just glaucoma and to get over the nausea of chemo. It wasn't that you had to sell seniors, you had to open the closet door and let them the hell out. Because they want marijuana, it happens to be true."

That's why it's important to reach out to that demographic first. Senior citizens stand to receive the greatest benefit from cannabis, possibly more than any other age group of consumers. The medical benefits for diseases that are often rampant among the elderly have made them marijuana's top recipients, yet so many senior citizens are cutoff from access to this affordable, safe, and proven drug.

According to Pollster.com, the very people who actively turn out to vote are in the highest age brackets, and these are the people who have the power to actually make real change in our country.

“It's all about who votes. Those that do win. Those that don't lose. The chronic losers in American politics are the young who famously turn out at low rates election after election.

“No age group 18-29 managed to reach 45% turnout in 2000, and only two made it in 2004. Not one single age group over 30 fell so low in either year. Despite a little noise for each group, the pattern is a strong rise in participation rates with every year of age at least until the late 60s, after which there is some decline. Yet even among those 85 and over the turnout rate remains above 55%, more than 10 points higher than among their 20-something grandchildren and great-grandchildren.

“So what are the implications? If you gave me a choice of being wildly popular with the young or moderately popular with the old, I'd take the old any day. They are far more reliable in voting, and while their population numbers are small they more than make up for it in over-representation thanks to turnout differences.”

Surprisingly, last year was the first year that a Gallup poll indicated that the majority of Americans are in favor of legalizing marijuana use, whether it’s medicinal or not. So if 58% of Americans believe that the current criminal implications for cannabis is wrong, why is it still illegal? Why are they not persuading their representatives to do something about it?

First, it’s due to the reasons outlined in this text, reasons like corporate greed, big pharma, and lobbyists that line politicians’ pockets. But that still shouldn’t be enough to keep the people’s voices from being heard and listened to.

It’s because they’re not speaking out. It’s not enough to believe in something or even to share a viewpoint with one's friends. You must vote to enact real change, or all is lost.

That's why the Silver Tour is focusing on encouraging senior citizens to put aside their prejudices and shut down the lies that agenda-driven individuals spread. The mission of the tour is to help spread awareness and understanding so that the people who actually do vote can finally have their voices heard in a way that supports their fellow citizens.

## **"United States: The Secret Weapon That Can Get Marijuana Legalized Nationwide"**

By Steve Elliott - Toke of the Town/Special to The Silver Tour

*What if I told you there is a secret weapon that, if understood and utilized by the cannabis reform community, could fairly quickly and very decisively decide the issue of marijuana legalization once and for all?*

*Everybody knows that cannabis legalization is very, very near the tipping point in the United States. Even the folks at Gallup, not exactly known for wild-eyed political statements, said this month after examining their latest poll results -- which showed that a record-high 50 percent of Americans support legalization – that, "If this current trend on legalizing marijuana continues, pressure may build to*

*bring the nation's laws into compliance with the people's wishes."*

*Drilling down into the results of that same Gallup poll reveals our potential secret weapon for marijuana legalization.*

*Support for legalizing cannabis is directly and inversely proportional to age, ranging from 62 percent approval among those 18 to 29, down to only 31 percent among those 65 and older.*

*Now, let's think about that for a moment. One of the age groups which would most directly and immediately benefit from marijuana legalization would be our senior citizens. Acquainting seniors with this fact, and energizing them politically to support legalization, could hasten the arrival of legal cannabis by years.*

*Right now, seniors in two-thirds of the U.S. -- 34 states -- don't have the option of using medicinal cannabis, even with a doctor's recommendation. National legalization would clear that roadblock out of their path quickly and effectively, so that senior citizens across the land could experience the palliative and curative properties of marijuana.*

*Now, if only we had a pitchman -- preferably, someone in the senior demographic -- who could bring that message to the over-65 crowd!*

*That's exactly where Robert Platshorn and the Silver Tour come in.*

*Platshorn is one of the few remaining old-school "pitchmen" in America -- in fact, I'd be comfortable saying he's likely the best pitchman in the country today. That's what he did for a living, in fact, for years. "Bobby Tuna" can sell an idea like nobody else, and we in the medical cannabis movement are lucky enough to have him on our side.*

*There is no more motivated spokesman than Platshorn; the guy served a brutal 29 years in federal prison on marijuana smuggling charges after having been convicted for bringing in tons of Colombian Gold in the 1970s. That makes him the longest-serving pot prisoner in U.S. history, so far.*

*And, with The Silver Tour, Platshorn already has the template in place to change senior's minds and open them up to the wonderful possibilities of cannabis legalization.*

*What's the Silver Tour? It is, quite simply, the way we can win over our Secret Weapon -- America's senior citizens -- to the cause of marijuana legalization.*

*"Last week's show in West Palm Beach confirmed the success we saw in Fort Lauderdale three weeks ago," Platshorn told Toke of the Town on Saturday. "At least 90 percent of the audience (all strangers to medical marijuana) leave the show with the intention of contacting their representatives to demand 'safe legal access' NOW. We provided letters, addresses and phone numbers to use in support of our state bill and Barney Frank's bill.*

*Robert Platshorn has the demonstrated ability and the desire to "sell" marijuana legalization to millions of seniors who might have never considered medicinal cannabis.*

*"I can organize and get people who would not normally expose themselves as activists, to take action," Platshorn told me. "I know how to do this and get results in a very short time.*

*"I have people pleading with me to bring The Silver Tour to almost every state," Platshorn said.*

*But, as we all know, taking that show on the road requires considerable cash -- and that's how you can help get this thing done.*

*Until now, Platshorn has provided almost all the seed money for The Silver Tour from book sales of his gripping autobiography, Black Tuna Diaries.*

*Federal medical marijuana patient and fellow Floridian Irvin Rosenfeld, author of My Medicine, has helped out by selling one of his tins in which the feds send him 300 ready-rolled joints every month.*

*"I was naive enough to believe that once I could show the type of results that no one else could match, the money would come flying in," Platshorn told me. "Wrong."*

*At this point in our movement's history, it would be a tragic and incalculable loss to let The Silver Tour die on the vine -- when the senior vote could put us over the top.*

But what exactly is The Silver Tour all about, and how does it operate? By providing accurate information, free food and informative get-togethers, along with a chance to meet patients, nurses, and doctors who have years of experience with medical cannabis, the tour educates older American voters through the Tuna's formula for turning seniors into advocates:

## We Can Legalize Cannabis Now

by Robert Platshorn, advocate, educator, and founder of The Silver Tour

*"For the past year, most of my income from Black Tuna Diaries, Square Grouper DVDs, and related memorabilia has gone to build and support The Silver Tour to teach senior voters the facts about medical marijuana. I realized two years ago that not a single national cannabis legalization organization was reaching out to educate the voting public. A few do valuable lobbying, others provide news and information to those folks who are already supporters, and when invited, organizations like NORML present our case in public debate. All of these functions are important, but leave a tremendous void in ending marijuana prohibition.*

*"After spending thirty years in federal prison for smuggling pot, the last thing I wanted to do was become an activist and risk the ire of the federal government at this late stage of my life. Sure, I wanted to see the law changed so that others wouldn't lose their freedom. But as I traveled the country speaking, doing book signings, and appearing at theater premiers of Square Grouper, what pushed me to take action was the plight of cannabis patients whose lives and quality of life depended on the availability of marijuana. I met people with MS, Parkinson's, cancer, epilepsy, Crone's Disease, chronic pain, and a host of common ailments that could be alleviated safely with a simple herb. Clearly, these people are patients, not criminals.*

*"Why me? Here comes the ego part. I have a unique skill and talent. The Village Voice website, Toke of the Town, called me 'The Secret Weapon that can get*

*marijuana legalized nationally.' For twenty years I was one of America's most successful pitchmen. According to the late Billy Mays, "Bobby Platshorn is a legendary pitchman and one of the all-time greats." In another words, I not only know what has to be done to reach main stream voters, I can actually do the job. If you saw the CNN coverage or the live stream of our last Silver Tour show, you know that people enter as skeptics and leave demanding "safe legal access" to the "kind herb." If you haven't seen this yourself, it is available at www.thesilvertour.org.*

*"Ask yourself, if the legalization movement had a spokesperson like Ron Popiel or Billy Mays, could this war on marijuana be over by now? Believe me, legalizing cannabis is a lot easier to sell than Ginzu Knives or Vita Mix blenders. Been there, done both.*

*"Although The Silver Tour is aimed at seniors (they vote), the story we tell appeals to a much wider audience. If you Google my name or The Silver Tour, you will see that we've gotten more positive national press attention in the last six months than all the national organizations put together. Our billboards drew dozens of national stories, including CBS, NBC, Newsweek's Daily Beast, and The Huffington Post. I've managed this much on less than a total of $20,000 in contributions. No national organization or major donor like George Soros or Peter Lewis has put in a penny. We've gotten this far on individual contributions and help from small businesses like Aqua Lab Tech in California and the producers of Square Grouper.*

*"Now it's time to finish the job. We are editing the Silver Tour show into a half hour format for TV. I'm an old hand at infomercials. I know how to buy half hour slots on local and national TV for a small fraction of*

*what an agency would pay for the same time slots. What will it cost? We can saturate Florida TV markets and make medical marijuana a reality for about twenty-five thousand dollars. Nationally? Under a million dollars will pay for a saturation national education television campaign that will create an unstoppable demand for the repeal of marijuana prohibition.*

*"That's what I can do. The proof of our success is already out there. Now it's up to you and the people you know who would like to see the end of the war on cannabis."*

*One of the chief mainstream media projects of The Silver Tour was a highly successful crowdfunding campaign through Kickstarter to produce a short film called Should Grandma Smoke Pot? Despite its kitschy title, the film is a highly informative look at the mission of The Silver Tour as it seeks to educate senior citizens on the benefits of medical marijuana while stripping away a lot of the myths, misconceptions, and outright fears associated with cannabis.*

*The campaign, which raised more than double its original goal for the production costs of the film, went on to share the message of cannabis' benefits through the final production.*

*"The Silver Tour will air this show hundreds of times on national and regional TV in thirty minute infomercial slots on major stations and networks. One network has cleared the show for airing and they love the concept. Two more networks have asked to see the finished show. It will be aired repeatedly in states that have legalization or medical marijuana bills on the ballot this year and states that need to begin educating voters with a view to future legislation," explain the show's creators in an update to their campaign.*

Throughout the film, renowned members of the medical community—not nameless men in white coats, but actual Harvard medical school personnel and doctors who've served both in patient care and research—stand up and proudly attach their names to their statements that cannabis is beneficial and harmless. Actual patients, including one man who was grandfathered in under previous government programs and therefore is allotted monthly shipments of cannabis by the US government, speak to audiences of concerned senior citizens, most of whom are not currently cannabis users but who do suffer from chronic medical conditions.

That is the demographic The Silver Tour is working to educate.

One of the show's creators explains repeatedly throughout the film that he is not encouraging or endorsing the concept of breaking the law. That is why the law must be changed. Marijuana is an incredibly valuable medical tool that stands to save lives and change the course of countless patients' diseases, but it can only happen if the law is changed. And as evidence has shown, the only voter block with the power to enact genuine, widespread change is the senior vote. That's why it's imperative that accurate information and sound medical opinion reach this important group of active voters and civic-minded citizens.

For more information on the film or to view it, watch *Should Grandma Smoke Pot?* on YouTube.

## The Silver Tour and SSDP Go to Washington

*By Bill Morrison*

*The chartered buses came from New Jersey, Pennsylvania and Maryland. "Grandma Lobbies for Medical Marijuana," advocates advancing on our nation's capitol and the halls of Congress to confront their representatives face to face. At issue is HB 499, a measure to bring federal cannabis laws in line with changes at the state level.*

*William Chegelis, chairman of the US Marijuana Party, spoke of being harassed, even in Colorado where cannabis is legal. He faced eviction because the apartment where he lives is partially funded by HUD and federal regulations don't recognize Colorado law. "It's crazy," Bill said. "People think we've got it good in Colorado, but we are still under the thumb of the feds." Colorado, with the most liberal marijuana laws on the books, still suffers under harsh federal penalties. Even though states are taking action, it isn't hitting the root of the problem—conflict with national policy. Until a national policy catches up with states', we will continue to risk our health, happiness, prosperity and erosion of our rights.*

*Later that day, Bill would be arrested, even though he's a registered medical marijuana patient and even though D.C. has approved medical cannabis.*

*On the bus, the conversation turned to dosage forms and current trends in MMJ therapy. Michael and Jeff, with Medical Cannabis Advocates of Maryland, had an animated discussion about vaporizer pen technology. This dosage form is emerging as a popular choice for patients because it's so convenient and discreet. Everyone had an opinion on what features were most important as well as which type of extract worked best.*

*Near the back of the bus, Connie Guy, an ex-mayor in Pennsylvania, talked a bit about politics. She said she came to make a point to her legislator – that marijuana as an issue wasn't going to go away and that the citizens in her state were watching. Her daughter Debra is the director of the Lancaster chapter of NORML, but couldn't make the trip. For every advocate who could free up a Monday to attend the all-day event, there were dozens, or even hundreds, who couldn't make it. The excited-to-be-here folks on the bus would speak for the unavoidably absent, the real majority who want this wasteful, ineffective and outdated policy updated.*

*As Vanessa Maria, also from Pennsylvania, told us: "We need to be relentless and determined. Real change takes time and you have to keep at it." She knows what she's talking about, having participated in several successful legislative efforts. "I tell them I'm going to keep calling, every week. I'm not going to go away."*

*Vanessa and Connie are hopeful, but realistic about getting marijuana legalized in Pennsylvania. There isn't enough support to get an issue on the ballot, and ballot measures are rarely used to good effect in the state. Instead, they hope to move a bill for legalization in the State House. Currently, their state-level bill is in the judiciary committee, awaiting action.*

*The conversations on the bus ride have been energetic – the stories compelling. But soon enough we arrive in D.C. The buses drop everyone off in front of the Capitol Building. Police regulations require it, and it's about a half-mile walk to the Longworth Building where everyone is gathering. The walk sorts us into groups, with those least mobile struggling to keep up until the frontrunners notice and wait. No one is faking here; the medical conditions are real and compelling. And that's one of the most powerful tools in our arsenal – the real stories of citizens who are suffering, and for whom cannabis offers relief.*

*This event was spearheaded by Robert Platshorn (of Black Tuna Diaries fame), who ran a funding campaign online. There were also representatives from the Students for Sensible Drug Policy, LEAP, and a dozen NORML affiliates. Reporters from The American Cultivator rode the bus from Baltimore and had a chance to hear the hopes and concerns of those attending. We wanted to know who these people were, where they'd come from and what they hoped to accomplish.*

### *Grandma Lobbies for Medical Marijuana*

*"Seniors are the doorway to legalization and Grandma is the key to that door," says Bob Platshorn, the engine behind this lobby day at the Capitol. He traveled a bumpy road between the idea and making it happen. The event was funded by online donations through GoFundMe, and Bob had been drumming up support for months. The effort topped its $10,000 goal shortly before the cut-off, but funds were just one hurdle. Arranging for buses, reserving space in the congressional cafeteria and scheduling speakers for an afternoon buffet are some of the highlights, but when he first decided to take the Silver Tour to DC, Bob didn't even know if he would be able to attend.*

*"I can't even leave South Florida to go to Tallahassee [the capital] without special permission," he said. Bob is under the thumb of the parole office and*

*his movements are tightly controlled – a legacy of his time spent incarcerated for marijuana offences.*

*Still, Bob's idea was powerful enough to grab the attention and support of advocates across the country. Some could only support it monetarily, but others wanted a chance to be part of this historic lobbying effort.*

*In partnership with Students for Sensible Drug Policy (SSDP), the total group numbered about 150. We met up at noon in the congressional cafeteria for an introduction and briefing before going up to meet with their Congressperson. Those who hadn't been able to get an appointment would still visit offices and make their presence known.*

## ***Meet and Greet***

*Our numbers brought energy and excitement. The effect was multiplied when we got to the cafeteria and saw how big the turnout was. With everyone wearing a lanyard and badge, it was easy to spot our fellow MMJ lobbyists. A hundred different conversations we going on, introductions and reconnections. Advocates were keen to share their stories and hear what others were up to or meet people face-to-face they only knew over the Internet.*

*The group took over almost a quarter of the cafeteria. No small feat in the gymnasium-sized room. The banners went up and informational literature was stacked for the taking. Unfortunately, this much publicity didn't sit well with the Capitol Police. It wasn't long before several officers showed up to pow-wow with group leaders. Apparently, signage is not allowed in the congressional office buildings and literature isn't allowed for distribution.*

*One officer, seeing The American Cultivator's latest issue stacked up, gave us a choice, "Take the papers outside or we'll confiscate them." The papers were surrendered in some faint hope and with the half-humorous request that the officer read one before throwing the stack in the trash. Other advocates were similarly affected and all the banners had to be put away.*

*The remarkable thing was, in spite of some small discussion about civil rights, no one really got upset. This wasn't the aggressive rabble-rousing you might expect from a bunch of protesting pot heads. Instead, it made you proud to see savvy advocates dealing with "the man" in a sober manner – never losing sight of the bigger picture and what we were here for. This attitude remained, even when the officers then informed us that filming wasn't allowed either. The Capitol area of D.C. is highly regulated. There's even a permit required to use a tripod outside.*

*After the dust settled, one further bit of law-enforcement-induced excitement was still to come. A half hour after the first round, an officer stepped forward and blew a loud whistle – the kind you imagine an English Bobby might use. The whistle killed conversations across the cafeteria and the officer addressed the whole room.*

*"If anyone received candy from this man, it may have contained marijuana. Please turn it in to an officer." The man they were referring to was "Wandering Bill" – who we'd met on the bus.*

*The story emerged that Bill had let his caring nature override caution. He'd offered a medicated edible to someone in a wheelchair, not in our party. His good nature led him to a compassionate act which backfired and he was arrested for a misdemeanor because of it. Not good, because it took attention away from our main objective – to present our case to House Members.*

### *Making an Impact*

*By two o'clock, advocates were dispersing to meet with their Congress members in person. Although we didn't attend any of the private meetings, we did see several chance encounters and "elevator pitches."*

*It's a thing of beauty to watch an informed, well-spoken advocate at work in the halls of power. More than once, I got to see Bob Platshorn, Irv Rosenfeld, and others in action. In one case, while on a smoke break, a representative from a Pennsylvania chapter of SSDP, just making conversation, found out the young man he was talking to was an intern for a Pennsylvania Congressman.*

*"I'm from Pennsylvania too," he said. "We're here to talk to Representatives about medical marijuana." They talk for a few minutes and part ways. Two young men, no more than a couple years apart in age, both wearing the suit and tie default uniform here. It's good to see, and this is just the kind of interaction Bob Platshorn knew would happen.*

*A week after the event, Platshorn comments, "It makes a huge difference. More than a hundred of us, all wearing the same lanyard and badges. They knew we were there."*

*He's talking about the difference between a rally or festival and taking the message to the People's House effectively. Platshorn knows it does little good to preach to the choir. What's needed is an outreach to those with the power to change the legal landscape.*

*The United States Capitol is intimidating, the authority on display overwhelming. The symbols of a rich and powerful nation are all around – the statues and slogans, the marble buildings and manicured lawnscapes. Outside the Rayburn building, there are two statues. They guard the grand staircase entry. On the left, the "Spirit of Justice." On the right, "The Majesty of Law." They seem ironic to those familiar with laws abused to push an anti-cannabis agenda.*

*Three of us have gotten lost in the Rayburn building. We were on our way to the buffet in room 369. But on the third floor, where we end up, all the room numbers are in the two thousand range. So we wander about a bit.*

*The corridors seem endless. Deserted at 4 o'clock on a Monday. They stretch into the distance – polished marble floors, huge, sculpted wooden doors and on each side of every door, a pair of flags. One is always the stars and stripes, the other changes and we see they are state flags. We've stumbled upon the real deal, the offices where the government elites live. But it seems no one is on duty. Perhaps the country is left to fend for itself on weekday afternoons?*

*Through one open door, we spot a huge white bear fur on the wall facing us. It's at least ten feet long, reaching from the floor to the high ceiling. The flag outside tells us it's an Alaskan Representatives office. We reach the end of one corridor, turn, and the same scene is repeated – a city block's worth of doors and flags and well-waxed marble. The excess is overwhelming, having never seen anything this elaborately ornate in person. Picking a door at random, a very nice secretary working for the state of North Carolina offers directions. She's the only living person we see on the entire floor.*

### *The Buffet*

*Everyone arrives in time and we grab sandwiches at the buffet. The speeches start with Aaron Houston, the executive director of SSDP. He's followed by Neill Franklin, Executive Director of LEAP, who would appear on a CNN talk show, Piers Morgan Live, a couple of days later.*

*The heavy hitters continue and Grover Norquist speaks about drug legalization. Norquist is a lobbyist famous for his "no new taxes" pledge and Tea Party affiliation. Then, the main speaker, Congressman Jared Polis (D-CO) talks about the collision between the new laws in his state and the existing federal laws. It seems particularly poignant, since Wander Bill, also from Colorado, was arrested earlier – a real world example of the problem.*

*We get a chance to interview a few attendees afterward, and I talk to Delbert and Karen Mullins from Florida. They share their story about Delbert's arrest in December of 2011.*

*He's wearing a neck brace, but the couple is excited to be here. Karen tells me about Delbert's fight to use cannabis after Medicare stopped paying for Marinol. She says the cops made her take him to jail in her car after the arrest – "They didn't want him vomiting in the squad car." She smiles when she says, "He medicated on the way to jail, with the cops following us."*

*By six, we are all drifting back to the bus pick-up area. Wandering Bill is still with the cops, so we head back to Baltimore one passenger light. The lessons learned are plain and powerful. Showing up matters. Being a respectful but relentless thorn in their side is the only way to get the attention needed, and, as Bob Platshorn said, the only way to effect change is to get off the computer and reach those who can do something about the problem. They need to be told, and told over and over, that they work for us, that we demand justice, and if they won't do their job, we'll find someone who will.*

**Robert Platshorn and Federal patient Irv Rosenfeld at House of Representatives**

**Robert teaches Congressmen about cannabis**

**RP with Carl Rove and Rep. Jared Polis in DC**

ARTHRITIS AND MARIJUANA

IT'S RAINING $2 BILLS

DOUG BENSON CANA-COMIC

The American Cultiv

GRANDMA RECLAIMS THE PEOPLE'S HOUSE

The Silver Tour and SSDP Go to Washington DC

WARNING FROM MICHIGAN

**The Silver Tour Goes to Washington and Seniors Speak to Law Makers**

Me and LEAP's Neill Franklin

They came by bus to change the law

Chris Goldstein leading NJ Silver Tour Bus to Congress

**Willie and the Tuna**

**The Movie Square Grouper featuring "Bobby Tuna"**

**With my good friend and bestselling author Greg Campbell**

Me on Jon Stewart's Daily Show

Petitioning for medical marijuana in FL

With Gary Johnson in San Francisco

**On stage at Hempfest in Seattle paying homage to the late great Jack Herer where I first got the idea for The Silver Tour**

**Fundraising for The Silver Tour Radio Campaign**

**Featured in the 35th Anniversary Edition of High Times Magazine**

**On the Cover of *Releaf Magazine***

**On the cover of *Young at Heart***

**High Times writes about me and I write for *High Times***

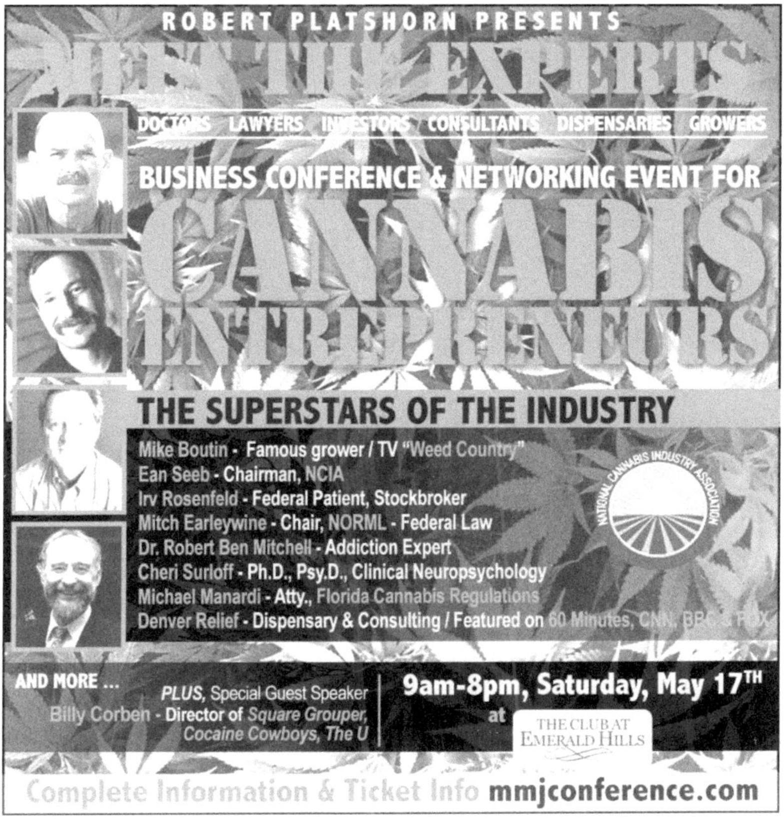


**My Meet the Expert Cannabis Business Conference**

# Chapter 12:
# The Times They Are A Changin'

Despite the constant barrage of negativity and power lobbed at efforts to keep marijuana illegal, there's hope springing up around the country. New measures and referendums are being introduced in a focused way, and lawmakers—especially at the local level—are beginning to see reason.

According to the work of the GeorgiaCare Project:

"The easiest way to become a marijuana activist is to start by spreading the message on the internet. There are thousands upon thousands of internet and social media users that can be reached with a bit tasteful "guerrilla warfare" online and I'm going to show you a few things you can do to help spread the message of cannabis law reform in the State of Georgia without even getting out of your chair.

- **Facebook:** Facebook is a fantastic platform for sharing the good news about cannabis. Simply sharing posts and photos from our Facebook page is a great way to get your feet wet and, more importantly, determine what sort of barriers from friends and family you are going to encounter during your activism.
- **Twitter:** Giving you the opportunity to change the world in just 160 characters, Twitter is a fantastic way to connect with others who are

interested in your subject. Use the right hashtags and watch the retweets roll in.

- **Forums:** Local internet forums are a *fantastic* way to get your message out to the masses, and can often be done anonymously. I have provided an example below of a message you can quickly post in your local internet forums, just modify it to fit the medium (and your tastes). Some examples of websites that run popular local forums include Topix, Patch and your local Craigslist. There are many many more, and running the search "forum +your town" will probably help you find even more.
- **Blog Comments:** Many people think of blogs as a one-way communication device, but it's actually a lot better than that. A well-worded (respectful) comment on a blog post can garner a website thousands of new visitors. If you are going to leave blog comments try to link to the GA CARE Project, both in the text of the post and, if allowed, in the "website" box that is usually just below your name in the form.
- **Write/Call Your Lawmakers:** Believe it or not lawmakers tend to listen when a large enough portion of their constituency rises up to make a point. Send your lawmakers a short, well-worded and respectful letter or email telling them how you feel about cannabis laws in the State of Georgia. If you need help finding your Senators or Representative please use our Congressperson Locator Tool. To find contact information for local lawmakers, such as State Representatives, State Senators or the Governor please use the Open:States lookup tool.
- **Letters to the Editor:** Most smaller towns and communities have local newspapers with very

open Letter to the Editor policies. If you are able, try writing a short letter to your local newspaper explaining why you think it's time to reform marijuana laws in the State of Georgia."

**Philly Mayor Agrees to Compromise, Will Sign Decriminalization Bill**

September 9th, 2014 by Morgan Fox as reported by Cannabis Activist Network

Yesterday, Mayor Michael Nutter announced that he had agreed to sign a bill to decriminalize marijuana possession in Philadelphia, with one small tweak. The bill was first introduced by Councilman Jim Kenney. In June, the City Council voted 13-3 to replace the current penalties of a $200 fine and an arrest record for possessing up to an ounce of marijuana, with a civil fine of $25. Mayor Nutter's compromise deal would still make smoking in public punishable by a $100 fine.

**A 2013 report by the ACLU** found that, although marijuana use is nearly identical across all races, African Americans in **Pennsylvania** are 5.2 times more likely to be arrested for marijuana possession than their white neighbors. Councilman Kenney estimates this measure could save the Philadelphia Police Department up to $4 million annually. **Some reports** estimate that the City of Brotherly Love would become the largest American city to adopt this sensible measure.

**NFL May Finally Change Its Outdated Drug Policy**

September 9th, 2014 by Alizeh Siddiqui

It appears as though the NFL is finally progressing towards changing its controversial drug policy.

According to a **NBC Sports story**, the NFLPA plans to vote tonight on proposed changes to the NFL's existing drug policy. The changes, if ratified, may include an increased threshold for which players are allowed to test positive for marijuana. However, the NFLPA first needs to get a proposal from the league itself. According to the *NBC Sports* posting, that has not happened yet.

*"The players are prepared to vote on a proposal from NFL tonight but they will need something to review well in advance of that vote," NFLPA spokesman George Atallah told PFT by phone. "As of right now, there's nothing yet. Players have been informed of the status of the league's proposal on an ongoing basis. [On Monday], [NFLPA president] Eric Winston and [NFLPA executive committee member] Brian Waters reiterated the importance of a fair due process for hGH testing, a line in the sand with respect to player discipline before a fair due process on DUIs, and also other issues that were important to them."*

The "other issues" include the manner in which players are processed through the substance abuse policy, amid much criticism and media attention regarding the use of marijuana and the Cleveland Browns wide receiver, Josh Gordon's, suspension.

*According to Nate Jackson, a* ***New York Times*** *op-ed contributor and former tight end that medicated with marijuana for most of his career, "Gordon has marijuana in his system. He broke the rules. I understand that. But this is a rule that absurdly equates marijuana with opiates, opioids, and PCP. The NFL's threshold for disciplinary action for marijuana is 10 times higher than the one used by the International Olympic Committee."*

The NFL rethinking their approach to marijuana is long overdue. Their current policy reflects outdated stances onmarijuana and pain management, penalizes players who seek an alternative to painkillers, keeps them in a perpetual state of injury and injury management, and risks creating new addicts.

*In the end, as stated by MPP's Morgan Fox, "**The NFL's harsh marijuana penalties do nothing to promote the health and safety of the players**." **[MPP emphasis added]***

It is important to note that this push for decriminalization is not relegated or reserved for a handful of people with pie-in-the-sky ideals about what constitutes good medical practice or natural, holistic healing. Law enforcement officers, politicians, and yes, even the UN's global report on drugs and crime have all said the same thing: genuine efforts at legalization are vital to moving forward.

According to the Global Commission on Drug Policy's September 2014 report, "Taking Control: Pathways to Drug Policies That Work," the need for better approaches to how we address drugs are required:

**Foreword From The Chair**

"The international drug control regime is broken. In our 2011 report we called on global leaders to join an open conversation on drug policy reform. We recommended that they immediately discuss alternatives to the failed war on drugs. In subsequent reports we drew their attention to the urgent need for reform to reduce the devastating epidemics of HIV and Hepatitis C. We asked policy makers to break the fifty year taboo on talking about more effective and humane ways to manage drugs.

"Today, three years later, we are pleased to see that a genuine debate on new approaches to drug policy is underway in an array of national and regional forums. Crucially, the discussion is based on evidence, and new, exciting innovations are spreading across the Americas, Africa, Europe, South and South East Asia, and Australia and the South Pacific. The discussion is truly global, and governments and civil societies are learning from one another, and testing out new approaches on the ground.

"The reality in 2014 is that governments and civil societies are not just talking, many are taking action. Drug policy reform is moving from the realm of theory to practice. Courageous leaders from across the spectrum are seeing the many political, social and economic dividends from drug policy reform. They recognize the critical mass of voices demanding a new course. And recognizing that change is inevitable, they are beginning to experiment with a range of solutions drawing from solid data and with an open mind. Informed approaches are trumping ideological ones and the results are encouraging.

"In this report, we set out a broad roadmap for getting drugs under control. We recognize that past approaches premised on a punitive law enforcement paradigm have failed, emphatically so. They have resulted in more violence, larger prison populations, and the erosion of governance around the world. The health harms associated with drug use have got worse, not better. The Global Commission on Drug Policy instead advocates for an approach to drug policy that puts public health, community safety, human rights, and development at the center.

"We need to be bold but pragmatic. There is no one-size-fits-all pathway to enacting drug policy reform.

We recognize that the shift will demand changes in domestic and international policy and practice. It will entail trial and error and an honest and critical engagement with results. But we are encouraged by the signposts that are emerging that can help governments and citizens take the right steps forward. They have momentum on their side, and can gather insights from the many positive developments around the world that have occurred since 2011.

"What is now needed is action by the world's multilateral institutions, first of all the United Nations (UN). We are delighted to see the quality of high level debate being generated from heads of state and senior UN figures. It is also encouraging to see important regional organizations contributing to positive reform. Reports supporting change from the Organization of American States, the West Africa Commission on Drugs, and the Global Commission on HIV and the Law, are all critical building blocks of drug policies that work. They are also openly challenging the international drug control regime and creating political space for new players to explore similar approaches.

"We are driven by a sense of urgency. There is a widespread acknowledgment that the current system is not working, but also recognition that change is both necessary and achievable. We are convinced that the 2016 United Nations General Assembly Special Session on drugs (UNGASS) is an historic opportunity to discuss the shortcomings of the drug control regime, identify workable alternatives and align the debate with ongoing debates on the post-2015 development agenda and human rights. The Global Commission encourages all UN member states and agencies to continue rethinking the question of drug policy reform. We encourage leaders to seriously engage with new challenges, not least new synthetic drugs appearing on the market almost daily, which demand more creative responses.

"A stale political declaration in 2016 that promises to 'solve the drugs problem' and make the world 'drug-free' is not going to be the answer the world needs. We reiterate that the international community needs to come to terms with the reality that easy answers to solve the drug problem do not exist.

"Our report does not offer the definitive solution. Rather, it provides a roadmap for pragmatic policy change we think will make the drug- related problems the world faces today much more manageable. We ask that countries take advantage of the 2016 UNGASS as an opportunity to finally start getting drugs under control."

--Fernando Henrique Cardoso, Former President of Brazil (1994-2002)

**LEAP: Law Enforcement Against Prohibition**

Despite the lucrative nature of making repeated arrests, seizing citizens' property, and taking government grant money to continue the relentless pursuit of cannabis patients, there are agencies even within the law enforcement industry that are working for the good of the public.

LEAP, which stands for Law Enforcement Against Prohibition, is an organization whose summary focus is to combat the harsh penalties and rampant prosecution of people who are simply trying to get well and manage their pain. At the risk of oversimplifying the issue, LEAP's work is to try to free up law enforcement personnel to actively do their sworn job, namely protecting and serving the public. There is nothing to protect the public from where a medical marijuana user concerned, yet police officers and sheriff's department officers are constantly held to investigating and arresting citizens instead of protecting the public from actual harm.

This is where agencies like LEAP are trying to create reform.

According to the organization's "After Prohibition" report, we have nothing to fear from decriminalization efforts, despite the hard-line approach to keeping a tight lid on the plant from corporate enemies.

"Law Enforcement Against Prohibition envisions a world in which drug policies work for the benefit of society and keep our communities safer. A system of legalization and regulation will decrease violence, better protect human rights, safeguard our children, reduce crime and disease, treat people suffering from drug abuse as patients rather than criminals, use tax dollars more efficiently, and restore the public's respect and trust in law enforcement." –LEAP mission statement

As Chief Norm Stamper (ret.) stated, "Think of this war's real causalities: tens of thousands of otherwise innocent Americans incarcerated, many for 20 years, some for life; families ripped apart; drug traffickers and blameless bystanders shot dead on city streets; narcotics officers assassinated here and abroad, with prosecutors, judges, and elected officials in Latin America gunned down for their courageous stands against the cartels; and all those dollars spent on federal, state, and local cops, courts, prosecutors, prison, probation, parole, and pee-in-the-bottle programs."

LEAP has made its position very clear: it is not the job of law enforcement to stop a human being from putting a substance into his body, especially one with lifesaving benefits like cannabis. If the end result of drug use becomes a crime such as violent or abusive activity, or a socially unacceptable behavior like driving a vehicle while impaired, then that certainly becomes an issue for law enforcement. But for the police to be charged with deciding that the behavior one individual is engaged in where others are not affected, that is a violation of privacy and a waste of taxpayer funding. It is a waste of time and manpower, especially when police forces are already suffering from more criminals than they can possibly handle.

It's interesting to note that the position LEAP takes in its mission statement and report is one of cautious acceptance. Nowhere does the statement say that marijuana is harmless or not addictive or even in any way beneficial. It is not a statement of support for marijuana. Instead, it is a plea to common sense and reasoning to say to America, look at the effects of Prohibition in the 1930s. It didn't work then, and it's not working now. Individuals' behavior cannot be taken down by force, and it's a tremendous waste to continue to fight an individual's activity.

In the case of cannabis, however, we're charging law enforcement with not only regulating individuals' behaviors when they do not have an impact on the public good, but we're also taking the time and money involved and using it to destroy the lives of desperately ill people. And LEAP has made its point very clear on where the real crime is in that situation.

## Taking Cannabis to Veterans in Need

New data has indicated that US military veterans commit suicide at a rate that has now reached 22 deaths per day. That's one suicide every 65 minutes. Early investigations into the suicide rate have pointed to health issues and a lack of access to medical care as part of the underlying issue, a fact that some veterans' groups and advocates are working 'round the clock to change.

A chilling section of the website MedicalCannabis.com outlines the horrors that veterans and active duty military have faced when trying to find real-world, viable solutions for severe pain, traumatic brain injury, post-traumatic stress, and more. These horrors have included demotions in rank and pay for failing random drug tests, being denied prescription to opiate-based pain medication due to prior failed drug tests for marijuana, and more.

One advocate, Al Byrnes, a combat counselor and co-founder of the organization Veterans for Medical Cannabis Access, described in detail his interaction with a former Marine sergeant who served two tours in Iraq. During his second tour as a rifleman, he was hit by an IED. He suffered a debilitating injury to his back, traumatic brain injury, and has now been diagnosed with PTS due to his combat service and injuries.

The soldier, whom Byrnes simply refers to as "Daniel," was helped by medical marijuana until it was discovered in a random drug screening. Due to his admission that he had used cannabis to treat his pain while still undergoing physical therapy, he was then denied any further pharmaceuticals containing an opiate-derivative. Now, he has no access to cannabis or to pain medicine, and is somehow expected to continue.

According to Byrnes, *"I have a letter in my possession written by the Undersecretary for Health, Department of Veterans Affairs, dated July 06, 2010, addressed to my co-founder of VMCA, in part it reads...*

*"'This is a follow-up response to your letter requesting clarification of the Veterans Health Administration's (VHA) policy regarding the practice of prescribing opioid therapy for pain management for*

*Veterans who provide documentation of the use of medical marijuana in accordance with state law.' (State law is an important factor now in treatment for all Veterans regardless of duty period or medical problem. I call it treatment by geography. A completely new medical concept, never tried before in human history, being experimented with on the wounded.)*

*"He continues, 'If a Veteran obtains and uses medical marijuana in a manner consistent with state law, testing positive for marijuana would not preclude the Veteran from receiving opioids for pain management in a Department of Veterans Affairs (VA) facility.'*

*"Dan did not while in the Marines and does not obtain cannabis legally now in KY. If KY were to allow cannabis used clinically, Dan would be okay.*

*"Who or what do you want to blame for this travesty? The CO for being a bureaucrat instead of a doctor. Kentucky politicians for being feckless cowards. The ER physician for sending a man in pain out on the street. His case worker at the VA for being a lemming instead of a real advocate. The entire Congress of the United States for sending the youth off to war and then abandoning them because they smoked a joint? They all could be stand up humans, but are not. Dan stood up, and they could treat him as a role model; instead, they don't treat him at all."*

According to the advocacy organization's website, "Veterans for Medical Cannabis Access is committed to protecting the rights of veteran patients and health care professionals by advocating for safe and legal access to cannabis (marijuana) for all appropriate therapeutic uses and to encourage research on cannabis as a treatment alternative."

Their goals include providing educational and patient advocacy resources on medical cannabis as it relates to veteran-specific issues, working with the Veterans Health Administration on cannabis policy in order to ensure that medical staff are well informed of the latest medical cannabis research findings, encouraging the federal government to reschedule cannabis under an appropriate drug control schedule, and most important, ensuring that state medical marijuana laws recognize medical conditions common to veterans, to include things such as chronic pain and PTSd.

Another advocacy organization has stepped in to fill a need, namely access to pain management and affordable relief in the form of free marijuana. Calling itself Operation Grow4Vets, this organization's intent is to provide free marijuana to veterans in need so that economic situations and personal finances are no barrier to much-needed relief for those who've served our country in the military:

"The mission of Operation Grow4Vets is to help reduce the staggering number of Veterans who die each day from suicide and prescription drug overdose. We provide Veterans with the knowledge and resources necessary to obtain or grow their own marijuana for treatment of their medical conditions."

Part of the dilemma involved is that doctors cannot yet legally prescribe cannabis to their patients. They can recommend it, they can support the use of it, they can even fill out required documentation in states that allow patients to possess a small amount. But as for writing an actual prescription that can be filled in a pharmacy and covered under health insurance or VA benefits, that's not how it works.

Even worse, the anti-legalization crowd has added a new misconception to its agenda-based propaganda, that marijuana causes mental disorders, especially paranoia. And the last thing a soldier with PTSD needs is a paranoia-inducing drug, right?

Wrong. There is no evidence at this time that there's any truth to that correlation, yet many states have already blocked medical marijuana as indicated for PTSD.

"An ever increasing number of medical studies have shown that marijuana is a safe and effective treatment for pain, Post-traumatic Stress Disorder (PTSD), and Traumatic Brain Injury (TBI). Despite this fact, some people maintain the belief that marijuana is nothing more than a dangerous drug. However, numerous recent polls indicate that well over 80% of all Americans support the use of medical marijuana. Other polls indicate that more than 50% of Americans now support full legalization and almost the same number support banning tobacco products.

"Regardless of their personal position on the use marijuana for medical purposes, there is virtually universal agreement that our Veterans deserve to have any and all treatment options available to them. Medical marijuana has allowed thousands of Veterans to either reduce, or completely discontinue the use of dangerous prescription medications."

And even though no link has been found and the medical community has dozens of studies to back up the support for medical marijuana to treat a wide variety of disorders, cannabis is still off limits to many patients who stand to benefit greatly from its relief due to "a widely publicized review study published in 2007 concluded that trying cannabis just once could increase the risk of schizophrenia and related psychotic disorders by 40%.

"On the other hand, these suggestions have never been confirmed by studies designed to evaluate a direct causal relationship. Instead, studies have only look back in time after schizophrenia was diagnosed to find that a disproportionate number of patients happened to be current or past marijuana users. As a result, the claim that marijuana use causes schizophrenia remains controversial and support among experts has gradually decreased as evidence of the contrary grows stronger." (Source: TruthOnPot.com, "Does Marijuana Cause Schizophrenia?" April 6, 2013)

And that's where Operation Grow4Vets comes in. While vets in many places cannot buy cannabis to treat their PTSD, it's perfectly allowable for an individual to give another legally of age individual a small amount of marijuana. The organization is working to provide adequate access to those who don't live in areas that have decriminalized recreational-use marijuana—like Colorado and Washington, where a veteran can purchase marijuana without a doctor's approval for his condition—and therefore aren't even eligible for the relief.

"While the current trend is moving in a positive direction," continues Operation Grow4Vets, "most physicians are still reluctant to prescribe medical marijuana for their patients. Recent directives issued by the Veteran's Administration have provided physicians with minimal latitude in allowing their Veteran patients to use medical marijuana in conjunction with the treatment being provided by the VA. However, VA physicians are still not allowed to prescribe medical marijuana to Veterans. This prohibition is directly tied to the unwillingness of the U.S. Government to accept reality. It is our position that this attitude reflects a callous disregard for the physical, mental, and emotional wellbeing of the brave men and women who have made incredible sacrifices to protect the freedom we love."

Sadly, the organization's efforts are being undermined in the media by a group that calls itself the Colorado Smart Approaches to Marijuana Coalition, or SAM, but that organization is anything but smart or working towards smart approaches to cannabis. On its home page, the site lists a photo and quote from none other than Kevin Sabet, the author and speaker who travels the country spreading unfounded statements that he refers to as the "seven myths of marijuana" to anti-legalization advocates and voters.

From the SAM homepage:

"To recap, the science is emerging on the effects of marijuana, but we can say with some certainty that marijuana use is significantly linked with:

- Addiction[31]
- Heart and lung complications (the jury is out on a connection to lung cancer, though) [32][33]
- Mental illness [34]
- Car crashes[35]
- IQ loss and poor school outcomes[36]
- Poor quality of life outcomes[37]
- Poor job performance[38]"

The first item in the list has been disproven since the earliest days of sworn testimony before lawmakers, and the car crashes specifically mentioned have also been disproven by the DOT. Yet SAM continues to spread debunked lies to concerned citizens and policy makers, while the studies cited on the SAM page are from agencies with a known and exposed interest in keeping marijuana illegal due to the money to be made from other sources for doing so.

# Epilogue

So you've seen the evidence. You've seen the history of criminal ties to marijuana. You've read the tales of abuse and horror in for-profit teen rehabs and prisons. You've seen the links to the evidence that says cannabis not only relieves the pain and suffering that so many patients feel during accepted medical treatments, you've seen the articles that say cannabis has actually been shown to treat illnesses and shrink tumors, not just treat the side effects.

Even worse, you've seen the evidence that clearly shows the horrible racial divide in this country where marijuana criminalization is concerned. The elected officials that you and I allowed to lead this country have taken bribe money to incarcerate children. They have arrested and convicted African-Americans at triple the rate of whites for the same exact crime. They have spent $13 billion a year of your money to prosecute non-violent offenders whose crime is indulging in a plant that has been a known and widely used medical treatment for thousands of years.

All of this has happened while you and I footed the bill. Your tax dollars have enabled the persecution of your fellow citizens while we went about our lives unaware of the true scope of the problem.

But now that you know, what are you going to do?

Where do you start? Now that you know that this all started with a conspiracy to prevent hemp from taking hold in the US, now that you know about a viable medication that was ripped from the medicine cabinets so a handful of people could line their pockets, what are you going to do?

If you're like most people, this isn't your problem. Given the statistics of both medical and recreational marijuana use, the majority of the citizens in this country don't even use it. So why should you even get involved?

Because it's the right thing to do. In the US, we've allowed a handful of people with an agenda—one that involves personal gain and greed—to block access to a lifesaving medication, and even worse, we're stripping our fellow citizens of their freedom. Our friends and neighbors are in danger of malicious prosecution and literally death, all while we get to rightfully claim it's not our problem because marijuana isn't our issue.

But it is our issue. These are our neighbors and coworkers and yes, even our family members who are suffering from medical ailments. They are forgoing a lifesaving medication because they're afraid of losing their jobs when they fail a drug test, jobs that they have to keep because they provide the health insurance that makes treatment even possible. At the same time, some of these same people are rotting in slave labor prisons while our children and grandchildren line up to cover the costs down the road.

So again...what do we do now? How do we make our voices heard, how do we speak up for those who clearly aren't being listened to? How do we help ensure that access to safe, healthy strains of cannabis are available to those in need without the fear of the arbitrary three-strikes laws?

You've already taken the very first step towards equality and care for your fellow people: you've bothered to read the truth about marijuana and cannabis and the insider issues that have led to criminalization. From here, it's just a matter of taking a few matters into your own hands.

First, it's absolutely vital that you help spread the word, that you spread the truth about these myths that so many anti-marijuana agenda pushers have fed the public. You've now seen documentation of the anti-weed agenda and you know it has nothing to do with keeping Americans safe, healthy, or clear-headed, and has everything to do with money.

Next, you can get involved in activism projects. It's understandable that everyday citizens may be reluctant to speak up on this issue. After all, whenever the mainstream media portrays the pro-cannabis crowd—whether it's for medical use or recreational use—they invariably trot out some emaciated, dreadlocked young man wearing a faded T-shirt emblazoned with a pot leaf. Who would want to be aligned with promoting the same agenda as that person? Right. That's exactly why they feature the stereotypes that we all fear.

They don't want to roll out footage of your church pastor quietly buying doctor-approved medication to take home to his cancer-stricken wife. Who could possibly have a problem with a well-loved "man of God" providing medically-approved relief for his dear wife? Or your elderly neighbor; who could take issue with an upstanding member of society, perhaps even a decorated war veteran, using medically indicated cannabis for a painful condition? Or a child whose doctors have tried every pharmaceutical chemical-cocktail they could think of to stop her seizures, but have found that marijuana oil is the only thing that works?

Of course you would vote for legalization if you saw frame after frame of competent, "normal" people who rely on cannabis for their health. But the people in charge of the issue just can't have that, so they spread images that have been fueled by nasty stereotypes since this war on drugs began.

### Stoners No More: Campaign Works to Change How Marijuana Users Are Portrayed in the Media

A new advertising campaign in Colorado is aimed at targeting the longtime stereotypes surrounding marijuana users, refuting many of the paid-for advertisements that have portrayed them as annoying losers. The era of a giggling stoner with a limited grasp of English and a lack of motivation are being replaced with sensible messages intended to help new users, especially those in younger demographics and those who are new to relying on medical marijuana now that they finally have semi-decriminalized access, make wise decisions about marijuana consumption.

Some of these ads, paid for with a $75,000 campaign sponsored in part by the Council for Responsible Cannabis Regulation, are working to expose the "fear mongering" associated with some of the earliest anti-drug abuse ads, many of which date back to the 1980s. This campaign includes taglines that read, "Decades of fear-mongering and condescending anti-marijuana ads have not taught us anything about the substance or made anyone safer." The ads end by reminding users to consume responsibly.

Other ads are already targeting the expected influx of people who plan to vacation in Colorado for obvious recreational reasons, and still others who are willing to travel to a state that has enacted these measures because their own states have yet to provide medical marijuana access to patients in need. While this might be an exciting time for the state tourism council and the chambers of commerce scattered around the state, law enforcement and health care officials are less than thrilled about the new arrivals who've traveled to Colorado for what they think will be unfettered access to recreational marijuana.

According to an article by Kristen Wyatt of the Associated Press, "The [Council for Responsible Cannabis Regulation] organized the 'First Time 5' campaign, which cautions that new users shouldn't eat more than 5 milligrams of marijuana's psychoactive ingredient, or half a suggested serving.

"The campaign warns users that edible pot can be much more potent than the marijuana they're smoking — and that the pot-infused treats on store shelves are much stronger than homemade brownies they may recall eating."

By sharing sensible messages and featuring everyday portrayals of average citizens in their ads, these advocacy groups hope to help individuals not only consume marijuana safely, but also change the image of the typical marijuana user.

Campaigns like this one are needed due to the barrage of obstacles that the anti-legalization agenda puts in place for patients in need. Those powers that be choose to roll out headlines about Mexican drug cartels, and further the trumped up lies about the rates of kids smoking marijuana. They sweep under the rug the news about doctored crime lab evidence that has already sent thousands of wrongly convicted, innocent people to jail. They even make unfounded claims that marijuana funds terrorist organizations within our country.

What they don't realize is that legalizing marijuana and putting government controls in place would strip away all of those threats, eliminating the power they think marijuana has for evil. Drug cartels and terrorist organizations frankly can't be funded by a drug that is readily and legally available from authorized, licensed dispensaries. It would be like trying to fund your crime ring based on street sales of aspirin. And surveys have already shown that teen marijuana use is dropping, and sociologists have already likened that trend to the fact that young people view marijuana as a medication...again, like aspirin?

This is where you come in. Put pressure on your representatives at the state and federal levels. Tell them that you sent them to the capital to represent you and to speak for the good of your state and your country. Remind them that you're sick of the wasted money and wasted lives that current legislation mandates. When the opportunity arises for medical marijuana legislation to come before lawmakers, be sure that your voice is heard and that you speak up for the people around you. If your state offers its citizens the opportunity to vote for legislation that would make this drug available to patients in need, don't stay home, don't think that this isn't your issue because you don't use it. Get out and vote so that others who do need it can have safe, legal access.

On the home front, you can be a voice of reason when your friends and neighbors spout garbage that has been spread courtesy of people like Kevin Sabet. You can expose the teen rehab industry for the profiteering kidnappers they are, corporate masterminds who've become rich from ripping children away from their families and locking them up for a drug that has been proven to not be addictive and therefore doesn't respond to the same rehabilitation programs that other drugs require. You can simply be a "normal" person who calmly and rationally explains the truth and encourages your citizens to investigate it for themselves.

This article by Bill Morrison for TheAmericanCultivator.com outlines the lengths that advocates and concerned citizens are currently going to in order to ensure that patients in need of effective, inexpensive, and lifesaving cannabis aren't subjected to federal penalties are seemingly arbitrary punishment under the guise of federal statue. These citizens, who advanced on Washington, DC, to speak to their representatives in Congress, were a part of an event known as "Grandma Lobbies for Medical Marijuana," a joint effort in which The Silver Tour and the SSDP took advocates from several states to the nation's capital to work for real change.

# Author's Note

Despite being the only organization using local and national mainstream media to educate seniors and mainstream America on the facts and benefits of marijuana, The Silver Tour is still without substantial funding.

No other organization has received the level of praise from the press and media. No other organization has changed so many minds in the course of successfully bringing seniors out of closet and onto the forefront of cannabis legalization.

The Silver Tour has placed billboards on busy highways, aired "Should Grandma Smoke Pot?" hundreds of times in a dozen states, and is now running a radio campaign in Florida to ensure passage of medical marijuana this November. You can listen to the radio campaign here:

**https://soundcloud.com/groups/silver-tour-radio-spots**

The Silver Tour has no paid personnel and is a 501(c)3 tax exempt organization. Please consider a generous tax deductible donation to The Silver Tour. It will without a doubt hasten the end of cannabis prohibition, make this important medicine available to millions of needy patients, and help to bring home thousands of innocent Americans languishing in prisons in every state. You can donate online at www.thesilvertour.org or send a check to: The Silver Tour, 254 Lake Constance Drive, West Palm Beach, FL 33411

# Appendix

**GA Guide to activism**

http://www.gacareproject.com/wp-content/uploads/2013/08/A-Guide-to-Enacting-Medical-Marijuana-in-Georgia.pdf

## Table I – Court filings involving Straight, Inc.

| Plaintiff(s) | Defendant(s) | Nature | Judgment |
|---|---|---|---|
| Lulu Corter | Dr. Miller Newton (formerly national clinical director Straight, Inc); Kids of North Jersey, and his psychiatrists | child abuse | $6,500,000 settlement |
| Rebecca Erlich | Dr. Miller Newton (formerly national clinical director Straight, Inc); Kids of North Jersey, and his psychiatrists | child abuse | $4,500,000 settlement |
| Administrative | Lucy | She had already been placed in SAFE on 3 separate Marchman Acts for observation. | Magistrate denied Marchman Act commitment |

| | | | |
|---|---|---|---|
| | | She escaped was now 18, and her dad , an attorney, tried to force her back in on 4th Marchman Act. | |
| Criminal | G. T. and J. P. old comers at Growing Together--a Straight-descendent program | In an apparent un-official rite of passage called the Naked Crusader, four old comers tried to orally sodomize a newcomer, masturbated on his back. criminal # for G. T. 97028770MMD02 | |
| Criminal | Straight-Cincinnati | sensory deprivations, sexual confessions, kids sitting in own defecation, kids carving on self. Atty. Richard Doyle 606-431-5683 , Cincinnati, led 3 year investigation. | Straight voluntarily closed on day of trial. Strangely, today Kids Helping Kids of Cincinnati --a Straight descendent program operates out of old Straight - Cincinnati facility |
| Administrative | | Growing Together. State investigation found that a GT client warned that he might commit suicide but his counselors thought he just wanted attention. The client did commit suicide and the state | |

| | | | |
|---|---|---|---|
| | | concluded that the client may still be alive had his warning been taken seriously | |
| | Straight President Walter Loebenberg and Straight Exec Dir Bernadine Braiwaite | Officers of Pembroke Pines Gen Hospital, prior to Straight, failed to pay back appx. $950K of Medicaid money. | outcome not known |
| Criminal | Straight counselor Arthur Nichol, age 40 | rape of two male teenagers, a Straight client and his friend | |
| Criminal | George Ross of Possibilities Unlimited--a Straight descendent program. Prosecutors announced they would seek jail time. | While Miller Newton is the highest Straight or former Straight official to pay out the highest civil award against a Straight or a Straight-like program, Dr. George Ross, Straight's former national education director, is the highest Straight or former Straight official to ever be prosecuted in a criminal court. (Miller Newton settled with the federal government by paying $45,000 for 254 fraudulent | Prosecutors were Phil Maloney and a Mr. Giles. Ross' attorney was the former states attorney. Ross was acquitted. |

| | | | |
|---|---|---|---|
| | | insurance claims in return for not being criminally prosecuted.) Ross was tried in Aug 1985 for physically holding kids in his program. Originally 5 people made charges against him but the judge dismissed 2 immediately. One of Ross' character witnesses was Helen Petermann, Straight's former clinical director, who herself has been accused of abuse. | |
| John Doe | Straight-Springfield, et al | Minor alleged was spat upon and not allowed to wipe off spit until he admitted he was a drug addict. He escaped and was run down and beaten by Straight old comers until a Virginia State trooper interceded. | Attorney Sandra Havrlik, of Fairfax County handled his case. Disposition is unknown. |
| Columbia Mgt, Inc | Straight, Inc. | Straight sued by its landlord sued for failure to pay $42,726.31 in rent. | unknown |
| Fairfax Food Services and Caterers | Straight, Inc. | Straight sued by a Pizza company for owing a $17,177.72 | "discontinued and stricken" |

| | | | |
|---|---|---|---|
| | | pizza bill. | |
| Christi Fortson | Straight Dallas | False imprisonment, physical and emotional abuse, she was "frightened, humiliated, embarrassed, and suffered severe physical pain and emotional anguish" | Defended by D. Gerry Orth of Chappel and Handy. Outcome unknown. |
| Michael Daniels | Straight-Saint Petersburg | sued for driving him insane | Daniels lost |
| Bill Fager | Straight-Springfield | sued for abusing him and driving him insane | Fager lost |
| Straight Dallas | Tempie Worthy (mother of Christi Fortson) | a gag suit to keep the mother from sounding off at protests of the Straight facility | see Christi Fortson |
| Sherri Slaughter | Straight Dallas | kidnapped | her atty asking $5 million. She independently settled for $2,000. |
| Frank L. Giocondo | Kids of Southern California | small claims case # SC316584 | |
| Khachik Toomian | Kids of Southern California | small claims case # B029996 | dismissed with prejudice 1-4-91 |
| Harriet I. Hermann | Kids of Southern California | small claims case # SC319545 | |
| Richard A. Hermann | Kids of Southern California | small claims case # SC319545 | Richard Hermann awarded $1303 plus $26 cost of court on 2-7-89 |
| Rykoff Sexton, Inc. | Kids of Southern | small claims case # B041973? | dismissed with prejudice 5-14-90 |

| | California | | |
|---|---|---|---|
| Randel Sherwood | Straight of Southern California | small claims case # B088158 | |
| Yorbi Linda Commerce Assoc | Straight of Southern California | case # 688552 | Straight ordered to pay $872,642.37 on 10-6-92. Appears to be for rent default. |
| Gibralta Products, Inc. | Kids of Southern California | case # 565557 | |
| Harriet Herman | Kids of Southern California | case # 584418 | |
| Altobar Dev. Co. Inc. | Kids of Southern California | case # 564182 | |
| Criminal | Straight counselor Ken Barker | allegedly kissed and touched client Beth Cline | trial date 1-8-91. resolution not known. |
| Scott Beatty | Straight Springfield, VA | spat upon, other abuses. | unknown |
| Administrative | | State health granted 90 day conditional license to Straights in Orlando and Saint Petersburg instead of the normal yearly license due to violations. | |
| Jeffrey Dewitt Mildrum and mother Rene H. Mildrum | Straight Saint Petersburg | abuse | Straight settled |
| Karen Norton | Straight, Inc.; Miller Newton | Miller Newton threw Karen Norton against a wall | $720,000 #85011481CI |
| Amy Craun | Straight-Springfield, | abuse | unknown |

|  | VA, |  |  |
|---|---|---|---|
| John Doe | Straight St Pete | had psychiatric problems--not drugs. Was beaten, starved, started carving on his body | Attorney Karen A. Barnett handled case. Straight settled for $15K and host family for $10K. |
| Eric Weaver | Straight Cincinnati | Claimed Straight made him so despondent he carved on his body. Parents say they were told by Straight staff that carving was normal part of detox. | Cincinnati attorney Jonathan Schiff was representing Weaver as of 10-16-86. |
| John Does 1, 2, 3, 4. | Straight-Cincinnati | Four youths fled Straight Cincinnati. | Cincinnati attorney Jonathan Schiff represented all four successfully and kept them from being sent back. |
| John Does 1, 2, 3, 4. | Straight Cincinnati | Filed in Ohio from 83 - 85 by Ohio attorney David J. Scacchetti complaining kids beaten, painfully restrained, held in small isolation rooms for long periods of time, denied food and sleep. | Two suits settled out of court; two pending as of 2/91. |
| Wendi Weidman | Straight Cincinnait | a teenager, alleged attacked and beaten at Straight and at host home | unknown |
| Benson Williams age 14 | Straight Sarasota | atrocities including beatings, hung by his | Sarasota attorney Larry Byrd handled case. |

| | | | |
|---|---|---|---|
| | | underpants carried about by his hair, mental and physical torture, deprivation of medical attention and schooling | |
| Lawrence Taylor Williams | Straight Sarasota | 15 years old at time of abuse. alleged being deprived of bathroom facilities and proper food. | Sarasota attorney Larry Byrd handled case. |
| Margaret L. Heath | Straight Sarasota | beaten, thrown to a concrete floor, and pinioned there for over 2 hours, deprived of adequate food, water, sleep pulled out of chair by hair, denied education, denied bathroom privileges. | unknown |
| Straight, Inc. | State of Florida | Straight sues for right to force teens into treatment | |
| Administrative | | Florida Health warns Straight to stop force therapy | |
| Administrative | | Florida Health orders straight to change its ways | |
| Michael T. Keen | Straight St Pete | assault, false imprisonment, etc | unknown |
| 5 teens rep by ACLU | Straight-Atlanta | inhumane treatment | |
| Arletha Schauteet | Straight-St Pete, Miller Newton | held against will, kidnapping, told by Newton her | writ of habeas corpus released her. Her atty William A. |

| | | | |
|---|---|---|---|
| | | mom would be put in jail for kidnapping if she did not co-operate. | Leffler. Straight settled-undisclosed amount. |
| Hope Hyrons | Straight-St Pete, Miller Newton | kidnapping, false imprisonment at sibling interview, restraint, (she's from Longwood, FL) told by Newton, I don't give a damn about your rights | Straight settled for undisclosed. Her atty William A. Leffler |
| Michael Daniels | Straight-St Pete | driving him insane | Daniels lost |
| Martin Brashears | Straight-Atlanta | he was an adult, false imprisonment | unknown |
| Criminal | Straight-Sarasota and specified counselors. | Sarasota states attorney James T. Gardner (principal assistant David Levin) issues damning 600 page report on Straight-Sarasota on kidnappings false imprisonments, threats to court order unless voluntarily sign in; enrolling those not drug dependent, hair pulling, neck grabbing, throwing clients against walls. Based on statements from Straight counselors In 1989, David Levin, | facing 24 criminal indictments Straight Sarasota voluntarily closed. |

| | | | |
|---|---|---|---|
| | | former Sarasota ass't state atty, said on West 57th Street--it was child abuse and torture directed by Miller Newton. | |
| Charles from Albuquerque | | transported to Straight by in leg irons by 2 private detectives. | judge ordered release because proper commitment procedures not followed and judge saw no sign of drug addiction. |
| Jacqueline Stallings | Straight Saint Petersburg | physical assaults and false imprisonment | case # 83012161CI. Straight found to have committed a "malicious act". Settlement for $37,500. |
| John Douglas | Straight Saint Petersburg | abuse | case 85001827CI. Straight found to have committed a "wrongful act". |
| Michael Keen | Straight-St Pete | false imprisonment | |
| Criminal | | criminal restraint and involuntary servitude served on Miller Newton | Bergen County Superior Court dismissed charges. |
| Criminal | | Bergen County prosecutors found black eyes, strip searches, sleep deprivation, solitary confinement and denial or right to leave at age 18 | prosecutors escorted out a number of kids over age 18 |
| Susan W. Milan AKA Susan White | Straight-Atlanta | Ms. Milan represented by ACLU. Alleged | awarded $37K for peanut butter diets |

| | | | |
|---|---|---|---|
| | | medical malpractice, false imprisonment, fraud, assault. ACLU contact President Bruce Morris | |
| Jennifer Woolston | Kids of Salt Lake City, et al | kidnapping, strip search, in trying to escape she fell from window and broke bones in feet and arms, dislocated shoulder, damaged cartilage/ligament in both knees | she was released by writ of habeas corpus on 9-21-89. She won her case for an undisclosed amount. |
| Administrative | | Miller Newton's franchise Kids of Southern California closed under state scrutiny. Straight occupied the facility the day Kids left and took over the Kids' clients. Just over a year later the state closed Straight down for child abuse. | |
| Criminal | | hospital records show bleeding from scalp and blurred vision for client Tony Mitchele. When he became an adult he left but staff member Tony K. | According to staffer Christy Johnston, Mitchele dropped charges after Kids promised never to take him back |

| | | | |
|---|---|---|---|
| | | was arrested for trying to kidnap Mitchele back to the program. | |
| Larry Clay | | a legal adult in home state of Texas held against will | taken out by an FBI agent with a subpoena |
| Criminal | | KIDS' staffer Alex Zdanow tells West 57th Street he and others were ordered to take two kids into a room and "throw them around" | no charges |
| Administrative | | Newark Administrative Judge Edith Klinger releases damaging 53 page report on KIDS saying Many of the deficiencies . . . create hazards to health and safety | state health officials ignored Judge's report and granted Kids a special license to operate for another 10 years! |
| John Doe | King E. Davis, Commissioner of Dept Mental Health, Virginia, Barry P. Craig, Dir of Licensure, Dept of Mental Health, VA, host home parents and Straight-Springfield, | 13 year-old sexually abused by old comer in host home bathroom. second offense for the old comer. Sandra Havrilak, the boy's attorney, sued Virginia | Virginia Commonwealth Atty determined that Commissioner Davis could not be sued. But Davis closed Straight after this for a record of child abuse. Outcome against Straight unknown |

| | | | |
|---|---|---|---|
| | Va. | | |
| Dianne Saccomani | Straight, Inc. | breach of contract. in her response she includes report of findings from Florida Protective Service System detailing abuses her son Larry Turner received | unknown |
| G. N. | Straight-Springfield, VA, | sodomized by curling iron by 3 old comers for failing to write diary. Sndra Havrilak thought to be her attorney | unknown |
| Criminal | Carlos Lugo, Michael O'Connor, George Clemence | KIDS' counselors Carlos Lugo, Michael O'Connor, George Clemence beat 17 year old Channery Soto | all three counselors convicted of assault. fined like $100. Michael O'Connor admitted that beatings were routine. Judge Emil DelBaglivo said it was "almost unbelievable" that the program director would condone violence. |
| Criminal | George Clemence | charged for assaulting Michael Siculietano. Clemence was convicted 3 years before for assaulting Channery Soto | prosecutors dropped charges without informing Siculietano |
| Criminal | Miller Newton, et al | Marilyn Kearns, age 23, filed police report charging | Hudson County did not prosecute, nor did the US Justice |

| | | | |
|---|---|---|---|
| | | kidnapping, false imprisonment after she attended sibling rap in Secaucus, NJ In 1997 a copy of the police report was handed to the FBI in Newark, NJ | Dept. |
| Criminal | Patricia Logan | assault on 13 year-old Celena Moore | convicted of simple assault Jan 1998 |
| Criminal | Jenny Logan, Erin Moss | assault on 13 year-old Celena Moore. Jenny Logan is listed as one of the defendants in Jennifer Woolston's civil suit against KIDS of Salt Lake City | no prosecution |
| Criminal | Erin Moss | Andrea Jones complaint against Erin Moss | no prosecution |
| Criminal | Miller Newton | Sharon Tyler files charges | no prosecution |
| Criminal | Miller Newton | Chrysis Johnson files charges | no prosecution |
| Administrative | | Essex County juvenile judge releases John Shaw from KIDS treatment after personal meeting with him | |
| Criminal | | Dr. Newton accused by federal prosecutors in Newark of insurance fraud. | Newton agrees to pay $50,000 to cover 254 counts of insurance fraud but does not have to plead guilty. Former KIDS psychiatrist Raymond Edelman |

| | | | admits that KIDS fraudulently used his rubber stamp after he left the program |
|---|---|---|---|
| Criminal | Layne Meechan, founder of Proctor Advocate, Salt Lake City--which is based, in part, on Miller Newton's Kids. | prosecuted apparently for allowing a girls' peers to abuse her | apparently convicted but overturned by a judge on a technicality. |
| Roger Rossano | KIDS, NJ | fraudulent insurance charges | KIDS apparently lost or settled |
| James Wright | Straight-St Pete, Carl Palumbo, and others | A Maryland judge sent Wright to Straight in lieu of jail. Wright said he entered Straight after 7 hour intake in which he was threatened with physical harm. claims he was later kidnapped by Calumbo who represented self as a cop, and others. He was hog tied and taken back to Florida, but escaped on the way. | Straight settled. outcome on others unknown. Fairfax Judge Bach, who had sent Fairfax Judge Crounce's son to Straight in lieu of jail., presided. Judge Crounce filed a writ of habeas corpus to see own son. |
| Father of Michael Calabrese | Michael Calabrese | Miller Newton had looked into his eyes and determined Michael was a drug addict. | |

| | | | |
|---|---|---|---|
| | | Father petitioned Orange Cty Court to have his son committed to Straight. | |
| Administrative | | HRS-Florida state health--issued report that Straight threatening kids to be court ordered or sent to psychiatric hospital unless voluntarily sign in. | |
| Kristina Mizerak | Straight-St Pete, et al | jumped or fell from 4th floor window trying to escape from host home or trying to commit suiicde. says she was sexually abused at Straight. got a broken back. Her attorney Julian M. Piper also handled Daniels case. | settlement. records sealed but St Pete Times sued in 83 to unseal and Judge did so. |
| Criminal | | US Representative C. W. Young from Florida announced he was investigating potential criminal misconduct of Straight-St Pete after receiving 3 complaints, presumably from out of state. | none |
| Criminal | | In Jan 1978 Florida health - | Bob Marshall fired from his job with |

| | | | |
|---|---|---|---|
| | | HRS- released a report stating that 30 allegations of abuse could not be substantiated. However, Bob Marshall later publicly stated the report had been toned down. The Florida Bureau of Criminal Justice & Policy Assistance did its own report and found that many of the 30 allegations had been substantiated. Mel Sembler admitted that some Straight people had called the Secretary of Health. The report also found that in 1.5 years Straight had admitted 460 kids but only 1 had been black! | state health. |
| Criminal | | St Pete Police Officer Hartz, nephew of Straight director Jim Hartz accused of threatening a kid at Straight by pulling out handcuffs. | investigated by Chief Mac Vines who found no wrong doing. Mac Vines was on Straight's advisory committee along with Lt David Milchan. After Bob Marshall fired from HRS Milchan worked for HRS before becoming Chief of Police for St Pete |

| | | | |
|---|---|---|---|
| | | | Beach. Straight co-founder Joe Zappala's residence. Later Lions Club has Zappala Policeman of the Year Award. |
| Criminal | | Gail Stepheson. Escaped form Straight, ran to a house asked to use phone, occupants said OK. Later Straight girls walked into the home without permission and drug Ms. Stepheson out. This launched a Congressional inquiry by Florida Congressman Bill Russell. Several people came forward and said they would testify, but James Russell--the states attorney did not investigate. Weeks later Stepheson announced she now wanted to stay in Straight. It was at this time that Mack Vines who became chief of police and Judge Dadswell joined a committee to study Bob | |

| | | Marshall, the HRS official investigating Straight. Marshall was fired. The same had happened in 1973 at the St Pete Seed with Roger Young, then to Jeff Bourgholtzer whose dad became a founding board member of Straight (Leonard Lubin, ACLU represented both boys), The same thing happened to a 16 year old girl who had been abducted from Saint Petersburg Catholic High School into The Seed with her mother's consent. All forced to The Seed in 1973, made the newspapers but James T. Russell, the states attorney who was on The Seed's advisory board took no action. Allen Allweis, Russell's chief investigator was on Straight's advisory board and later became a | |
|---|---|---|---|

| | | | |
|---|---|---|---|
| | | director on Straight's board of directors. Attorney Myron Mensch was also on Straight's advisory board and his brother Richard was an assistant state's attorney. | |
| David F. White | | kidnapping, strip search, assault, illegal search, invasion of privacy, released by writ of habeas corpus, boys dad is prominent area attorney Jack E. White, who may have later become a judge | unknown |
| | | Jerry Vancil escaped from Straight in 1977, got to press and said he had been beaten. Press investigated and found that an incident had occurred. Jerry Vancil disappeared and state investigating official Bob Marshall was fired. | |

## Table II

| Party 1 | Case | Action | Date | Party 2 | Section | ID Nmbr |
|---|---|---|---|---|---|---|
| STRAIGHT INC | 93000807CO | ENF FOR JDG | 02/09/93 | SCHREIBER MARK T MD | 040 | 99799 |
| STRAIGHT INC | 93000216FJ | FOREIGN JUDGMENT | 05/19/93 | YORBA LINDA COMMERCENTE R ASSOCIATES | 008 | 99899 |
| STRAIGHT INC | 93000220FJ | ENF FOR JDG | 05/25/93 | ADVANCE NOTICE INC | 904 | 99799 |
| STRAIGHT INC | 93000221FJ | ENF FOR JDG | 05/25/93 | ADVANCE NOTICE INC | 904 | 99899 |
| STRAIGHT INC | 93000236FJ | FOREIGN JUDGMENT | 06/07/93 | SCHREIBER MARK T MD | 905 | 99899 |
| STRAIGHT INC | 93000807CO | ENF FOR JDG | 02/09/93 | SCHREIBER MARK T MD | 040 | 99699 |
| STRAIGHT INC | 94000481CI | FOREIGN JUDGMENT | 01/26/94 | GORDON STEVEN G | HOC | 99899 |
| STRAIGHT INC | 96002682CI | MTG FORECL | 04/29/96 | BANK OF AMERICA NATIONAL TRUST AND | | 99698 |
| STRAIGHT INC | 96006511CI | MTG FORECL | 10/16/96 | PRINCIPAL MUTUAL LIFE INSURANCE COMPANY | 019 | 97599 |
| STRAIGHT INC SOUTHER N CALIFORN IA | 91009241CI | REPLEVIN | 05/28/91 | BELL ATLANTIC TRICONTINENT AL LEASING | 021 | 99899 |
| STRAIGHT INC | 92002969MF | MTG FORECL | 10/05/92 | FIRST UNION NATIONAL BANK OF FLORIDA | 019 | 99599 |
| STRAIGHT INC | 92003087CO | CONTRACT | 05/21/92 | DEMMI JOSEPH M SR | 039 | 99999 |
| STRAIGHT INC | 92003644MF | MTG FORECL | 12/11/92 | FEDERAL NATIONAL MORTGAGE ASSOCIATION | 021 | 99399 |
| STRAIGHT INC | 92004041SC | CONTRACT | 06/22/92 | FARRELL ROBERT E JR | 044 | 99999 |
| STRAIGHT INC | 92004443CO | CONTRACT | 07/21/92 | RUSSELL PATRICIA M | 042 | 99999 |

| STRAIGHT INC | 92005995SC | CONTRACT | 09/18/92 | SEALE ALBERT F | 045 | 99899 |
|---|---|---|---|---|---|---|
| STRAIGHT INC | 92006831SC | GOODS S SOLD | 10/29/92 | DRAGTON DEBRA L | 045 | 99899 |
| STRAIGHT INC | 92006832SC | GOODS S SOLD | 10/29/92 | DRAGTON DEBRA L | 045 | 99899 |
| STRAIGHT INC | 93000040FJ | FOREIGN JUDGMENT | 01/29/93 | YORBA LINDA COMMERCENTE R ASSOCIATES | 906 | 99899 |
| STRAIGHT INC | 93000040TJ | | | | | 99899 |
| STRAIGHT INC | 92000067FJ | FOREIGN JUDGMENT | 03/10/92 | BSI TEMPORARIES INC | 019 | 99899 |
| STRAIGHT INC | 92000961CI | CONTRACT | 02/20/92 | ECKERD JACK CORPORATION | 021 | 99999 |
| STRAIGHT INC | 92001253CI | SLANDER | 03/06/92 | BRADBURY RICHARD | 008 | 99899 |
| STRAIGHT INC | 92001387CI | CONTRACT | 03/16/92 | FLEET CREDIT CORP | 019 | 99899 |
| STRAIGHT INC | 92001556MF | MTG FORECL | 05/11/92 | SECRETARY OF VETERANS AFFAIRS | 007 | 99299 |
| STRAIGHT INC | 92001672CO | CONTRACT | 03/17/92 | FRUHMORGEN JOHN C | 040 | 99999 |
| STRAIGHT INC | 92001802SC | RENT | 03/16/92 | FLOYD BOBBY R | 045 | 99899 |
| STRAIGHT INC | 92002194CI | CONTRACT | 05/07/92 | SEAGRAVES BARBARA | 008 | 99999 |
| STRAIGHT INC | 92002251CI | CONTRACT | 05/12/92 | MEISS KATHERINE K | 013 | 99999 |
| STRAIGHT INC | 92002852CO | CONTRACT | 05/12/92 | TANT BARBARA D | 039 | 99999 |
| STRAIGHT INC | 91003600CI | CONTRACT | 03/05/91 | BARRANCOTTO CHARLENE | 013 | 99999 |
| STRAIGHT INC | 91003601CI | CONTRACT | 03/05/91 | MILLER LINDA | 011 | 99999 |
| STRAIGHT INC | 91007216CO | CONTRACT | 11/06/91 | ORTA MAGDIA | 039 | 99999 |
| STRAIGHT INC | 91007217CO | CONTRACT | 11/06/91 | EDWARDS DEIDRE SUSAN | 039 | 99999 |
| STRAIGHT INC | 91007218CO | CONTRACT | 11/06/91 | WILLIAMS MARIANNE | 054 | 99999 |
| STRAIGHT INC | 91007219CO | CONTRACT | 11/06/91 | DASHLER JANICE | 054 | 99999 |
| STRAIGHT INC | 91007220CO | CONTRACT | 11/06/91 | BESTER LISA KELLY | 054 | 99999 |

| | | | | | | |
|---|---|---|---|---|---|---|
| STRAIGHT INC | 91015173CI | CONTRACT | 08/26/91 | BELL ATLANTIC TRICONTINENTAL LEASING | 018 | 99899 |
| STRAIGHT INC | 91019305CI | CONTRACT | 11/06/91 | JONES WANDA S | 011 | 99999 |
| STRAIGHT INC | 91019306CI | CONTRACT | 11/06/91 | SMITH SHARON LEE | 013 | 99999 |
| STRAIGHT INC | 91000521CO | CONTRACT | 01/23/91 | MILLER LINDA | 054 | 99999 |
| STRAIGHT INC | 91000680CO | CONTRACT | 01/28/91 | WINRIGHT KENNETH | 040 | 99999 |
| STRAIGHT INC | 91000754SC | CONTRACT | 01/28/91 | PARKER CHERYL A | 046 | 99999 |
| STRAIGHT INC | 91001357CI | CONTRACT | 01/24/91 | FORD MARY ANN | 008 | 99999 |
| STRAIGHT INC | 91001437CI | CONTRACT | 01/25/91 | HEATH CHRISTINE | 018 | 99999 |
| STRAIGHT INC | 91001440CI | CONTRACT | 01/25/91 | ORTA MAGDA | 008 | 99999 |
| STRAIGHT INC | 91001509SC | CONTRACT | 02/25/91 | MASON MARILYN | 044 | 99999 |
| STRAIGHT INC | 91001607CO | CONTRACT | 03/06/91 | MESSER LEWIS C | 054 | 99999 |
| STRAIGHT INC | 91002728CI | CONTRACT | 02/18/91 | YORBA LINDA COMMERCENTER ASSOCIATES | 018 | 99899 |
| STRAIGHT INC | 91003098CI | CONTRACT | 02/25/91 | FLEET CREDIT CORP | 019 | 99899 |
| STRAIGHT INC | 90019976CI | CONTRACT | 11/27/90 | INGERSOLL DEBORAH LYNN | 019 | 99999 |
| STRAIGHT INC | 90019977CI | CONTRACT | 11/27/90 | TOWLER JANE | 013 | 99999 |
| STRAIGHT INC | 90019980CI | CONTRACT | 11/27/90 | VOGENEY WILLIAM E | 018 | 99999 |
| STRAIGHT INC | 91000514CO | CONTRACT | 01/23/91 | PIERSON ROGER | 040 | 99999 |
| STRAIGHT INC | 91000515CO | CONTRACT | 01/23/91 | BARRANCOTTO CHARLENE | 040 | 99999 |
| STRAIGHT INC | 91000516CO | CONTRACT | 01/23/91 | SEAGRAVES BARBARA | 054 | 99999 |
| STRAIGHT INC | 91000517CO | CONTRACT | 01/23/91 | MINEO SHARON | 054 | 99999 |
| STRAIGHT INC | 91000518CO | CONTRACT | 01/23/91 | SCHWALM CHERYL S | 039 | 99999 |
| STRAIGHT INC | 91000519CO | CONTRACT | 01/23/91 | MCVAY DONALD | 039 | 99999 |

| | | | | | | |
|---|---|---|---|---|---|---|
| STRAIGHT INC | 91000520CO | CONTRACT | 01/23/91 | MEANS E MIRANDA | 054 | 99999 |
| STRAIGHT INC | 90018258CI | CONTRACT | 10/24/90 | KELLY GERALD | 019 | 99999 |
| STRAIGHT INC | 90018259CI | CONTRACT | 10/24/90 | SWAN HELEN J | 019 | 99999 |
| STRAIGHT INC | 90018260CI | CONTRACT | 10/24/90 | DUNN JAMES W | 009 | 99999 |
| STRAIGHT INC | 90018261CI | CONTRACT | 10/24/90 | KING TINA RIDENOUR | 018 | 99999 |
| STRAIGHT INC | 90018262CI | CONTRACT | 10/24/90 | GRIMES MYRNA | 019 | 99999 |
| STRAIGHT INC | 90019233CI | CONTRACT | 11/13/90 | FOWLER MERRILL | 018 | 99999 |
| STRAIGHT INC | 90019234CI | CONTRACT | 11/13/90 | MCKAY BARBARA J | 019 | 99999 |
| STRAIGHT INC | 90019236CI | CONTRACT | 11/13/90 | EDMONDS NANCY | 008 | 99999 |
| STRAIGHT INC | 90019698CI | CONTRACT | 11/20/90 | CROUCH ELAINE M | 017 | 99999 |
| STRAIGHT INC | 90019974CI | CONTRACT | 11/27/90 | GLENN MARY LOU | 019 | 99999 |
| STRAIGHT INC | 90017358CI | CONTRACT | 10/09/90 | SACCAMANI DIANE | 011 | 99999 |
| STRAIGHT INC | 90017359CI | CONTRACT | 10/09/90 | KILEY RICHARD | 019 | 99999 |
| STRAIGHT INC | 90017360CI | CONTRACT | 10/09/90 | HIDBRADER LILLIE | 019 | 99999 |
| STRAIGHT INC | 90017361CI | CONTRACT | 10/09/90 | MARTIN TERRY | 017 | 99999 |
| STRAIGHT INC | 90017362CI | CONTRACT | 10/09/90 | EVERETT MARSHA JANELLE | 011 | 99999 |
| STRAIGHT INC | 90017363CI | CONTRACT | 10/09/90 | HALL WILLIAM T | 009 | 99999 |
| STRAIGHT INC | 90017364CI | CONTRACT | 10/09/90 | ANDERSON ROBERT B | 008 | 99999 |
| STRAIGHT INC | 90017365CI | CONTRACT | 10/09/90 | BUXTON DONALD F | 018 | 99999 |
| STRAIGHT INC | 90017366CI | CONTRACT | 10/09/90 | MULCAHY JOSEPH | 013 | 99999 |
| STRAIGHT INC | 90018257CI | CONTRACT | 10/24/90 | ANNEOVA HILDEGARD | 008 | 99999 |
| STRAIGHT INC | 90009126SC | CONTRACT | 10/26/90 | COLACIELLO WENDY | 044 | 99999 |
| STRAIGHT | 90009127SC | CONTRACT | 10/26/90 | KORMAN | 044 | |

| INC | | | | NICHOLAS | | 99999 |
|---|---|---|---|---|---|---|
| STRAIGHT INC | 90009128SC | CONTRACT | 10/26/90 | PENCE THERESA | 044 | 99999 |
| STRAIGHT INC | 90009699SC | CONTRACT | 11/16/90 | HUGHES JULIA | 045 | 99999 |
| STRAIGHT INC | 90009814SC | CONTRACT | 11/20/90 | JUSTICE LAWRENCE K | 045 | 99999 |
| STRAIGHT INC | 90009815SC | CONTRACT | 11/20/90 | FIORE KATHLEEN | 045 | 99999 |
| STRAIGHT INC | 90009816SC | CONTRACT | 11/20/90 | SURI PETER | 045 | 99999 |
| STRAIGHT INC | 90009817SC | CONTRACT | 11/20/90 | GILBERT MARALYN N | 045 | 99999 |
| STRAIGHT INC | 90010056SC | CONTRACT | 12/03/90 | SETTLE NANCY CAMERON | 044 | 99999 |
| STRAIGHT INC | 90010057SC | CONTRACT | 12/03/90 | CANTOR NANCY | 045 | 99999 |
| STRAIGHT INC | 90006418CO | CONTRACT | 11/27/90 | GREENE ROBERT | 040 | 99999 |
| STRAIGHT INC | 90008547SC | CONTRACT | 10/09/90 | HOGAN PETER | 046 | 99999 |
| STRAIGHT INC | 90008548SC | CONTRACT | 10/09/90 | FERRIS RICHARD E | 046 | 99999 |
| STRAIGHT INC | 90008549SC | CONTRACT | 10/09/90 | MALEK ROBERT | 046 | 99999 |
| STRAIGHT INC | 90008550SC | CONTRACT | 10/09/90 | KEELE ARTHUR H | 046 | 99999 |
| STRAIGHT INC | 90008551SC | CONTRACT | 10/09/90 | NOHL JENNYNE S | 045 | 99999 |
| STRAIGHT INC | 90009122SC | CONTRACT | 10/26/90 | CRAVENS ROD | 046 | 99999 |
| STRAIGHT INC | 90009123SC | CONTRACT | 10/26/90 | OWENS AUTUMN | 045 | 99999 |
| STRAIGHT INC | 90009124SC | CONTRACT | 10/26/90 | PHILLIPS JAMES | 046 | 99999 |
| STRAIGHT INC | 90009125SC | CONTRACT | 10/26/90 | HALLMAN KATHLEEN | 045 | 99999 |
| STRAIGHT INC | 90005695CO | CONTRACT | 10/25/90 | CARVAJAL NADINE GARCIA | 040 | 99999 |
| STRAIGHT INC | 90005696CO | CONTRACT | 10/25/90 | SAYLOR MARY | 040 | 99999 |
| STRAIGHT INC | 90006039CO | CONTRACT | 11/13/90 | BAKER DEBORA | 040 | 99999 |
| STRAIGHT INC | 90006260CO | CONTRACT | 11/20/90 | WYNNE JAMES R SR | 040 | 99999 |
| STRAIGHT | 90006261CO | CONTRACT | 11/20/90 | HOLTAN | 040 | |

| INC | | | | RICHARD A | | 99999 |
|---|---|---|---|---|---|---|
| STRAIGHT INC | 90006411CO | CONTRACT | 11/27/90 | JAGGERS BLAINE | 039 | 99999 |
| STRAIGHT INC | 90006414CO | CONTRACT | 11/27/90 | RICHARDSON TERESA HESLER | 039 | 99999 |
| STRAIGHT INC | 90006415CO | CONTRACT | 11/27/90 | MUSTIPHER RENA BELL | 039 | 99999 |
| STRAIGHT INC | 90006416CO | CONTRACT | 11/27/90 | WILLIS JEANNE B | 040 | 99999 |
| STRAIGHT INC | 90006417CO | CONTRACT | 11/27/90 | WILSON HAROLD R | 054 | 99999 |
| STRAIGHT INC | 90005235CO | CONTRACT | 10/09/90 | BAILEY EDWARD G | 054 | 99999 |
| STRAIGHT INC | 90005236CO | CONTRACT | 10/09/90 | BEHUNIAK PATRICIA M | 040 | 99999 |
| STRAIGHT INC | 90005237CO | CONTRACT | 10/09/90 | GUARINO BARBARA A | 039 | 99999 |
| STRAIGHT INC | 90005238CO | CONTRACT | 10/09/90 | AMORE CHARLES | 054 | 99999 |
| STRAIGHT INC | 90005514CO | CONTRACT | 10/29/90 | TIMES PUBLISHING COMPANY | 042 | 99899 |
| STRAIGHT INC | 90005690CO | CONTRACT | 10/25/90 | MCCALLION ROBERT E | 054 | 99999 |
| STRAIGHT INC | 90005691CO | CONTRACT | 10/25/90 | LICATE DARLENE | 039 | 99999 |
| STRAIGHT INC | 90005692CO | CONTRACT | 10/25/90 | ORCUTT GERALD | 040 | 99999 |
| STRAIGHT INC | 90005693CO | CONTRACT | 10/25/90 | POWERS JAMES R | 039 | 99999 |
| STRAIGHT INC | 90005694CO | CONTRACT | 10/25/90 | NEUMANN PATRICIA | 040 | 99999 |
| STRAIGHT INC | 83012161CI | MALICIOUS ACT | 10/14/83 | STALLINGS JACQUELINE A | 019 | 99899 |
| STRAIGHT INC | 85001827CI | WRONGFUL ACT | 02/07/85 | DOUGLAS JOHN E JR | 025 | 99899 |
| STRAIGHT INC | 85011481CI | NEGLIGENCE | 08/12/85 | NORTON KAREN | 019 | 99899 |
| STRAIGHT INC | 85014022CI | CONTRACT | 09/30/85 | STPAUL PROPERTY AND LIABILITY INSURANCE COMPANY | 019 | 99999 |
| STRAIGHT INC | 86013400CI | WRONG ACT NEG | 09/03/86 | MILDRUM JEFFREY DEWITT | 025 | 99899 |
| STRAIGHT | 87016188CI | CONTRACT | 11/03/87 | STPAUL FIRE AND | 019 | |

| INC | | | | MARINE INSURANCE COMPANY | | 99999 |
|---|---|---|---|---|---|---|
| STRAIGHT INC | 90005231CO | CONTRACT | 10/09/90 | GREENE REX | 039 | 99999 |
| STRAIGHT INC | 90005232CO | CONTRACT | 10/09/90 | MACFARLANE DONNA J | 040 | 99999 |
| STRAIGHT INC | 90005233CO | CONTRACT | 10/09/90 | WALKER DAWN M | 039 | 99999 |
| STRAIGHT INC | 90005234CO | CONTRACT | 10/09/90 | WILLIS GARY M | 040 | 99999 |
| STRAIGHT INC | 77009022CI | HABEAS CORPUS | 09/30/77 | | 000 | 99799 |
| STRAIGHT INC | 77011901CI | MALICIOUS ACT | 12/21/77 | | 000 | 99799 |
| STRAIGHT INC | 78002848CI | HABEAS CORPUS | 03/20/78 | | 000 | 99899 |
| STRAIGHT INC | 78002849CI | HABEAS CORPUS | 03/20/78 | | 000 | 99899 |
| STRAIGHT INC | 79000764CI | NEGLIGENCE | 01/19/79 | | 012 | 99899 |
| STRAIGHT INC | 81001605CI | HABEAS CORPUS | 02/11/81 | | 014 | 99899 |
| STRAIGHT INC | 83005318CI | NEGLIGENCE | 05/05/83 | DANIELS MICHAEL | 011 | 99899 |
| STRAIGHT INC | 83011761CI | WRONGFUL ACT | 10/06/83 | KEEN MICHAEL T | 013 | 99899 |
| STRAIGHT FOUNDAT ION INC | 92003644MF | MTG FORECL | 12/11/92 | FEDERAL NATIONAL MORTGAGE ASSOCIATION | 021 | 99499 |
| STRAIGHT FOUNDAT ION INC | 93000807CO | ENF FOR JDG | 02/09/93 | SCHREIBER MARK T MD | 040 | 99899 |
| STRAIGHT ADOLESC ENT DRUG AND REHABILI TATION CENTER | 93000040FJ | FOREIGN JUDGMENT | 01/29/93 | YORBA LINDA COMMERCENTE R ASSOCIATES | | 99898 |
| | | | | | | |

Praise for *Black Tuna Diaries*

“This is a true account of the life of America's most written about marijuana smuggler. Between the accounts of his smuggling adventures, Robert tells his life story. Life as a member of "The South St. Gang", his years as an actor, a famous pitchman, a successful entrepreneur in America and England, Bull Fighter in Spain, TV producer, smuggling pilot, big game fisherman, and federal inmate. This book is different than many, or even most, novels you read about drug smuggling, let alone the supposedly true ones. It reads true, and Platshorn's propensity to display the entire picture, warts and all, is both commendable and a refreshing touch. Even the dedication page in this book is different from the usual vapid or sometimes maudlin dedications one sees in books today, and is worth a read...”
–Lou Novachek, *The Book Review*

“I love it! It's my kind of story. I'm going on a book tour and I'll tell my readers that I'm reading your book.” –Greg Campbell, author of *Blood Diamonds, The Road to Kosovo*, and *Flawless.*

“I spent Christmas Eve catching mahi mahi and tuna off the coast of Costa Rica and finishing your book. It was a riveting tale.” –Lazlow, author of *Grand Theft Auto, The Game*

Read a sample and order autographed copies at BlackTunaDiaries.com.

Want to end cannabis prohibition? Five good reasons to support the Silver Tour today:

1. Live Silver Tour shows in senior communities, auditoriums, churches and synagogues.
2. Our TV show, "Should Grandma Smoke Pot?" aired hundreds of times in dozens of cities.
3. Powerful billboards placed on major streets and highways.
4. Saturation radio campaigns designed to educate on the benefits of cannabis.
5. The Silver Tour donations are tax deductible. We are a federal 501(c)3.

The Goal - To educate and inform seniors on the benefits and exciting discoveries in the medical cannabis field. To encourage activism for legalization and create demand for safe access. *Seniors vote and they talk to their representatives.*

It's very simple. Millions of seniors make up the vast majority of those that will actually vote in an election year.

That's where The Silver Tour comes in. For the past four years, The Silver Tour has successfully convinced millions of seniors to demand safe legal, access to medical marijuana. We did this with live Silver Tour Shows, our TV show "Should Grandma Smoke Pot?" and by bringing busloads of seniors to the House of Representatives in Washington DC.

Do it now! Please donate to The Silver Tour at TheSilverTour.org.